# VITAL GODLINESS:

## A TREATISE

ON

## EXPERIMENTAL

AND

## PRACTICAL PIETY.

BY WILLIAM S. PLUMER, D. D., LL. D.

PUBLISHED BY THE
AMERICAN TRACT SOCIETY,
150 NASSAU-STREET, NEW YORK.

IF THIS BOOK SHALL AID ANY ONE

IN MAKING

HIS CALLING AND ELECTION SURE,

TO

THE EVER BLESSED NAME

OF

The Father, the Son, and the Holy Ghost,

BE GLORY IN THE HIGHEST,

World without end.

# CONTENTS.

## CHAPTER I.



## CHAPTER II.



## CHAPTER III.



## CHAPTER IV.



## CHAPTER V.



## CHAPTER VI.



## CHAPTER VII.



## CHAPTER VIII.



## CHAPTER IX.



## CHAPTER X.



## CHAPTER XI.

# VITAL GODLINESS.

## CHAPTER I.

### GENERAL REMARKS ON RELIGIOUS EXPERIENCE.

THE test of real character is to be sought in each man's experience. He who has never exercised faith, repentance, love, humility, hope, and joy, cannot be profited by his theories and speculations on these subjects. All knowledge which is unfelt and inoperative puffs up the mind and hardens the heart. It is better to have the workings of gracious affections than to be able to define them, or to speak ever so learnedly respecting them. The great use of a large part of divine truth is rightly to affect our minds and hearts, and so to control our practice.

It is often doubted whether the present age is remarkable for depth of religious feeling. In many cases ministers preach a low experience.

The consequence is painful laxity in religious practice. Among many professors there is a manifest disinclination to converse on vital subjects in religion. This is a great evil. Although hypocrites may babble on such topics, yet true Christians should not thereby be deterred from telling what God has done for their souls, or from diligently seeking to discover and commend the highest style of holy living. Perhaps on all branches of these subjects there is less preaching than formerly. A minister of this generation said that he had received many hundreds of printed sermons sent out by his brethren, and that among them all he remembered but one on the subject of experimental religion. Yet it is noticeable that when a preacher of ability and sound discrimination discusses any branch of this subject, he is always highly acceptable to the best class of professors.

The testimonies to the necessity of experimental piety are exceedingly numerous. Almost every fit form of expression is employed by inspired writers to teach us this great truth. Thus says David, "O taste and see that the Lord is good; blessed is the man that trusteth in him." Psa. 34:8. "Come and hear, all ye that fear God, and I will declare what he hath done for my soul." Psa. 66 : 16. So Elihu said, "Suffer me a little, and I will show thee that I have yet to speak on God's behalf." Job 36 : 2. Often in the Scriptures religious experience is expressed by hungering and thirsting, by eating and drinking. Isa. 55 : 1; Matt. 5 : 6 ; Song 5 : 1; John 6 : 53–58. Job, David, and Isaiah all inform us of the power of religious experience in their own case. Job 42 : 5, 6 ; Psa. 51; Isa. 6 : 5.

Nor is the testimony of uninspired men on this point less harmonious. Richard Baxter says, "The way to have the firmest belief of the Christian faith is to draw near and taste and try it, and lay bare the heart to receive the impression of it; and then, by the sense of its admirable effects, we shall know that which bare speculation could not discover. Though there must be a belief on other grounds first, so much as to let in the word into the soul, and to cause us to submit our hearts to its operations, yet it is this experience that must strengthen it and confirm it. If any man will do the will of Christ, he shall know that the doctrine is of God. John 7 : 17. The melody of music is better known by hearing it than by reports of it, and the sweetness of meat is known better by tasting than by hearsay, though upon report we may be drawn to taste and try. So is there a spiritual sense in us of the effects of the gospel on our own hearts, which will cause men to love it and hold it fast against the cavils of deceivers or the temptations of the great deceiver."

John Owen says, "Experience is the food of all grace, which it grows and thrives upon. Every taste that faith obtains of divine love and grace, or how gracious the Lord is, adds to its measure and stature. Two things therefore must briefly be declared: 1. That the experience of the reality, excellency, power, and efficacy of the things that are believed, is an effectual means of increasing faith and love. 2. That it is the Holy Ghost which gives us this experience."

John Newton says, "Experience is the Lord's school, and they who are taught by him usually learn by the mistakes they make that they have no wisdom, and by the slips and falls they meet with that they have no strength."

Charles Buck says, "The report of the blessings of the religion of Christ, or the intelligence that provision is made for guilty man, can be of no avail without a real participation of them. We must not perceive only, but we must feel; and feeling, of course we experience."

President Edwards the elder says, "A gracious experience arises from operations and influences which are spiritual, from an inward principle which is divine, a communication of God, a participation of the divine nature: Christ living in the heart, the Holy Spirit dwelling there in union with the faculties of the soul as an internal vital principle, exerting his own proper nature in the exercise of those faculties. Now it is no wonder that that which is divine is powerful and effectual, for it has omnipotence on its side."

The late Dr. John M'Dowell says, "If we be Christians, we shall delight to meet with our fellow-Christians, and engage with them in conversation on experimental piety. And true religion must either be very low or be entirely wanting in the heart of that person who seldom speaks on the subject, or extends not his conversation beyond the doctrines and forms of religion, or speaks in an uninterested or heartless manner. The Scripture saints, as appears from their history, engaged much in religious conversation."

Yet it is to be regretted that but few modern books treat of this subject. Doctrinal discussions, treatises on the history of the Bible, on branches of Scripture morals, and on church government, are numerous. But rarely do we find able men turning their attention to the work of God in the soul. It was not always so. In the seventeenth century the ablest productions of the greatest minds were on experimental religion. The exceeding popularity of a few books, first published in our own age, shows that so far as there is piety, such reading is in great demand. This will be more and more so as true religion shall prevail.

It is admitted that the subject of experimental religion is not free from difficulties. But most of these are theoretical, rather than practical. Yet those which grow out of the deceitfulness of sin and the temptations of the great adversary, should be carefully studied by all persons, by religious teachers in particular, and the consolations of God sought out and administered accordingly. It is also worthy of notice that the best treatises in this department of religious literature are often narratives of the dealings of God with particular persons. Religious biography constitutes a very useful and popular part of a well-chosen library. If the time shall come when the memoirs of Halyburton and Brainerd shall be unwelcome to the great body of God's people, then indeed the glory will have departed.

John Newton remarks that "it is to be lamented that in this enlightened age, so signalized by the prevalence of the spirit of investigation, religion should by many be thought the only subject unworthy of a serious inquiry; and that while in every branch of science they studiously endeavor to trace every fact to its proper and adequate cause, and are cautious of admitting any theory which cannot stand the test of *experiment*, they treat the use of the term *experimental*, when applied to religion, with contempt."

The tendency of this age is to become vague and superficial. In giving an account of the work of God on one or many, there is a proneness to deal in generals and avoid particulars. In some cases there may be reasons of delicacy for saying little; nor is it necessary to present individuals by name or description of person before the community. But how refreshing it would be to meet with a recent narrative like that which President Edwards has given of one who is now understood to have been the person who afterwards became his wife. In their narratives of revivals of religion, the old magazines often present quite a contrast to many of our modern journals. This deficiency has sometimes been noticed and a desire for a change expressed, but we seem to be getting further and further from the old paths.

Yet let us not be discouraged. Let us labor to banish unreasonable prejudices against this subject as a proper topic of familiar or religious conversation. This will be no easy task. So many ignorant men have spoken things which they ought not, so many weak men have uttered folly, and so many bad men have obtruded their erroneous views upon the attention of others, that some have been quite disgusted with the whole matter. Thus it has come to pass that even in the free church of Scotland a candidate for the ministry is not examined as to his acquaintance with experimental religion or his motives for seeking the sacred office. But it is never safe to argue from the abuse of any thing against its use.

Not only in preaching, but in their private walks, pastors might exert a happy influence on this subject. Let them converse freely and fully with those seeking admission to the Lord's table. In their pastoral visits let not this subject be forgotten. Sometimes it may be well to leave particular questions to be answered or talked over on a subsequent interview. It would also be well if all that class of able works which have handled the different branches of this subject were brought into general use in our churches. John Newton has long been a favorite. His writings on experimental religion contributed much to the revival of piety in the latter part of the eighteenth and the early part of the nineteenth centuries. John Owen on Indwelling Sin is more profound than any thing Newton ever wrote. One of the best works on the whole subject is Guthrie's Trial of a Saving Interest in Christ. Dr. Archibald Alexander on Religious Experience is admirably suited to awaken a fondness for this kind of reading.

But more than any thing else, we always need in the church a copious outpouring of God's Spirit on the hearts of his people, giving them a zest for spiritual things and a great desire for a full assurance of understanding, of faith and of hope. Many real Christians have made but low attainments, and are too little dissatisfied with their present state. One who should speak and act with the zeal and ardor of Paul, of Knox, of Welsh, of Whitefield, or of Henry Martyn, would by the thoughtless world be esteemed mad. But wisdom is justified of her children. The truly regenerate and growing Christian will not be offended at sound views on this subject.

It may encourage us to study this subject, to remember that, though in unessential particulars there is an endless diversity in the experience of men, yet in all that necessarily belongs to vital piety there is a substantial agreement. Perhaps a more striking contrast could hardly be found between two men, than between John Newton and Occum the Indian preacher. Yet Newton says of the latter, that "in describing to me the state of his heart, when he was a blind idolater, he gave me in general a striking picture of what my own was in the early part of my own life; and his subsequent views of the gospel corresponded with mine as face answers to face in a glass."

John Owen also says, "As sin worketh in

one, so doth it in another; as grace is effectual in one, so is it in another; as he that prayeth longeth for mercy and grace, so do they that join with him. Of the same kind with his hatred of sin, his love to Christ, his laboring after holiness and conformity to the will of God, are also those in other believers. And hence it is that persons 'praying in the Spirit' according to their own experience, are oftentimes supposed by every one in the congregation rather to pray over their condition than their own."

Nor is there any way of preserving men from falling into error respecting the true nature of religion, but by bringing them to feel its power. "The head may be strengthened till the heart is starved." Indeed, infidelity itself will be sure to gain a footing in a community where vital godliness is not experienced. John Owen truly says, "The owning of the Scripture to be the word of God bespeaks a divine majesty, authority, and power to be present in it and with it. Wherefore, after men who have for a long time so professed, do find that they never had any real experience of such a divine presence in it by any effects upon their own minds, they grow insensibly regardless of it, or to allow it a very common place in their thoughts. When they have worn off the impressions that were on their minds from tradition, education, and custom, they do for the future rather not oppose it than in any way believe it. And when once a reverence unto the word of God on account of its authority is lost, an assent unto it on account of its truth will not long abide. And all such persons, under a concurrence of temptations and outward occasions, will either reject it or prefer other guides before it."

There is not a doctrine of revelation the power of which ought not to be felt in the human soul. If God is revealed to us in a trinity of persons, as the Father, the Son, and the Holy Ghost, it is that we may love and serve and worship him just as he is revealed. If Jesus Christ made a vicarious atonement, that great doctrine is revealed to us that we may rest the whole weight of our salvation upon it. If men are totally depraved, that truth ought to be known and felt, that the whole salvation of the gospel may be sought and secured. Nothing therefore can be more unphilosophical than to charge that experimental religion and wild enthusiasm are synonymous terms.

If men dead in sin are ever to be restored to spiritual life, they must be the subjects of a mighty work of grace; they must be taught of God; they must be born from above; they must be called out of darkness into God's marvellous light; they must be renewed in the inner man.

The advantages of experience are felt in all the affairs of life. The truths we know by experience are worth more to a wise man than all he can learn from the demonstrative sciences or the reasonings of others. In all the departments of life, he who has experience has qualifications denied to the mere theorist or scholar. Religious experience puts us on our guard against the snares of the world, the flesh, and the devil. It teaches us modesty, self-distrust, and humility. It causes us to abound in all prudence. It gives us a delightful confirmation in the truth. It fits us for doing good to an extent far beyond what we could ever attain by instruction in the letter of God's word.

All the friends of true religion ought carefully to guard against the abuses of religious experience. They should be very careful to avoid all vain boasting, a sin into which men easily fall. They should learn wisely to discriminate between the genuine and the spurious, between effects produced by divine truth on the one hand and by nervous temperament on the other. They should be especially careful not to rely on any past attainments which do not produce present good fruit. Any exercise of the mind which leads us to dulness in devotion, to carelessness about holy living, to want of zeal for the salvation of men, is not gracious. It may be well here to state that there is nothing gained by substituting, as some seem disposed to do, the term *consciousness* for that of *experience*. There is no word better explained in religious literature than the word experience, and such a change of terms is likely to induce confusion.

## CHAPTER II.

### EARLY RELIGIOUS IMPRESSIONS.

The early exercises of a soul turning to God have unusual interest, because they are connected with the setting up of Christ's kingdom in the heart. The mind of man has a peculiar delight in contemplating the origin of things, and in seeing them rise to vigor. This is so in the growth of grain, plants, and trees, in the beginning of revolutions, in the founding of empires, and in the early struggles of mind to rise to worth and greatness. But the early history of religious impressions has vast interest, from the fact that it is the *soul* that is then saved and restored to communion with God. Cecil says, "The history of a man's life is to himself the most interesting history in the world, next to that of the Scriptures." The reason is that it is a detailed account of what he has learned in the school of experience.

#### AWAKENING.

The work of God for the recovery of the soul of man begins in what is fitly spoken of as an *awakening*. A revival of religion a century ago was often so called. It was a good name. It described an effect produced both on saints and sinners. The term seems to be scriptural. "It is high time to awake out of sleep." "Awake to righteousness, and sin not." "Awake thou that sleepest, and arise from the dead, and Christ shall give thee light." Rom. 13:11; 1 Cor. 15:34; Eph. 5:14. The peculiar fitness of this mode of speaking arises from the fact that the stupor of a sinful state is aptly compared to sleep. That sleep is guilty. It is also profound. It is like the sleep of death, from which none awake but by the power of God. Indulged a little longer, it will prove fatal. There is a time when every subject of divine grace is awaked from spiritual lethargy. This awakening is sometimes so gentle, that its commencement can hardly be fixed to any date. Again, it at once arouses the whole soul. It has often been noticed, that in some cases it is preceded by peculiar thoughtlessness, or even by outbreaking wickedness. But when God's time has come, he effectually arouses the soul, and makes his arrows sharp in the heart of the King's enemies. The means employed to this end are various.

God often puts great honor on the very words of Scripture. "The word of God is quick, and powerful, and sharper than any two-edged sword, piercing even to the dividing asunder of soul and spirit, and of the joints and marrow, and is a discerner of the thoughts and intents of the heart." Heb. 4:12. "The law of the Lord is perfect, converting the soul." Psa. 19:7. Sometimes the mere reading of God's word is blessed to this end; and if men could be prevailed on to examine and ponder its truths more than they do, they would oftener begin the search for a Saviour. Even of the darkest book of the New Testament it is said, "Blessed is he that readeth, and they that hear the words of this prophecy, and keep those things which are written therein." Rev. 1:3. Some writers of the seventeenth century notice the fact that God honored the phrase, "And he died," which occurs so often in the fifth chapter of Genesis, to the awakening of a great sinner. It is an interesting exercise in which little circles, composed of religious people, sometimes engage, to inquire what portion of God's word was thus first deeply impressed on the mind of each one.

The word of God preached is still more

frequently blessed to the same end. Thus many thousands were awakened on the day of Pentecost. Modern times give us instances of many hundreds impressed under one gospel sermon. The church of God still sings, "How beautiful are the feet of them that preach the gospel of peace, and bring glad tidings of good things." "Faith cometh by hearing, and hearing by the word of God." Rom. 10:15, 17.

Uninspired writings, which contain sound Bible principles and urge divine things on the attention with great tenderness and solemnity, are often greatly blessed to men's salvation. They awake them out of sleep, and bring into exercise all their faculties. It is therefore a good thing to circulate good books. The author has known five persons in one neighborhood brought to deep concern, and finally to a hope in Christ, by reading the first part of Doddridge's Rise and Progress of Religion in the Soul.

Sometimes God arouses men from their guilty slumbers by some startling providence or some awful judgment. The sudden death of some loved one starts in the mind of the survivor the question, Where should I now be, if I had been called so soon or with so little warning? "When thy judgments are in the earth, the inhabitants of the world will learn righteousness." Isa. 26:9. Personal affliction is sometimes sanctified to the same end. In a respectable Christian church, not long since, every official member was known to have been a thoughtless worldling until God's hand was laid heavily upon him. Many a child of God now says, "Before I was afflicted I went astray; but now have I kept thy word. It is good for me that I have been afflicted; that I might learn thy statutes." Psa. 119:67, 71. "In their affliction they will seek me early." Hos. 5:15. Manasseh went heedlessly and brutally on in a course of crime and cruelty until dreadful calamities overtook him. Then he "prayed, and God was entreated of him." 2 Chron. 33:13.

Sometimes a pious conversation, a kind and friendly admonition, a hint dropped in love, a word fitly spoken, has the same effect. A profane oath, an act of injustice, a debauch, or some other sin, has filled a man's soul with such horror that he has had no peace until he fled to Christ. To show his power, God may make any of our sins to flash condemnation in our face, thus fulfilling the scripture, "Thine own wickedness shall correct thee." Jer. 2:19.

A powerful means of arousing men to attend to their souls' affairs is the conversion of their fellows, and especially of notorious sinners. Our Lord himself speaks as though he regarded this as the loudest kind of call: "The publicans and the harlots believed John; and ye, when ye had seen it, repented not afterward, that ye might believe him." Matt. 21:32. When rightly considered, the conversion of a fellow-creature is well suited to call up the attention of every candidate for eternity.

Frequently, however, men can give no minute account of the causes or beginnings of their increased attention to religion. Nor is it necessary that they should. A man may not know the steps or causes of his recovery from sickness, and yet he may now be a well man. Often too there is at first nothing very clear in the state of mind of one who is beginning to turn to God. Nothing indeed so much interests him as the general subject of salvation. He sees its importance; he owns its necessity. The mind also often spends its chief thoughts for a season on one sin, or one point of truth, and this serves as a key to many others.

In this state of awakened interest, the course of thought pursued is as much in accordance with the laws of mind, and is in this sense as natural, as in any period of one's history; so that the man greatly wonders that he never before saw things on this wise. He greatly marvels, and well he may, that his mind could so long be utterly dead to the things of salvation. Although he may not yet be the subject of a *saving* change, yet the frame of his soul is very different from what it was. Never before was he in such a state, for he has now fairly entered upon a course of

### RELIGIOUS REFLECTION.

The power of reflection is that which chiefly distinguishes a man from a brute; and the habit of reflection, more than any thing else, distinguishes a wise man from a fool. He must be given over to folly who never looks at the remote bearings and consequences of his actions. Things may easily be done which can never be undone. The silliest may plunge himself into ruin. There is no wise man who is not considerate. The rash, light, heedless must expect in all weighty matters to go astray. Reflection is important in proportion to the gravity of the matter on which we are called to exercise it. As religion is the most important theme on which the human mind is ever fixed, so above all other topics human salvation calls for thought, care, reflection. True religion is as reasonable as it is necessary. To be pious without thoughtfulness is not possible. No one acts so wisely as he who counts the cost, looks well to his state, and entirely consecrates himself to God. In their most solemn appeals, the Scriptures address man as rational: "O that they would consider." "Thus saith the Lord of hosts, Consider your ways." "I speak as to wise men; judge ye what I say." Deut. 32:29; Hag. 1:7; 1 Cor. 10:15.

Every stage of serious reflection is liable to many interruptions. Yet where God has begun a work of grace in the soul, the mind will not fall into continued thoughtlessness. God will employ suitable means to keep the attention awake. Perhaps he will make the example of the righteous at once a reproof and an encouragement, and that of the wicked a warning and a cause of alarm to the soul ready to settle on its lees. The conduct of the worldly or profane is often held before the mind as a mirror, in which one sees reflected the wickedness of his own life. If God has not yet shown to the soul the beauty of holiness, he at least enables one to see that the truly pious possess many advantages, and awakens a desire to secure them. It is a point gained when one clearly perceives that the servant of God is the better man. So that in the midst of company and lawful employments one often finds his thoughts eagerly turned to everlasting things. This is proof that God has not abandoned him to the power of all evil. Under such circumstances the talkative man will be inclined to silence and seriousness. He will look at the past, think of the life he has led, recount God's mercies to him, review many parts of his conduct with pain, and say, If I had my life to live over again, I would not do as I have done. I am an unhappy man. My state is sinful. Possibly I may be nigh to a miserable death or an undone eternity. I cannot justify my present course of life. I am not fit to die. I am not holy. Sin is deeply rooted in my nature. Without a great change of character, I shall never be what I ought.

Looking at the future, he remembers that he must live for ever, that ere long death will summon him into the presence of his Maker, and that without a change in his character and prospects, he must pass from the solemnities of his lone interview with God to the retributions of an unblessed eternity. By this time he has probably become a habitual reader of the Bible and of other religious books. Although sinful shame has still much power over him, yet he thinks prayer useful and obligatory. A fit place of retirement, suitable words to be used, and more than all, a suitable frame of mind, seem to him to be wanting. It will be well for him if Satan does not prevail on him at first quite to restrain prayer. A young man under serious impressions once retired to his room, locked his door, closed the shutters, and was about to pray, when he thought some one might see him through the keyhole. He went to cover that, when a band of music began to play under his window. His attention was drawn off. He offered no prayer then. His seriousness left him. Let men be warned by such a case. Men must call upon God or perish. "Let sinners learn to pray." He who is effectually diverted from prayer, is hopelessly involved in guilt.

Led by God's Spirit, a soul thus awakened

and brought to reflection finds out much of the vanity of earthly things. His sense of their fleeting duration, and of their unsatisfying nature, is deep and strong. Once he called them the chief good. Now he sees that they are vain, empty, delusory. He sees that his pursuit of them has been both foolish and sinful. The merriment which once filled him with delight now grieves him to the heart.

By this time he begins to wonder what these things mean, and how they will terminate. Preaching has a strange effect on him. The words of truth have a peculiar pungency. He is surprised to find another exactly describing his thoughts and feelings. Sometimes he suspects that some one has informed the minister of Christ of his unhappy state. At times he feels a momentary anger that the secrets of his heart should be thus exposed; but a good conscience will show him that the fault is in himself.

Not unfrequently one in this state is beset with sceptical thoughts. They are a great annoyance to him; but his efforts to get rid of them are unsuccessful. They are the natural fruit of his corrupt and unbelieving heart. Nothing belongs more properly to an unregenerate state. He has wickedly cherished them for a long time. The habit of unbelief has grown inveterate.

The best means to be used for overcoming these infidel temptations will be hearty prayer and the simple reading of God's word. The gospel is its own witness. The word of God is life and spirit. Nothing so directly and forcibly attacks sin. Yet no means possess inherent and adequate efficacy. God alone can cast out this devil of uncleanness and scepticism. Hence the necessity of fervent prayer. If the Lord should leave one in this doleful state of unbelief, his destruction would be inevitable, but it would be just.

One who has been brought thus far may be sorely tempted to give up both the hope and the pursuit of salvation. Seeing himself very far short of what he ought to be, he fears that he may never become a Christian. Should such fears prevail, he will sink into the inertness of despondency. Yet if God purposes to grant him salvation, he will not allow him to consent to the tempter. A kindly influence in his heart will urge him to flee from the wrath to come. He will feel that he cannot turn back. Nor can he stand still. He is afraid of the avenger of blood. He has hope that he shall yet be in the city of refuge. Sometimes fears almost overwhelm him; but yet they are not allowed quite to prevail against him. This state of mind is followed by religious inquiry.

## CHAPTER III.

### EARLY RELIGIOUS IMPRESSIONS—CONTINUED.

### RELIGIOUS INQUIRY.

Religious inquiry naturally succeeds reflection. The three thousand converted on the day of Pentecost were all honest and earnest inquirers: "Men and brethren, what shall we do?" Acts 2 : 37. The same was true of Saul of Tarsus: "Lord, what wilt thou have me to do?" Acts 9 : 6. So also the jailer cried, "Sirs, what must I do to be saved?" Acts 16 : 30. It cannot be otherwise with the truly awakened. Any man in deep distress and ignorant of the true method of deliverance, will naturally and earnestly desire instruction. The truly anxious soul will cry to God for divine guidance: Teach me thy statutes; lead me in a plain path; let me not err from thy ways; my Father, be thou my guide. He will also search the Scriptures with a sincere desire to know their teachings. He will ask the pilgrims to Zion and the ministers of the gospel to show him the way to the hill of the

Lord. Sometimes he finds poor counsellors, who but perplex or mislead him. But the best directions that can be given him are either not understood or not followed, until he is led by the Spirit of all truth. I have known an intelligent man to send seven hundred miles for a printed sermon which had been useful to one of his friends, in the hope that it might show him also the way of life.

The chief ingredient of this inquiry, when it is likely to result in saving good, is its sincerity. The young ruler asked our Lord a very weighty question and in a very earnest manner; but as soon as he got the full answer, he went away exceeding sorrowful. Saul of Tarsus cried, "Lord, what wilt thou have me to do?" As soon as he received the answer, he obeyed the voice of Christ. There is no substitute for genuine sincerity. The lack of it spoils every thing.

True, hearty inquiry is soon followed by

### GOOD RESOLUTIONS.

Within the present century some have taught that a change of the governing purpose was the great essential of salvation. The practical result on many was a belief that if they resolved to be Christians, they were

Christians. This greatly damaged the cause of Christ and injured men's souls. In opposing it, perhaps some went to the opposite extreme. It is not consistent with the laws of the human mind to undertake and execute any great work without a purpose of heart so to do. Accordingly he whose case we are considering, resolves to forsake some known or open sins, to avoid profane language, company, and practices, or to perform certain known duties. But he now learns how difficult it is for him, who is accustomed to do evil, to learn to do well. The usefulness of forming resolutions depends very much on the state of heart accompanying them. When made in a spirit of self-righteousness, or under a vain persuasion that we may thus commend ourselves to God, they are of no use. Purposes formed in a spirit of self-dependence vanish before temptation as walls of snow melt away before a vernal sun. Resolutions formed in gross ignorance, in thoughtlessness, or in vainglory, profit not. We should never resolve to do an impossibility. Yet no man amends his ways without forming a purpose to that effect. A sound mind first lays its plan, and then executes it. Only madmen live without method.

The prodigal's return to duty and the home of his youth was preceded by the resolution, "I will arise and go to my father." The resolutions of the elder President Edwards doubtless exerted a happy influence on his subsequent life. They are remarkable for sobriety. John Caspar Christian Lavater, an eminent servant of Christ, died at Zurich in Switzerland, A. D. 1799. He has left some sober and practical resolutions, which are but little known. They are:

"I will never, either in the morning or evening, proceed to any business, until I have first retired, at least for a few moments, to a private place, and implored God for his assistance and blessing.

"I will neither do nor undertake any thing which I would abstain from doing if Jesus Christ were standing visibly before me, nor any of which I think it possible that I shall repent in the uncertain hour of my certain death. I will, with the divine aid, accustom myself to do every thing without exception in the name of Jesus Christ, and as his disciple I will sigh to God continually for the Holy Ghost to preserve myself in a constant disposition for prayer.

"Every day shall be distinguished by at least one particular work of love.

"Every day I will be especially attentive to promote the benefit and advantage of my own family in particular.

"I will never eat or drink so much as shall occasion to me the least inconvenience or hinderance in my business. Wherever I go, I will first pray to God that I may commit no sin there, but be the cause of some good.

"I will never lie down to sleep without praying, nor, when I am in health, sleep longer than eight hours at most.

"I will every evening examine my conduct through the day by these rules, and faithfully note down in my journal how often I offend against them."

The Scriptures tell us of many who formed solemn resolutions. Joshua said, "As for me and my house, we will serve the Lord." The Psalms abound with solemn purposes: "I will love thee, O Lord, my strength;" "I will call upon the Lord, who is worthy to be praised;" "I said, I will take heed to my ways, that I sin not with my tongue;" "I will hope continually, and will yet praise thee more and more;" "I will remember thy wonders of old. I will meditate also of all thy work, and talk of thy doings;" "I will call upon him as long as I live;" "I will keep thy statutes." If you form resolutions, there can be no valid objection against writing them down. If formed, they should be intelligible, humble, well weighed, well understood, practicable, and adopted with caution, prayer, and deep solemnity. When a resolution is made, it should be kept. "Vow and pay unto the Lord." He hath "no pleasure in fools."

But a soul, in its first drawings towards divine things, finds it easier to resolve than to execute. Its resolutions seem in a great measure to fail. One washes himself in snow-water, but God plunges him in the ditch, and his own clothes abhor him. He finds that an external remedy will not cure an internal disease. Under the pungent preaching of the truth, his sins appear fearfully numerous and heinous. He loses the boasting spirit of self-exaltation which he once had. His eye gives way when you speak to him of serious matters.

Even with his kindred, his chief thoughts relate to salvation. If any of them are pious, he will seek an opportunity to disclose his state of mind. If they are ungodly, he will be pained by their wickedness. His thoughts on the lessons of piety taught him by his parents deeply affect him. If any of his friends have died in faith, he thinks of their example, and would fain follow their footsteps.

Meanwhile the world recedes from his view, and his prospects for the future seem to be under an eclipse. Once all seemed gay and dazzling before him; but now the things of time are growing less and less. As the coast of his native land fades from the view of the mariner going out to sea, so the scenes, the business, the attractions of earth are one by one lost to the view of a soul under the growing influence of divine truth. Such a process awakens feelings of sadness and desolation. By night, on his bed, he is restless and uncomfortable. His sleep is neither sound nor refreshing. Sometimes he is afraid to go to sleep, lest he should not awake in this world. He is troubled in visions of the night. And when he awakes, his heart is still heavy. The subjects of sin and salvation still press upon him and hold his attention. At night he wishes it were morning, and in the morning he wishes it were night.

Sometimes he is suddenly surprised into

sin, and finds that all his hopes of being already beyond the reach of evil are vain. He is amazed at his own weakness and inability to resist temptations. He mends his wall and daubs it with untempered mortar as before, and the Lord again rends it, and makes his soul sick at its own follies. But it is almost impossible to cure him of the belief that he can yet do something to purpose.

In this state of mind he wishes the pious would converse with him on his soul's affairs, and yet he has a dread of such a thing. He is willing to be instructed, and yet he is reluctant to walk in the way when he knows it. Sometimes he thinks he would give any thing for a new heart, and yet he will not make a full surrender. He would like to wear the linen white and clean, but he will not cast away the filthy rags of his own righteousness. In fine, his mind seems to be in a very contradictory state. He seems greatly humbled, but he will not take upon him Christ's yoke. He seems much inclined to the service of God, and yet he is led captive by sin.

If any ask what will be the result of all these thoughts and exercises, the answer is that they will either lead to peace with God, or to deeper guilt than ever before rested on the soul. These thoughts will either lead the soul to Christ, or they will leave it oppressed with unutterable criminality. He who thus feels will soon be a child of God, or twofold more the child of evil than ever. He will soon have a broken heart, or a heart fearfully hardened; a will sweetly submissive to God, or fearfully perverse and obstinate. Such influences as he is now under cannot be felt and the soul remain unaffected. They will produce vast good or prodigious evil.

Nor can any thing but great wickedness prevent a sound and speedy conversion to God. Self-murder, self-murder will be the awful sound that will ring for ever in the ears of such as are moved in the manner described, and yet shall die impenitent. "O Israel, thou hast destroyed thyself; but in me is thy help."

It is always safe and scriptural to urge persons thus exercised to make direct and immediate application to the Saviour. Let them come, though blind and naked, vile and guilty, helpless and miserable. Let none wait in an idle expectation that the terms of salvation will be altered. God draws all his true people, but he will drag none to heaven contrary to their wills. The promise is, "My people shall be willing in the day of my power." The invitations of the gospel are to the needy, the wretched, the lost. But let no man who is still in his sins suppose that he is willing to come to Christ, and that Christ is not willing to receive him. The reverse is the truth.

Let not persons thus concerned about eternal things be scared away from the whole matter of piety if they find their own hearts desperately wicked. Every man's heart has always been more wicked than he ever thought it to be. He who will not permit his wounds to be probed, must expect to die. Henry Martyn tells us that when awakened to divine things, he refused to read Doddridge's Rise and Progress of Religion, because he found the first part of it so humiliating. A discovery of one's sinfulness will not make him sinful, but it may lead to salvation.

Let all beginning a religious life expect sore trials. Satan is always most busy with those who are struggling to escape from his dominion. Men see their own want of heart, and Satan would persuade them that all religion is hypocrisy.

It is to be regretted that persons who

are seeking salvation should be brought too much into public notice. It is to be feared that many talk away their religious impressions, or allow others to do it. It is when one "sitteth alone and keepeth silence" that he is likely to "put his mouth in the dust; if so be there may be hope." Lam. 3 : 28, 29. In the twelfth chapter of his prophecy, verses 9–14, Zechariah describes the effect of a general outpouring of God's Spirit as inclining all classes to weep *alone*.

Let inquirers after salvation beware of bad company. "If sinners entice thee, consent thou not." "The companion of fools shall be destroyed." Even in good company there may be excess. But all bad company is dangerous. To avoid all commerce with the wicked is neither obligatory nor practicable. But between civil intercourse and companionship there is a wide difference.

It would be a great thing if those who are not Christians could be led to entertain some just sense of the evil of sin. Oh that the wicked knew the import of those words of Francis Spira: "Man knows the beginning of sin, but who bounds the issues thereof?" It is easy to do mischief, but who can undo it? To sin is natural; but to escape from it requires atoning blood, and the supernatural agency of God's Spirit.

It is always a duty to urge men to immediate faith and repentance. "Behold, now is the accepted time; behold, now is the day of salvation." Call on men to do with their might whatever their hands find to do. In his lives of great men, Plutarch says of Hannibal, that when he could have taken Rome, he would not; and when he would have taken Rome, he could not. It is true of many, that when they can secure a title to God's favor, they will not; and when they wish to do it, they cannot because they have misspent all their days of grace.

## CHAPTER IV.

### FURTHER STRIVINGS OF THE SPIRIT.

Some account has been given, of a soul beginning to shake off its guilty slumbers, and to turn its thoughts to the unspeakable concerns of sin and duty, immortality and glory, salvation and perdition. One who has had the exercises of mind thus described is certainly under the teachings of the Holy Spirit. Yet he may have many such thoughts and emotions without knowing their origin or Author. In giving this history of the mind's operations and discoveries, it is proper to state that ere this a suspicion, if not a conviction, that God's Spirit is now at work in the heart, takes possession of the mind. Nor is this without foundation. The fact is, that none but the Holy Ghost could have brought about this great change of views and purposes. It is not easy to tell what a solemn awe fills the mind when first a man is persuaded that he is the subject of supernatural and divine influences. The soul, like the patriarch, says, "Surely God is in this place, and I knew it not." Such a view hushes the soul into stillness. It remembers God and is troubled. He who feels thus is inclined to silence, lest he should do something wrong, and is afraid lest he should be deceived, or lest by thoughtlessness he should grieve the Spirit far from him, and relapse into former carelessness and iniquity. In this state of mind he will cry, "Cast me not away from thy presence, and take not thy Holy Spirit from me. Uphold me with thy free Spirit." He will now give a decided preference to pious company. He looks on the children of God as the excellent of the earth. Yet intercourse with them deepens discoveries of sinfulness in his own heart. When they speak of joys, he longs for the same. He feels as if he had nothing whereof to rejoice. The review of his past life affords him no pleasure. It is all a dark, unillumined retrospect. It is gloomy, like the shades of death. He sees how vain and empty has been every thing which he once called happiness. He has now found out that the world is a cheat. His impression is that true religion would make him a happy man, and he is right. Sometimes his expectation of a speedy change becomes strong. He hopes he shall soon be a

Christian. He has an inextinguishable thirst for something which he has never had. To keep him from despair, a little light sometimes beams upon his path.

Then again, all his hopes of deliverance seem to forsake him. His affections seem to grow cold. Even his desires for any thing good appear to be languid. He is a mystery to himself. He exceedingly doubts whether he shall ever be a child of God. Thus hope and fear alternate. He is restless and unhappy. He deeply regrets that he did not long since become a Christian, when his heart was less depraved and his will less stubborn. It cuts him to the heart to remember that all this sorrow over time misspent and opportunities lost is unavailing. He fears lest his present call should pass away unimproved. Nor are his apprehensions wholly without foundation, for notwithstanding all his efforts, his sins hang over him in all their guilt, number, and aggravations. Nay, they seem to be multiplied and magnified. The mote has become a beam, the molehill a mountain, the rivulet a torrent. These things incline him to solitude, and he goes mourning all the day. He has no heart for the mirth of the wicked, for he sees something of the evil of sin. He is not a partaker of the joys of the righteous, and therefore he feels not as if between him and them there was any warm or close fellowship. Go where he may, he feels wretched and self-condemned. He wonders that God has not long since destroyed him. He marvels that he does not now cut him down. Yet he hopes that this drawing of the Spirit is a token for good. He knows that his case is hopeless only when God totally and finally abandons him to the power of his sins and to the guilt of his iniquities. Thus every motion of the Spirit in his heart is an argument against despair.

Should his wicked companions discover or even suspect his state of mind, some of them will shun him, others will be alarmed, and yet others will scoff at him. These will raise the old cry, "Wilt thou also be his disciple?" Some will ask him if he is willing to give up all his pleasures; others will seek to allure him into forbidden paths; others will say, He is beside himself. But if God intends to bring him to a settled and renewed state, these things will deepen his distress and his views of the state of sin and misery into which he is plunged.

At the commencement of his seriousness he had many crude opinions. Perhaps he thought he never would become a member of the church, but that he would be religious in a private way. Now he wishes that he was fit to be numbered among God's people. Or he once thought that if any great change ever came over him, it must be either very suddenly or very gradually. Now he would be happy to be converted in any way that the Lord might choose. He now probably supposes his failure is owing to the want of more system in his plan of proceeding; and so he adopts a rule for reading so much every day, or he determines to pray with more frequency, or with more outward signs of humiliation. But all proves unsatisfactory: he finds he can no more chain his thoughts than he can bind the wind; that he can no more bend his will than he can grasp the sun; that he can no more repent or believe than do the most impossible thing, if he is wholly left to his own energies. He is now experiencing what Paul felt: "I was alive without the law once; but when the commandment came, sin revived, and I died. And the commandment which was ordained to life, I found to be unto death. For sin, taking occasion by the commandment, deceived me, and by it slew me." Rom. 7:9–11. The law, like a lamp brought into a dark and filthy room, has disclosed the wretched state of the soul. What the law requires is found to be wanting. What it forbids is seen to be present. Sin begins to be regarded as sinful. It alarmingly abounds. One thus distressed, feeling the bitterness in his own soul, is almost sure that others must know his sad state. He wonders that Christians do not speak to him of his spiritual interests. He says, "No man careth for my soul." Like the prodigal, he is ready to perish, and no man gives unto him. He is amazed that some professors should be so absorbed with trifles and vanities of earth, while things of eternal moment press on his mind with such weight.

Should he fall in with a bigoted sectarian, more intent on making a proselyte to a party than on saving a soul from death, he may for a while be perplexed; but unless God should forsake him, he will not in the end be much influenced by him. The necessities of a soul thus pressed with guilt are too urgent to permit it to be absorbed with forms and names and pomps and shadows. The fiery sectary will soon be shunned. He was asked for bread, and he gave a stone. He was asked for a fish, and he gave a serpent. A poor soul, like the hunted hart on the mountain, is thirsting for living waters, and cares not for the strifes of words and the disputes of proud reasoners. He who is dying of thirst wants water, and nothing else. It is a glorious sight when God's Spirit triumphs over the efforts of bigotry and formalism and fanaticism, and brings a soul safely through their enticements.

One thing is now apparent: it is that God's word is no longer a dead letter. It has power and pungency. There is a disposition to apply the truth. Texts which once exerted no power over the mind have a keen edge. It seems to this man strange that he should not long since have yielded to the force of considerations which now have so vast an influence over him. Preaching has great point. Indeed, it seems to him that sermons are laying open the secrets of his heart. Sometimes he suspects ministers of indulging in personalities, when they know nothing of his sore distress.

He will now seek any book that he hears of as suited to his state of mind. But if it is sound and discriminating, while it enlightens it also distresses him. He wishes he could be exempt from worldly cares, that he might give undivided attention to more important concerns. When he hears of others obtaining a joyful hope in Christ, he is tempted to have hard thoughts of God because he finds no relief. But if God intends to bring him to a saving experience, he will show him the wickedness of all such charges against his Maker and his Sovereign. "Be still, and know that I am God." "The Lord is greatly to be feared."

He now finds himself involved in doubt and darkness. He knows nothing as he ought to know it. He longs for a guide, yet through unbelief rejects the only infallible teacher. He says, I am brought into darkness, and not into light; I look for light, but there is none; I feel after God, but I cannot find him. He asks the watchman to direct him, but he is still lost and bewildered. He finds that his case is wholly unmanageable by human skill and efforts. His heart, which until lately he regarded as good, he finds to be hard, corrupt, and stubborn. The cry of the Shunamite's child was, "My head, my head!" but the lament of this man is, "My heart, my heart!"

He finds it so unfeeling that he readily joins with the poet, and says,

"Of feeling all things show some sign,
But this rebellious heart of mine."
"My heart, how very hard it is,
How heavy here it lies;
Heavy and cold within my breast,
Just like a rock of ice."

To remove this hardness, he will bring before his mind images and denunciations of God's displeasure against the wicked. But it "shakes not at the wrath and terrors of a God." When he would melt it by tender reflections on God's love, he finds it still full of revolt; and even the scenes of Calvary often make it the more stout and defiant.

A sense of personal vileness may be strong and painful, and he may cry, "Create in me a clean heart, O God, and renew a right spirit within me." Yet oftentimes this prayer seems to have no heart in it. He does indeed long for purity of nature; but perhaps it is only that he may have something whereof to boast before God, or some righteousness of his own—to come before God with a price in his hand.

The author of these new views and emotions is the Spirit of God. These are the strivings of Him who was promised to convince the world of sin, of righteousness, and of judgment. He is now calling the soul to forsake sin and turn to God. The fears which torment his soul are the natural result of recent discoveries of God's amazing mercy and holiness, justice and power, which have all been slighted and contemned. Though no terrors will change the heart, yet they may be useful in driving the soul out of itself and away from its false refuges. He who is thus exercised ought to know that the kingdom of God is come nigh unto him; that now is his time to turn and live, while the Spirit strives. Should he withdraw, all is lost. Without his influences, we can no more move heavenward than we can sail a ship without wind.

That God's Spirit may call men to repentance, and be resisted, and take his final departure, is clear. The Scriptures say, "My Spirit shall not always strive with man." Gen. 6:3. "Ephraim is joined to idols; let him alone." Hos. 4:17. The word of God also gives us cases in which men have been greatly affected by divine things, and have had awful and pungent distress, and yet have drawn back to perdition. In the Old Testament, Saul and Ahab, in the New, Herod, Simon Magus, Felix, and Agrippa, are illustrations of the fearful abandonment of God. Men thus left to their own corruptions will inevitably perish. They will work out their own damnation with greediness. One of the greatest points of danger is found in the fact that a man may grieve away the Spirit without any fixed purpose of bringing his soul into such guilt. Obstinate resistance, continued unbelief, and refusal to obey the call when given, are often all that is necessary to quench the heavenly fire within us, and consign us to the coldness of death.

Hardly any thing is more offensive to God than an all-absorbing engagedness in worldly pursuits. This often causes the Spirit of God to forsake a man and leave him to the power of evil. "If any man love the world, the love of the Father is not in him." "They that will be rich fall into temptation and a snare, and into many foolish and hurtful lusts, which drown men in destruction and perdition." 1 John 2 : 15, and 1 Tim. 6 : 9. If a man prefers the present to the future, earth to heaven, riches that perish to riches which endure to eternal life, he offers an insult to God of so aggravated a nature as itself to justify God in leaving him to himself for ever.

Others indulge in a dangerous levity of mind. They are too frivolous to take hold of eternal things with any earnestness. To them solemnity is torment. They might be religious, if they might retain a light and trifling state of mind. But they regard the heavy demands made on their sobriety as enormous and unreasonable. So they lose their souls in a laugh. They jest and make a mock of awful things. They trifle with Scripture. Even their prayers do not partake of any profound awe.

Some men perish through a wild conceit, a fancy of their own, a whim that they will not surrender. On no subject are men so full of crotchets and quibbles as on religion. They sport themselves with their own deceivings. They are often better pleased with a phantom than with a reality. Error is sweeter than truth to the carnal mind. If men will prefer any thing to God's word, they must go down to death.

The angry passions, envy, hatred, malice, spitefulness, resentment, are all exceedingly offensive to God's Spirit. Pride and fretfulness are no less his abhorrence. He who hates his brother is a murderer. He who will not forgive shall not be forgiven. The only visible shape in which the Holy Ghost ever descended was that of a dove; and a dove is the very emblem of peace and gentleness, and flies from strife and noise and war. Therefore Paul says, "Grieve not the Holy Spirit of God;" and adds, "Let all bitterness, and wrath, and anger, and clamor, and evil-speaking be put away from you, with all malice; and be ye kind one to another, tender-hearted, forgiving one another, even as God, for Christ's sake, hath forgiven you." Eph. 4:30–32.

Too much company, and even too much attention to the public means of grace, may be unfriendly to the continued presence and power of God's Spirit in the heart. He loves to allure the soul, and bring her into the wilderness. In solitude the Spirit often pours his clearest light into the mind. It has been observed that meetings long protracted often exhaust the energies of the mind, and leave it in a state of apparent callousness. Bad company must of course be avoided. It has destroyed many. It ruined Herod. For his oath's sake, and for the sake of them that sat at meat with him, he took the life of the very man whose ministry had so deeply impressed him.

Sins of the appetite, such as gluttony and drunkenness, though they be not carried to the greatest lengths, have a brutalizing and hardening effect on the mind. All sensuality is followed by like consequences. He whose god is his belly cannot choose the God of heaven for his portion. He who is given to the bottle may have redness of eyes, but cannot have a penitent spirit. A devotion to the carnal is closely allied to the pursuit of the devilish. The sensual easily break all their good resolutions. They pamper the flesh. They grieve the Spirit. They yield to temptation, and are soon plunged into many dreadful sins.

It is to be feared that some allow their religious impressions to run too much in the way of sentimentalism. It is possible for men to weep away all their convictions. It is natural for distress to pass away in floods of tears. The Spirit strives not merely to induce men to shed some tears, but to lead them to forsake sin and turn to God. Till this result is gained, nothing is effectually accomplished. To come short of this, is to resist Him who calls us to a new life, to new hopes, to salvation.

Others harden themselves in sin by refusing the means of grace. They will not read and study God's word; they will not pray; they avoid religious conversation; they conceal the state of their minds; they are careless or irregular hearers of the gospel; above all, they refuse to practise what they already know, and so they make no progress. They do nothing except as they are moved by fears or remorse. They seem quite inclined to religion when pangs are upon them. They cry, and even roar under the terrors of God; but they never frame their doings to please him. If God leave such to utter hardness, it will be no wonder.

Sometimes men seal their doom by resolving to give their chief attention to outward things and external reformations, neglecting the religion of the heart. Some years ago a wicked man, in great distress about his soul, said, "I have made up my mind to amend my speech, and afterwards to attend to my heart." It was the signal of his ruin. His seriousness forsook him. He lived several years a hardened, foul-mouthed man, and then died a violent death. The Scripture rule is, first make the tree good, and then the fruit shall be good; purify the fountain, and the stream shall be sweet. He whose main desire is to cleanse the outside of the platter, even if he were successful, might yet die without hope.

Continued unbelief and impenitence, under any conceivable circumstances, may and must cause us to be given over to blindness of mind and hardness of heart. Many whose morals were blameless, who fully intended to lead a religious life but never did, who shed many tears and bore many terrors, have at last uttered the cry, "The harvest is past, the summer is ended, and I am not saved." He who called them suddenly forsook them. Wicked men are often surprised at finding themselves deserted by their serious thoughts, and unmoved by any tender impressions.

Against an issue so fatal there is no protection till one casts himself at the feet of Jesus. The longer this is deferred, the worse will be the sinner's state and the more imminent his peril. Already sin, like a gangrene, has spread its roots into every vital part. Unless there is a sovereign remedy, all is lost. Unless that remedy be applied, it were as well for him that it had never been provided. Whoever is the subject of divine influences is in a fearfully critical state. To use a figure understood by all, he has come to the forks of the road. The right way is narrow, steep, and difficult, but it leads to God and glory. The other leads to death.

Nor does any man know whether a soul once forsaken of God will ever be called again. Thousands have succeeded in stifling convictions and shaking off impressions, which proved to be the last effects of the Spirit's strivings. There is no more fearful state than that of a soul meditating the rejection—for what proves to be the last time—of the blessed Spirit of God.

As God has no other Son to give for our salvation if we reject the Lord Jesus, so he has no other Spirit to send into our hearts and call us to repentance if we reject the Holy Ghost. And if any man fails to secure illumination, regeneration, and sanctification by this divine Agent, those mercies will never be his. Every good thought, every right affection, and every holy desire come from him alone. A ship may have ten thousand yards of sail spread out, but that will never carry her into port unless the wind blows.

Let none forget that the Spirit of God is most loving and merciful. This is proven by all Scripture and by all the Spirit's work.

None is more kind, none is more gentle. A young lad had been resisting the calls of mercy. At last he opened the door and admitted the heavenly Stranger. His soul was so overcome with a sense of his vileness in so long resisting such mercy, that he said nothing had ever seemed to him so wicked, so ungrateful. He was right.

Urge all inquirers to make immediate submission to Christ, immediate application to the Saviour for mercy. Many years ago, a young man in distress for his soul revealed the state of his mind to an eminent minister, and then said, "If I should die to-night, do you think I should be saved?" The minister replied, "I have no sufficient reason for supposing that you love Christ; and if you do not, then you cannot be saved." "Then," said the young man, "I will sleep no more this night;" and he went out and spent the whole night in prayer. As the day began to break, he returned to the house where the minister was, rejoicing in hope of the glory of God, and saying, "I have found Christ precious to my soul." Oh that all men were in good earnest in seeking their own salvation.

# CHAPTER V.

## A SENSE OF WRETCHEDNESS.

A WRITER who flourished more than a thousand years ago reckons up two hundred and eighty-eight opinions of the ancients respecting the way of happiness. The fact is that man's want of happiness results from the most powerful causes—causes not capable of being removed but by an almighty Friend. So long as man and society remain in themselves what they are, more or less misery is inevitable. For wise purposes God denies us any cup of pure, unmixed pleasure in this life. Every generation endures a vast amount of misery. Poverty, disease, bereavements, commotions, make many sigh. Many, like Job, are weary of life. Yet mere suffering, without the grace of God, is unprofitable. One of the most painful thoughts connected with a sight of the woes of many is, that present sorrows are but preludes to those which shall be eternal. Most men mourn their want of health, wealth, honor, or success. How few deplore their unconverted state and their multiplied offences. But here and there one seeks deliverance from sin, which ought to be felt as the most grievous of all burdens. Indeed, how few have any deep, settled conviction of their own vileness. While this is so, they will not cry for mercy.

But now and then we find an exception. At first, indeed, the oppression of the spirit may not be great; but he who has just views of the nature of sin, will hardly stop short of great carefulness in seeking salvation. A slight view of ill-desert, united with a conviction of personal depravity, may awaken the first uneasiness. But divine grace has a tendency to develop clear views of spiritua things; and he who begins with very indistinct views, will find out by degrees great wonders in himself. At such a time a man easily discovers also that this world is a very unsubstantial good. It is not a saving, but to one rightly affected it is a profitable lesson, that all in this world is vanity of vanities. Men may indeed see the emptiness of earth, and sink into despair; but men wholly satisfied with this world will hardly seek a better country.

Right views of one's real character and

standing in God's sight as a sinner must be more or less painful and mortifying. So God says of Ephraim, "I have surely heard Ephraim bemoaning himself thus: Thou hast chastised me, and I was chastised as a bullock unaccustomed to the yoke: turn thou me, and I shall be turned." Jer. 31:18. This bemoaning one's self is the same state of mind elsewhere described in God's word as a weariness, an oppression of the soul. God often subjects those whom he would save to a training and discipline none the less salutary because very grievous. They are made to smart for their follies. They are sensible that they are out of the right way. They are disconsolate, and have no comforter. Things which lately attracted them are stripped of their bewitching splendor, and the heart is emptied of all that once charmed it. Such will soon be found writing bitter things against themselves. Every one thus exercised will say, "I am more brutish than any man, and have not the understanding of a man. I neither learned wisdom, nor have the knowledge of the holy." Prov. 30:2, 3. A sense of his own weakness and blindness takes possession of him. He is not hard to be persuaded that others know more than himself. He has learned that so many of his views are erroneous, that he has lost confidence in his judgments of religious matters. Such a discovery is to him of the highest importance. Had he remained in his former self-ignorance, he would have utterly perished in his own corruptions.

Such things are attended with a perception of his vileness and unworthiness, and like some of old, he arises in his heaviness and falls on his knees, and spreads out his hands unto the Lord, and says, "O my God, I am ashamed, and blush to lift up my face to thee; for mine iniquities are increased over my head, and my trespass is grown up unto the heavens." Ezra 9 : 5, 6. Or he feels as David once did: "Innumerable evils have compassed me about: mine iniquities have taken hold upon me, so that I am not able to look up; they are more than the hairs of my head: therefore my heart faileth me." Psa. 40 : 12. The number of his sins is so great, that he sees it is quite beyond his power either to subdue them or wash them away. Nor is he mistaken. Unless God undertakes for him, his undoing is everlasting. Like the publican, he stands afar off, and does not so much as lift his eyes to heaven, but smites on his breast, and says, God be merciful to me a sinner.

Nor is it only the number of his sins, but also the evil nature of sin itself, that deeply affects him. He now sees that sin is a horrible evil, a deadly poison, a desperate malignity, an incurable wound, a foul leprosy. In this state he will be sensible of his want of proper feelings towards God. His efforts to work himself up to a proper regard for his Maker are entire failures. His heart refuses to do any thing which his conscience declares obligatory. He finds his affections all disordered. He can love his friends, his family, his country; but he is amazed to find that he cannot love God. His heart is an iceberg for coldness, an adamant for hardness, a cage of unclean birds for vileness. Sometimes his affections seem somewhat enkindled, but they do not go forth to his satisfaction. When he weeps, it is soon over. His tears seem not to flow from a penitent spirit.

Frequently his external circumstances perplex him. Every thing goes wrong. His attention is distracted by various calls. Every thing seems to conspire against him. To release himself is impossible. To obtain help from God is his wish, but he knows not how to find him. In reading the Scriptures he finds difficulties. Some things are hard to be understood. Others, though plain, are in his view stern and severe. Against some his heart stoutly rebels. Although this alarms him, yet his efforts at repressing such wicked thoughts are quite unsuccessful. Things forbidden in God's law he lusts after. For many things sinful he finds in himself a longing, which seems to himself both strange and unnatural. Divine prohibitions seem only to inflame his unholy desires. Things commanded he has no heart for. The more he tries to control his desires, the more they torment him. The law commands; but his nature, in spite of him, leads him into disobedience. Temptations are strong, and he is weak. He is a helpless captive. All his efforts are in vain. His prayers seem to him a mockery. His strength is weakness.

Now his soul is "like the troubled sea, when it cannot rest, whose waters cast up mire and dirt." He has no might to do good. He cannot still the agitations of his own bosom. To peace he is a stranger. He remembers God, and is troubled. He has no access to the Father of spirits. He says, "Oh that I knew where I might find him; I would come nigh to his seat; I would order my cause before him; I would fill my mouth with arguments." He pleads for mercy and pity. His moisture is turned into the drought of summer. His bones wax old through his roaring all the day long. Day and night God's hand is heavy upon him. He forgets to take bread. His appetite fails him. His sleep is short and disturbed. God holds his eyes waking. At midnight he is sometimes heard sighing, or found weeping. Or "dry sorrow is drinking up his blood." His spirits and energies begin to fail. He mourns sore like the dove, and chatters like the swallow. He greatly fears that he is about to perish in his sins. In real distress he says, What shall I do? What shall I do to be saved?

> "I die with hunger here, he cries;
> I starve in foreign lands."

It seems to him that none pities his case, and that God has forgotten to be gracious. Yet he chides himself for such unbelief. His impression is that his own heart defers the relief he needs.

"Oh, who can tell what days, what nights he spends
Of tideless, waveless, sailless, shoreless woe!
When thus he lies,
Forlorn of heart, withered and desolate
As leaf of autumn, which the wolfish winds
Selecting from its falling sisters, chase
Far from its native grove, to lifeless wastes,
And leave it there alone, to be forgotten eternally."

To one in this sad state the cheerfulness of God's people but brings increase of wretchedness. And the thoughtlessness of the wicked but reminds him of the heathenish or brutish character of his former life. To exhort him to embrace the offered grace of God but dejects him. He says,

"The promise meets my eye,
But does not reach my case."

Sometimes it seems to him that he must give up all as lost for ever; but something holds him back from utter despair. He is led and upheld by an invisible hand. One, of whom he has yet no saving knowledge, is dealing with his soul, and will not let him go. Yet he sees no use in all his pains and efforts, for every struggle seems to sink him the deeper in sin and misery. He wishes his load of sin were gone, but it presses harder and harder. He is weary of his way, weary of heartless efforts, weary of his own want of stability, weary of his burdens, and sometimes almost weary of existence.

Now if any one is in such a case as this, let him turn his longing eyes to the Lamb of God, who taketh away the sin of the world. Let him look to Jesus, the author and finisher of faith, the author of eternal redemption, the only physician who can do a sinner good. Let sinners come to him. Come and welcome, ye perishing. Hospitals are *designed* for the sick, the lame, the mangled, the homeless. Water is for the thirsty, bread for the hungry, and a couch for the weary. Jesus Christ is the very Saviour man needs, and he is exactly suited to our wants. He is chosen of God, and precious. He was set forth to be the propitiation for our sins. He is the one Mediator between God and man. To him all the condemned and dying should resort. His mission into this world was that he might seek and save that which was lost. To that end he lived; to that end he died; to that end he rose again; to that end he intercedes above; to that end he sends the Spirit of all grace to convince the world of sin, of righteousness, and of judgment. Should the Lord Jesus fail to save sinners, he would lose his reward; his sufferings would be without fruit; nothing would be left him but the shame, the spitting, the cross, the spear, the crown of thorns, and the total failure of the hope that was set before him, when he endured the cross, despising the shame.

### WHAT IS IT TO COME TO CHRIST?

What is faith in him? How does one feel when he lays hold of the Saviour?

"Justifying faith is a saving grace wrought in the heart of a sinner by the Spirit and word of God, whereby he, being convinced of his sin and misery, and of the disability in himself and all other creatures to recover him out of his lost condition, not only assenteth to the truth of the promise of the gospel, but receiveth and resteth upon Christ and his righteousness, therein held forth, for pardon of sin and for the accepting and accounting of his person righteous in the sight of God for salvation."

As a definition, this is full and clear. True saving faith receives Christ, and rests on him to the exclusion of all other ground of confidence in the matter of salvation.

It may aid some minds to have this truth illustrated by several figures drawn from Scripture.

A soul under a sense of its lost condition may be compared to the dove which Noah sent out of the ark. It feels itself unhoused, unsheltered, unsupported. It wanders up and down, sometimes thinking it sees before it a spot where it may rest, but on trial its expectations are disappointed. At length, wearied almost beyond endurance, its false hopes all disappointed, its energies enfeebled, its spirit humbled, it resolves on seeking the ark. It seeks and finds it; and to its great joy the spiritual Noah puts forth his hand and takes it in. Then for weariness it finds rest, for a waste of troubled waters a sure abode, and for howling tempests settled quiet.

Or suppose one out in a vast desert. He sees a little cloud rising. At first it gives him no apprehensions. But it continues to spread and to blacken. It mutters heavy thunders; it shoots out its forked lightnings; it seems exceedingly angry, and wraps up every thing in gloom. Every minute makes it more and more manifest that exposure to its peltings will be distressing and dangerous. The weary traveller looks around for shelter. Sometimes he thinks he descries a place of protection. He tries it, but finds it will answer no good purpose. He tries another and another; but they are all insufficient. Meanwhile his apprehensions of danger increase. The storm seems ready to rend every thing in its fury. Now his eye is directed to a shelter that is near him. It seems inviting. It is capacious. In it is room for all that will come. It is not hedged about nor barred. Jesus says, "Behold, I have set before thee an open door." It is just such a refuge as he needs. Just as he supposes the storm is about to pour its fury upon him, he runs into this shelter and is safe. This newly discovered refuge is Christ. Thus "a man"—the divine man Christ Jesus—"shall be as a hiding-place from the wind, and a covert from the tempest, as rivers of water in a dry place, as the shadow of a great rock in a weary land." Isa. 32:2. The man sees this place, and wonders that he saw it no sooner. It is so near, and so accessible. "Say not in thy heart, Who shall ascend into heaven? that is, to bring Christ down from above; or who shall descend into the deep? that is, to bring up Christ again from the dead. But what saith it? The word is nigh thee, even in thy mouth and in thy heart; that is, the word of faith which we preach: that if thou shalt confess with thy mouth the Lord Jesus, and shalt believe in thy heart that God raised him from the dead, thou shalt be saved." Rom. 10: 6–9.

But the soul thus affected has many difficulties.

The author of "Quiet Thoughts for Quiet Hours" gives the following questions and answers respecting one in the state just described:

"How shall I come to God, for I am a sinful creature?

"Jesus said, 'I am the way; no man cometh unto the Father but by me.' John 14: 6.

"But how can I feel sure that Jesus will receive me?

"'Him that cometh to me I will in no wise cast out.' John 6: 37.

"I have nothing that I can bring to him.

"'I will give unto him that is athirst of the fountain of the water of life freely.' Rev. 21: 6.

"But should I not first endeavor to purify my soul from sin?

"'Who can bring a clean thing out of an unclean? not one.' Job 14: 4. 'Without me ye can do nothing.' John 15: 5.

"How then shall I come?

"'By a new and living way, which he hath

consecrated for us through the vail, that is to say, his flesh.' Heb. 10:20.

"Is God sure to receive me? Can he love me?

"'I will receive you, and will be a Father unto you, and ye shall be my sons and daughters, saith the Lord Almighty.' 2 Cor. 6:18.

"What should be the object of my life?

"'Ye are bought with a price; therefore glorify God in your body, and in your spirit, which are God's.' 1 Cor. 6:20.

"Can my unimportant actions in any way glorify the everlasting God?

"'Herein is my Father glorified, that ye bear much fruit.' John 15:8.

"What do you mean by fruit?

"The fruit of the Spirit is love, joy, peace, long-suffering, gentleness, goodness, faith, meekness, temperance.' Gal. 5:22, 23.

"Does God then take notice of my daily conduct?

"'I know the things that come into your mind, every one of them.' Ezek. 11:5. 'He that planted the ear, shall he not hear? He that formed the eye, shall he not see? He that teacheth man knowledge, shall he not know?' Psa. 44:10.

"I am very ignorant; who shall instruct me?

"'Search the Scriptures.' John 5:39. 'The holy Scriptures, which are able to make thee wise unto salvation, through faith which is in Christ Jesus.' 2 Tim. 3:15.

"But I have so many evil habits to combat; what shall I do?

"'Gird up the loins of your mind.' 1 Pet. 1:13. 'Fight the good fight of faith.' 1 Tim. 6:12. 'For he hath said, I will never leave thee, nor forsake thee.' Heb. 13:5.

"But there are trials and temptations in my way which others have not.

"'There hath no temptation taken you but such as is common to man; but God is faithful, who will not suffer you to be tempted above that ye are able; but will with the temptation also make a way to escape, that ye may be able to bear it.' 1 Cor. 10:13.

"I wish I had some friend who could understand all the trials of my spirit.

"'We have not a High-priest which cannot be touched with the feeling of our infirmities; but was in all points tempted like as we are, yet without sin.' Heb. 4:15.

"It is my desire to walk uprightly, but I feel I have no strength.

"'He giveth power to the faint, and to them that have no might he increaseth strength.' Isa. 40:29.

"May I go and ask him, then?

"'If any of you lack wisdom, let him ask of God, that giveth to all men liberally and upbraideth not, and it shall be given him.' Jas. 1:5.

"How will God give me wisdom?

"'I will put my Spirit within you, and cause you to walk in my statutes, and ye shall keep my judgments and do them.' Ezek. 36:27.

"When trouble comes, what shall I do?

"'Call upon me in the day of trouble: I will deliver thee, and thou shalt glorify me.' Psa. 51:15.

"Need I not fear the hour of death?

"'When thou passest through the waters I will be with thee.' Isa. 40:2.

"Nor the day of judgment?

"'Who shall lay any thing to the charge of God's elect? It is God that justifieth. Who is he that condemneth? It is Christ that died.' Rom. 8:33, 34.

"Oh, I will cast in my lot with God's people, for they only are happy.

"'We are journeying unto the place of which the Lord said, I will give it you; come thou with us, and we will do thee good.' Num. 10:29.

"'The Lord bless thee, and keep thee; the Lord make his face shine upon thee, and be gracious unto thee; the Lord lift up his countenance upon thee, and give thee peace.' Num. 6:24–26."

Truly it is kind to invite men to Christ. Let them come boldly, in the confidence of faith, at once, without delay. Well and wisely did Paul desire that he might "be found in Christ, not having his own righteousness, which is of the law, but that which is through the faith of Christ, the righteousness which is of God by faith." Phil. 3:9. Only thus can the soul be set at liberty.

If you will come to Christ you shall have rest—rest to your souls, however weary, however burdened—a holy rest from the servitude of sin and Satan—a rest from tormenting fears, from corroding cares, from an accusing conscience. The unholy quietness of unrenewed nature is but the precursor of wrath, as an unusual stillness precedes the earthquake. But the rest of the soul in Christ is like that of the Israelites when, after their long journeyings and wars and troubles, they were enfeoffed and settled in Canaan.

Vespasian the Roman emperor gave a great reward to a person who came and professed a great love for him. Come to Christ, thus proving that you love him, and he will give you blessings whose value can never be adequately estimated by a finite mind. He will receive you. "Him that cometh unto me I will in no wise cast out." He will give you an indisputable title to imperishable glory.

Let no one hesitate what choice to make. No man can afford to sustain the loss of his soul, the loss of the divine favor, the loss of the smiles of Christ. Men must be saved in him, or they will be ruined for ever.

You can but die if you come to Christ, and you must die if you do not come. Every man is naturally like the four leprous men spoken of in 2 Kings 7:3–11. Let him but arise and go trustfully to Christ, and all will be well.

## CHAPTER VI.

### CONVICTION—CONVERSION.

Attention has been directed to the earlier stages of religious concern—the first thoughts, purposes, temptations, failures, relentings, burdens, sorrows, and struggles of a soul in its attempts to flee from the wrath of God. It may be proper here to make a few general remarks, explanatory of what is often the state of a sinner's mind immediately before conversion.

He discovers that the Bible is a revealer of the secrets of his soul, a discerner of the thoughts and intents of his heart. He is ready to say, Come see a book which hath told me all things that ever I did. At such times God's word is as a glass, in which a man beholds his natural face. It reflects his image, and shows him his sad deficiencies and his great deformity. He finds his heart to be exceedingly depraved. He is convinced that the imaginations of the thoughts of his heart are only evil continually. In this state of mind David compared his pains to "broken bones." If you have ever had a broken bone, you may have an idea of his meaning. Thoughts of it occupy the mind day and night. For a moment company may seem to create a diversion of the thoughts, but soon they revert to the fractured limb. Such a one awaking at a dead hour of the night, immediately thinks of the injured part. All attempts to shake off reflection concerning it are fruitless. In another place David says, "My sin is ever before me." His mind dwelt upon his transgressions. Like a vast army of men, they were continually passing in solemn review. In this state of mind, one feels that God has a right to have mercy on whom he will have mercy, and to have compassion on whom he will have compassion. Whatever may be his theory on the subject, his heartfelt conviction is, that without wrong to him, God may withhold all the blessings of salvation. Yea, he feels that God would be justified in condemning him for ever, and be clear in driving him to outer darkness. He says,

> "Should sudden vengeance seize my breath,
> I must pronounce thee just in death:
> And if my soul were sent to hell,
> Thy righteous law approves it well."

Sometimes one in this state is greatly annoyed with wicked and even blasphemous thoughts. The object of the tempter seems to be, to banish all hope of reconciliation with God. It sometimes happens to such a soul as to that young man of whom we read, "And as he was yet a coming, the devil threw him down and tare him." Luke 9 : 42. When his prey is about to be taken from him, the old lion is greatly enraged. He cannot bear to witness the escape of a single soul.

One thus exercised will discover that the belief which he has hitherto had of the Bible is unavailing. It has been merely historical, cold, and powerless. Or it has been the faith of devils, and has merely filled his soul with terrors. He now feels the need of a faith which is "of the operation of God." And even in the surrender which he is about to make, there is so much timidity and such a sense of unworthiness, that commonly the most he can say is, "Lord, I believe; help thou mine unbelief." Boldness in coming to the throne of grace is seldom enjoyed even by young converts.

One who has advanced thus far will probably be more than ever beset by the evil one. The Hebrews never fared so hard as just before they left Egypt; and never were so hated as after they began to march towards Canaan.

He is sadly disappointed that the measures he has adopted for relief have but sunk him the deeper in misery. Like that woman in the gospel, he has spent all his substance on physicians, and is no better, but worse. Prayer, hearing the word, reading, conversation, and resolutions have all been found ineffectual, and even worse; they have brought more wrath on the soul, because of the sin attending them.

In this state one might adopt the language of the psalmist: "My soul is full of troubles... I am as a man that hath no strength... Thou hast laid me in the lowest pit, in darkness, in the deep. Thy wrath lieth hard upon me, and thou hast afflicted me with all thy waves.... I am shut up, and I cannot come forth... Mine eye mourneth by reason of affliction. Lord, why castest thou off my soul? Why hidest thou thy face from me? Thy terrors have cut me off." Psa. 88. He feels that God must help him, or he must die in his sins. Like Peter sinking, he says, "Lord, save me." Or like Hezekiah he exclaims, "Mine eyes fail with looking upward. O Lord, I am oppressed; undertake for me." Isa. 38:14.

Such a man will grieve because he cannot grieve, and mourn because he cannot mourn, and weep because he cannot weep. He is astonished at his guilt and at his hardness of heart. He is convinced that an entire change of heart is in his case necessary to happiness here and hereafter. He also sees that if he shall ever be saved, it must be by an act of free, rich, sovereign grace. His boasted ability is found to be nothing. His strength is weakness. His merits are now not named. He feels that he deserves no good thing. His righteousnesses are as filthy rags. He is ready to come before the Lord with the language of self-condemnation. He feels like Benhadad's servants, when they put sackcloth on their loins and ropes upon their heads, and went to the king of Israel, thus confessing that their lives were in his hands and at his mercy. 1 Kings 20 : 31.

This state of mind is conviction, which involves always a sense of five things: sinfulness, guilt, ignorance, helplessness, and misery. This conviction is of course not alike pungent in all cases; nor is it necessarily accompanied with extreme agitations or terrors; but it is a clear view of one's state as demanding the remedy provided in the gospel. If the work of conviction should proceed, and hope never come to the relief of the soul, the result would be the impenetrable gloom of despair, as in the case of the damned. Let a man see his lost estate, and not see the Saviour as he is freely offered, and he will be a desperado in the government of God. Often the sinner desires that his convictions may proceed, because he looks upon them as punishments for sin—as punishments richly deserved. If he had his way, he would not even now come to Christ. If he could weep and mourn and grieve and be melted as he wishes, he would be satisfied without any other atonement than that which he could thus make. At least, he would seek no other. In all his dealings with him, God's plan is to shut him up to the faith of Christ; that through the law he may be dead to the law, that he may be married to Christ.

Ask such a one if he thinks he is under conviction, and he will probably reply in the negative. His views on that subject are very vague and erroneous. Indeed, he has no distinct idea of what conviction is, except that he believes it is a step towards salvation. He thinks he has no such feeling as in anywise prepares him for a change. It seems to him that he is losing instead of gaining ground.

The nearer he approaches to salvation, the further does he seem from it. The darkest hour is just before day. It was midnight when Pharaoh dismissed Israel. Exod. 12:30, 31. In his Almost Christian, Meade gives a salutary warning: "Never rest in convictions till they end in conversion. This is that wherein most men miscarry; they rest in their convictions, and take them for conversion, as if sin seen were therefore sin forgiven; or as if a sight of the want of grace were the truth of the work of grace." Conviction, however deep or distressing, is not saving. This brings us to consider

CONVERSION.

On this subject, let a few things be premised.

1. All conversions are not alike in their circumstances, though they produce like results. They lead to the forsaking of sin, to the acceptance of Christ, to holiness of life, and finally to glory. But the steps by which this is done are various. Some conversions are extraordinary, as that of the thief on the cross and that of Saul of Tarsus. Even in ordinary conversions there is a great variety. Some are sudden, some are gradual, some are

preceded by many terrors, some are marked by extraordinary views of the tenderness of God. No one therefore will here expect an account of the peculiar exercises of any one person, but rather such statements as may suit most cases of ordinary experience.

2. Nor will the reader expect an account of the manner in which the Spirit of God operates on the heart. No man has this information. Of course an attempt to give it is presumptuous. Solomon says, "Thou knowest not the way of the Spirit." Eccl. 11:5. Paul says, "What man knoweth the things of a man, save the spirit of man which is in him? even so the things of God knoweth no man, but the Spirit of God." 1 Cor. 2:11. God has not informed us how he operates in any matter; but his methods of proceeding are wisely and necessarily concealed from human ken. So our Saviour clearly taught, John 3 : 8.

3. If what has been said be true, then in speaking on the subject of conversion, the greatest modesty becomes us, lest we should hastily lay down principles which might on the one hand discourage some of the true children of God, or on the other, encourage false hopes in those who are aliens from the commonwealth

of Israel. To guard against both these extremes is no easy task. Many ignorant persons are forward in such matters. But let us distrust ourselves where we have not a "Thus saith the Lord" to guide us. Let no man lay down any thing as essential, unless in his word God has made it so.

4. It is not uncommon for one to think, that if he shall obtain relief, it will be in some particular manner, such as he has devised in his own mind, or heard of in the case of others. One under conviction is ready to fall into superstitious imaginings. But when the Lord intends to grant deliverance, he will save from fatal delusions. Naaman had a plan of being cured of leprosy; but his was not God's plan. Conversion is always different from the conjectures of a carnal heart. It is well it is so. The Scriptures fairly teach us so. Isa. 42:16.

When the soul is duly humbled in its own eyes—when it has renounced self-will and self-righteousness, and despaired of helping itself, and God's Spirit is savingly at work, some glimpses of Christ are afforded. The soul has a desire to lay hold on him, but unbelief is too strong for reason or for conviction to cure. The soul now sees, approves, and accepts some of the truths of the gospel in a way it never did before. It gets some glimpses of Him who is the way, the truth, and the life. The clouds begin to break, and a star of hope appears;

"It is the Spirit's rising beam."

As the natural sun does not from midnight darkness in a moment burst upon the world, so in most cases the Sun of righteousness rises gradually upon the soul. "His going forth is prepared as the morning." At first, he who has been sore troubled is comforted by his new discoveries. Hope begins to gild his path, and he is for a time relieved of a great burden. But often this state of mind does not last long, and he begins to fear that his deep impressions are leaving him. He is alarmed to find himself becoming cheerful. He tries to recover his painful feelings, but often fails. Sometimes he has his wish, and then his soul drinks in the wormwood. He then cries anew to the Lord for mercy, and the light of God's countenance begins to shine upon him more fully and clearly. He may soon be more than ever at a loss respecting the work of grace within him. He cannot be sad as he was, because the Lord is making him joyful. He is afraid to rejoice, except with trembling, for his soul has not forgotten his late experience. An interruption of the pleasant view of divine things he had enjoyed awakens great desires for its return. But to regain lost comforts is not always easy. Once gone, the soul fears lest it has offended God by not more highly prizing them. But when the light returns, it is commonly with increased brightness. Thus light and darkness often alternate, until at length the soul is brought to a more settled peace. Fears no longer prevail. Hope is in the ascendant. The soul sees salvation flowing from the cross of Christ, and begins to apprehend the spiritual import of such phrases as, "through Christ," "in Christ Jesus," "by Jesus Christ," "in the name of Christ." The plan of redemption now delights him, though his views are very imperfect; yet he wishes no other prophet, priest, or king than the Lord Jesus. He rests upon him alone for salvation. He trusts the whole weight of his soul on Him who bled and died on Calvary.

Were you to ask him whether he supposed he was converted, he would probably say, No. Yet he thinks he is getting into the right way. Or perhaps he would say, "I do not know whether I am converted or not; but one thing

I know, that whereas I was blind, now I see. Behold, all things are become new." He looks on time and eternity, sin and holiness, truth and error, the Bible, the Saviour, the pious, the world, life and death, things present and things to come, in a new light. In particular, he is pleased with the fulness, freeness, power, kindness, and glory of Christ. He loves and admires the Saviour for what he is, for what he was, for what he shall be, for what he has done, for what he is doing, and for what he shall yet do to save perishing men. He loves what Christ loves, and hates what Christ hates. He can look back a short time, when such and such portions of Scripture were brought home to his soul with power and sweetness. He is greatly surprised and mortified at a review of his past life. He wonders with unutterable wonder how he could have remained in sin so long. And then he weeps tears of joy and gratitude that He who made him has had mercy on him.

The peace now found is solely in the merit of Christ. The soul wholly rejects all thoughts of salvation by another. The gospel way is so honorable to God and so safe for the sinner—it so perfectly satisfies the demands of the law for a perfect satisfaction and a perfect righteousness, that the most enlightened sinner says, Here I end my quest; I need no other Saviour; now by faith I enter into rest.

In the same way the soul obtains purity. God has inseparably united pardon and purity, justification and sanctification. No man is freed from God's displeasure without being cleansed in his own nature also. Only this difference should be noted: pardon and acceptance are perfect at once; purification is gradual and progressive.

When the soul is thus sheltered in Christ, how pleasant it is to consider that this is of old the hiding-place of the penitent; that on this refuge, two thousand years ago, beat the awful tempest of God's wrath; but even at the height of the storm, the dying thief here found shelter and salvation. The soul that is thus in Christ cannot perish. It was weary and heavy-laden; it has now found rest. It was exposed and doomed; it is shielded and saved.

Such a soul would gladly recommend Christ to others. He wishes that all might know him and find refuge in him. His spirit is tender and benevolent. "When the Holy Ghost descended upon the Son of God, he borrowed not the semblance of a bird of prey, but of the mourning and tender dove." And when he now descends to "stamp his image on the heart, the impression which he leaves is not that of fierceness or bitterness, but of gentleness, tenderness, and good will to all men." To such the Sanctifier becomes the Comforter. "As the dove conveyed to Noah's ark the intelligence of the subsiding of the waters, so will the heavenly Dove convey to the soul the glad tidings that the tempest of eternal wrath no longer sweeps over her path." Every soul that comes to Christ receives the earnest of the Spirit. Terror has given way to heavenly peace; fear has yielded to hope; distress has been succeeded by tranquillity; darkness has fled before the brightness of the rising of the Sun of righteousness.

As to the question whether a man knows the time of his conversion, it may be stated that some have known it. The thief on the cross, Zaccheus, the jailer, Paul, and the three thousand converted on the day of Pentecost, evidently knew the time of their great change. So in modern times men may be able to point out the day of the happy saving change. If so, very well. But it should be observed, that many who think they know the time are mistaken. This is true of those boasting hypocrites who never were converted at all, as their wicked lives show. It is also true that many humble, diffident persons had met with a saving change long before they ceased to write bitter things against themselves, or ventured to cherish the hope that they had already passed from death unto life.

Let not any who know not the time of their conversion be cast down, if they now have evidence that they do truly love the Lord Jesus, if they now keep his commandments. It is nowhere said in the Bible, ye must know the time of your conversion; but it is said, Ye must be born again. The change, not the time of its occurrence, is the essential thing. If we pass from death unto life by the power of God's Spirit, it cannot endanger our salvation to be in doubt or in ignorance of the time when that happy event occurred.

Again, one must judge of his own state by the fruit he bears; and fruit that is ripe in an hour will perhaps be rotten as soon. A godly life is the infallible evidence of conversion. When our fruit is unto holiness, we know that the end shall be everlasting life. Every one who hopes that he is converted to God should examine himself and prove his own work, and then he shall have rejoicing in himself alone, and not in another. In judging of piety, there is no substitute for a holy life. The great peculiarity of God's people is that they are "zealous of good works." In spring many a tree is covered with beautiful blossoms, which are not in autumn followed by any good fruit. We are Christ's disciples if we do whatsoever he commands us. We are the servants of the wicked one if we do the works of the flesh. We may boast of discoveries, of raptures, and ecstacies, but all is in vain if a consistent life be not the result. So that many who say that they know the time and place of their conversion are unquestionably deceived.

Whether a man knows the fact of his conversion is a matter that admits of similar remarks. If any knows that he is converted, let him be humble, not proud. If God has favored him with unusually bright evidences, let him not despise his brethren who are in painful doubt about their state. Humility is an excellent virtue. There is indeed a sense in which a man cannot be converted without knowing it: namely, he cannot undergo any change in his views and affections without being conscious of the exercises and emotions of his mind and heart thus changed. But surely one may have the exercises of a new-born soul without knowing that these are the exercises of a renewed nature. The miser knows what passes in his own mind, but he does not know these things prove him a wretch. The self-conceited man is conscious of all his mental exercises, but is far from seeing that they mark him out as a poor weak creature. So the convert cannot know that his views and feelings prove him a child of God until he is correctly informed by the Bible what constitutes piety. So that a man must first search the Scriptures to see what they require to prove piety, and then search himself to see whether he has what is thus required by God's word. The result of such examination may be satisfactory. If so, a good foundation is laid for permanent peace of mind.

In corroboration of this view, it may be stated that with cautious minds nothing is harder than to believe as one wishes. With what difficulty did the disciples believe that Christ was risen from the dead. Luke 24:41. How often do we hear the saying, The news is too good to be believed. It was so with the Jews released from Babylon: "When the Lord turned again the captivity of Zion, we were like them that dream." Psa. 126:1. Should any say, Is it possible for one to have his chains taken off, the prison doors opened, himself brought out and set free, and he not know it? the answer is, Yes. This may be done literally and corporeally. Peter was sleeping in prison between two soldiers, and bound with two chains, when the angel of the Lord smote him on the side and awaked him. His chains then fell off, and he girded himself, and put on his sandals, and cast his garment about him, and followed the angel, as he was bid to do. And yet Peter "wist not that it was true which was done by the angel; but thought he saw a vision." Nor did he come to himself, nor was he satisfied of his deliverance until they were past the first and second ward, until they had passed the iron gate which led unto the city, and which opened to them of its own accord, and until they had passed through one street, and the angel had departed from him. Acts 12:6–11. Here we have a man going through the entire process of being awaked out of sleep, of hearing the angel's words, of dropping his chains, of girding himself, of putting on his sandals, of throwing his garment about him, and following the angel, and yet doubting the reality of the whole matter. The release was so marvellous that he could not believe it true. Much more then may a soul be brought out of its prison-house, have the chains of its terrible condemnation removed, come out of darkness into the marvellous light of the gospel, and yet doubt whether the change is not an illusion, a phantom, a dream. He says, "But yesterday I was a wretched outcast, a child of wrath, forlorn and guilty. Can I now be a child of God, an heir of glory, with my sins all pardoned, and myself accepted and regenerated? It cannot be so. The thought is too pleasant to be indulged." He who is truly enlightened and converted has had his eyes opened to see the exceeding excellence and importance of divine things, and if he is to be assured of his interest in them, he must have solid grounds of hope.

If any ask for the infallible signs of a saving change, a sound conversion, we must again refer them to a godly life. But there are some very strong points in which a genuine conversion is always distinguished from a spurious change. Guthrie notices three particulars in which all are deficient unless they are real Christians:

"1. They are not broken in their hearts, and emptied of their righteousness.

"2. They never took up Christ Jesus as the only treasure and jewel that can enrich and should satisfy, and therefore have never cordially agreed to God's device in the covenant, and so are not worthy of him, neither has the kingdom of God savingly entered into their heart: 'The kingdom of heaven is like unto a treasure hid in the field; the which when a man hath found, he hideth, and for joy thereof selleth all that he hath, and buyeth that field.'

"3. They never in earnest closed with Christ's whole yoke without exception, judging all his will just and good, holy and spiritual, and therefore no rest followed on them by Christ: 'Take my yoke upon you, and ye shall find rest unto your souls.'"

If any thing else needs to be added, it is that the self-deceived are as much like Christians at the first as at the last. They do not grow in grace, for they have none. They may increase in outward manifestations and professions, but never in a godlike temper. "True grace is a growing principle."

Where conversion is genuine, it will prove itself more and more. Especially do the Scriptures insist much on the possession of a childlike temper and disposition. Thus a little child is humble. The child of the king and of the beggar, left to themselves, would meet on the same level and freely mingle together. So the true convert has such a sense of his own vileness that he readily esteems others better than himself. A proud Christian is a contradiction.

In like manner he is meek. So far as he is like Christ, he is not disposed to strive, or cry, or lift up, or cause his voice to be heard in the streets. He is not boisterous nor clamorous nor contentious. To this his previous training has brought him. God has dealt with him as he has, that he may remember and be confounded, and never open his mouth any more because of his shame, when the Lord is pacified towards him for all that he has done. His soul is even as a weaned child. Ezekiel 16 : 23 ; Psa. 131 : 2.

So also a child is teachable. It is not inflated with self-conceit. It claims not to be wise in things it knows nothing of, but sits at the feet of teachers and learns its lessons. So the true convert sits at the feet of Jesus and learns from him the lessons of heavenly wisdom. God's word binds his conscience, but he calls no man master. None is more free from drinking in notions and forming opinions without good cause, but on the veracity of God he rests with entire confidence.

In the same spirit a child looks to its parent for protection, for food and raiment, and for comfort in distress. So the child of God casts his care upon an almighty arm, hides himself under the shadow of the Lord's wings, and trusts him for all. He calls upon the Lord. "Behold, he prayeth." It is not more natural for a living child to breathe than it is for a living Christian to pray.

Little children must also obey their father. So all true converts sincerely and heartily do the will of God. Neither fancy nor pleasure nor habit nor convenience nor ease nor public opinion, but God's known will must be our guide. After conversion it is our guide. Every true convert says, "Lord, what wilt thou have me to do?"

> "Faith must obey her Father's will,
> As well as trust his word."

He who has met with such a change shall not perish, but shall enter into the kingdom of heaven. No power in heaven will hinder him, and no power in earth or in hell can hinder him in achieving a final victory. Speaking of such, Paul says, "I am persuaded that neither death, nor life, nor angels, nor principalities, nor powers, nor things present, nor things to come, nor height, nor depth, nor any other creature, shall be able to separate us from the love of God, which is in Christ Jesus our Lord." Rom. 8 : 38, 39.

The change thus described is essential to salvation. Unless we are turned from sin to holiness, iniquity will be our ruin. We are naturally sunk down into sin; yet "without holiness no man shall see the Lord." It is only by a sound conversion that we acquire any genuine Christian virtue. This is a very solemn and weighty truth. It should alarm the wicked. It should make all men diligent in working out their salvation with fear and trembling. He who is to be the final Judge of quick and dead has said, "Except ye be converted, and become as little children, ye cannot enter into the kingdom of heaven." Here is something declared to be absolutely necessary. Less wealth, less public honor, less pleasure, less health than men now possess may fall to their lot, and yet they attain to the highest end of existence. A dying man called his son to him, and said, "Hold your finger in the blaze of that candle for one minute." The son refused. Then said the father, "Do you refuse to hold your finger there for one minute for me? and I, because I have spent my life in heaping up riches for you, shall endure the flames of hell for ever." Men must be converted. Without that great change they are eternally undone. There is no safety out of Christ. There is no salvation without turning to the Lord. Personal dignity, natural amiability, official sanctity will save no man.

## CHAPTER VII.

### CASES OF RELIGIOUS DISTRESS.

It is not uncommon for persons to have some experience in religion which is highly unsatisfactory to themselves. They have distressing and prevailing apprehensions that they have never closed in with Christ; nor has a good hope through grace ever filled their hearts to overflowing with joy and peace; and yet they are not careless on the subject. At times they are deeply exercised and sore vexed. The case of such calls for the tenderest concern of those who care for souls, as well as the liveliest interest on their own part. Their views of their lost and undone condition are not too strong. Their hearts are as unclean, their guilt is as great, their enemies as numerous as they have ever supposed them to be. They are beset with difficulties. They see the way, but are unable to walk in it. They approve but do not relish the things that are more excellent. Their hopes are crossed; their souls are grieved.

To meet such cases in all their variety is a

binding and difficult part of ministerial duty. To state all the shades of grief and temptation is not possible. But there are general principles of religion which are more or less suited to many cases. Besides, religious biography has shed much light on this whole subject. It is greatly to the relief of many minds to find that no temptations have befallen them but such as are common to men.

Sometimes one is full of fears lest he may have committed the unpardonable sin. Not unfrequently this apprehension is distressingly impressed on the mind by means of some portion of Scripture. Often will you hear cited that text, "For ye know that afterward, when he would have inherited the blessing, he was rejected; for he found no place of repentance, though he sought it carefully with tears." Heb. 12:17.

As this is a very important case, and often causes deep anguish of mind, it should not be lightly dismissed. Some have thought that the unpardonable sin could not be committed since miracles have ceased. But the Scriptures will not bear out such a statement. It is true the sin was no doubt often committed when the truth was visibly demonstrated by undeniable signs and wonders. But it may also be committed when these miracles have passed away.

Others have thought that, though the sin may possibly be committed in our day, yet the cases in which this is actually done are very few. Whatever definition is commonly given of this sin, this opinion seems to be without good foundation. Sound writers are pretty well agreed that the unpardonable sin is an act of one who is much enlightened and at the same time highly malicious against God. Light and malice are both essential to its existence. The light here spoken of respects spiritual things. The malice is directed against the person, work or offices of the Holy Ghost. Thus by the power of the Holy Ghost, which was given him without measure, Jesus Christ wrought miracles. The Jews, who beheld these wonders, knew that they could be the product of none but divine power. But they so hated the Lord Jesus that they ascribed his miracles to a Satanic influence, and thus committed the sin which hath never forgiveness, neither in this world, nor in that which is to come. Matt. 12:22–32.

If this view be correct, it follows that no

reason can be given why this sin may not be committed in this day. We may not have all the occasions for its commission which the Jews of Christ's day had; but we never lack occasions when we have dispositions to commit this kind of sin. Indeed, as the present is an age when the light of truth in many places shines very clearly, and as the minds of many thus enlightened seem very bitter and malicious against religion, it is to be feared that many commit this sin. Some have thought that there never was an age when the unpardonable sin was more common. But this cannot be proved. Yet in wonderful displays of grace and mercy in revivals of religion, how many who witness the most affecting scenes, and are themselves powerfully wrought upon, do yet harden their hearts until they even scoff at sacred things, laugh at the work of the Spirit, and call all vital religion fanaticism and the work of Satan. If such have the light which in many cases they profess to have, how does their case differ from that of the Pharisees when they saw Christ's miracles? In many ways men may commit the unpardonable sin; so that he who would not sin beyond forgiveness, must take heed how he trifles with holy things. This thought should produce in men a salutary alarm.

As to the question whether a distressed soul has actually committed this sin, it is proper to enter into several inquiries. Let one thus distressed look at the state of mind in which he did that act which he now fears was the unpardonable sin. Was it done wilfully, spitefully, knowingly? Did he intend to renounce God's Spirit for ever? To explain a little. Peter denied his Master, knowing that he was thus uttering falsehood. But he did it through fear of man, and not through malice against Christ. Therefore his denial of Christ was not the unpardonable sin. On the other hand, Saul persecuted the church maliciously. He breathed out threatenings and slaughter. He was exceeding mad against all Christians. But he did all this "ignorantly in unbelief." He knew not what he was doing. Therefore his zeal against Christians was not the unpardonable sin. But if Peter had, together with his knowledge of the matter, denied his Lord with the malice with which Saul persecuted the church; or if Saul, with all his malice, had persecuted the church with the knowledge with which Peter denied his Lord, then in either case the unpardonable sin would probably have been committed. Therefore let any one who fears his guilt in this matter, ask himself if the deed which brings such terror to his mind was accompanied with this light and malice. If not, there is no evidence that the soul has sinned beyond repentance.

Again, let one inquire what state of mind followed the act that creates such apprehensions. Was it "a certain fearful looking for of judgment?" Did the door of hope seem to be quite closed? Did the desire of reconciliation with God fully leave the soul; or was the dreadful act followed by utter insensibility, stupidity, and a seared conscience? Did you become wholly indifferent to salvation? Did you have no wish to be made pure and holy, humble and penitent? Such desires are not given to the God-forsaken. He who has committed this sin never after hungers and thirsts after righteousness. Such a state of mind shows that the Holy Spirit has not finally deserted the soul. Good desires are as truly from heaven as any other good thing ever enjoyed.

It is proper to add, that unworthy partaking of the Lord's supper, unless done with despite to the Spirit of grace and with contempt of all sacred things, cannot be proven to be the unpardonable sin. Although unworthy communion is a sin to be repented of, yet it may be and often has been forgiven.

It is doubtless sometimes in our power to know when one has sinned beyond forgiveness. This is implied in the words of John: "If any man see his brother sin a sin which is not unto death, he shall ask, and he shall give him life for them that sin not unto death. There is a sin unto death; I do not say that he shall pray for it." 1 John 5:16. Yet we should use great caution in such a matter. Some one expressed the belief that Bunyan had committed this sin. This statement had an exceedingly dreadful effect on his mind for a while; but God would not let him perish, and made him a chosen vessel in his church. Yet cases may occur in which good men will feel no liberty in praying for an offender. The number of such is larger than some suppose.

The last remark on this point is, that if you desire salvation through the blood of Christ and by the power of the Holy Ghost, it is clear that God has not given you up, though your sins may be both numerous and aggravated.

The air we breathe, the water we drink, is not more free than is gospel grace. The cry is, "Ho, every one that thirsteth, come ye to the waters, and he that hath no money, come ye, buy and eat; yea, come, buy wine and milk, without money and without price." Isa. 55:1.

Another state of mind, accompanied with great depression and much difficulty, is where one stoutly argues from his own wickedness of heart that his salvation is impossible. A man sometimes says, "I would go to Christ, but he is so holy and I am so sinful; he is spotless, and I am all pollution and guilt." In dealing with one thus afflicted, several things may be said. One is, that evil imaginations are the natural product of the carnal mind. "Out of the heart proceed evil thoughts, murders, adulteries, fornications, thefts, false witness, blasphemies." Matt. 15 : 19. There is no form of wickedness too strange or dreadful for an unsanctified heart. He who now complains so bitterly of his corrupt thoughts and affections, is not a worse man than he was formerly, but God is teaching him how wicked he has been. The great difference between present and past states of mind is this, that now the man sees how vile his heart is, whereas once he took no notice of the swarms of evil thoughts which passed through his breast. The present is not the only sinful state to be repented of. The prayer should ascend, "Remember not against me the sins of my youth; make me not to possess the iniquities of former years." It may also be stated that the exercises of such a one may now be less criminal than formerly, and this for two reasons. One is, that he now offers a sincere though inadequate resistance to evil thoughts, whereas formerly he welcomed them. Another is, that from his manifest distress at them, it is evident that they are the temptations of the wicked one. We are guilty in so far as we entertain the suggestions of the wicked one, and not merely because we are made to feel the annoyances of his temptations. But grant that any man's heart is far worse than it ever was before, or than he even now sees it to be, this is a good reason for applying to Christ. It is no reason for staying away from him. When one sees the wickedness of his own heart, it is evident that God has not yet delivered him up to ruin, for he is showing him his sins. These heart troubles show that nothing short of a thorough, internal, powerful change of nature can ever fit the soul for the abodes of the blessed in heaven. And this very corruption, so much lamented, should be a powerful argument for making speedy application to Christ for pardon and peace, for reconciliation and purification. But from such a state of mind to conclude that one may not come to Christ and plead for mercy is wholly unscriptural. It is entirely opposed to the gospel offer. This very state of mind and heart calls for the interposition of almighty power and amazing grace; and to exercise these is the delight of the redeeming Son of God. Though one be more vile than tongue can express—though the heart be a sink of sin, a fountain of iniquity, yet he may safely trust his cause with Jesus Christ. He came to set at liberty them that are bruised, to give life to the perishing, and salvation to the lost. Let every soul be persuaded to come to Jesus Christ.

He who thus complains of the wickedness of his heart, may the next hour complain that he has no just sense of his great sinfulness in the sight of God. This state of mind is not inconsistent with that last spoken of, though an ignorant person might so think. One reason why many a sinner is desirous of seeing more of his wickedness, is that he thinks there is some merit or profit in having distressing views of his undone condition. But this is surely a mistake. There is no more merit in a bad man seeing his vileness, than there is in a good man seeing his own uprightness. But suppose a man should see the worst of his case, and view his depravity as God views it, would it not drive him to despair? With the clearest views of the fulness and freeness of Christ ever attained on earth, it would probably be impossible to keep any man from giving up all hope if he saw his sins in all their guilt and number, baseness and aggravations. God is therefore very merciful in permitting us to see enough of our lost condition to make the gospel offer glad tidings to us; but he is no less merciful in withholding such views of our sins as would drive us to despair. And if any one would have a clearer and more salutary view of his own wickedness, let him repent of all the sin he sees chargeable to him and obtain pardon through the blood of Christ, and in due season his wish shall be gratified. No man will make very rapid and profitable attainments in the knowledge of his own wickedness until he has fled to Christ, and in good earnest begun the work of "mortifying his members which are upon the earth." Col. 3 : 5. In good earnest begin this work, and you will soon find that you are carnal, sold under sin, and that all former views of your lost estate were very defective.

Another distressing state is where there is a continual tendency in the mind to despair. Satan would have all men presumptuous or desperate. In the human heart are many elements which favor his designs. The language of perfect despair is, "There is no mercy for me; others may be saved, but my case is peculiar; my soul is lost." But there are various degrees of hopelessness, or of tendency towards it. To drive away all hope, Satan often greatly terrifies one by a view of his sins, points him to the holiness and inflexible justice of God, and tells him that he ought to know that with such a God there is no mercy for him. He reminds him of the length of time he has been seeking the Lord, and has not found him. He reminds him of others who in less time have attained a comfortable hope and settled peace. These and many other things does the adversary urge, that he may cut off all hope and leave the soul palsied with despondency. Sometimes he has fatal success. Sometimes he but harasses it for a season, and then follows deliverance. When he succeeds entirely, the soul becomes stubborn, hardened, and fearfully rebellious; and a less degree of the temptation of the adversary may be highly injurious for the time. When the prisoner of hope becomes the prisoner of despair, he is gone; and when he sees things in a very gloomy light, he may be sore vexed.

Let all who are tempted to despair well weigh the following things: Unbelief is the only sin by which a hearer of the gospel will seal his own ruin, and despair is the perfection of unbelief. To refuse to rely upon Christ's finished work is to reject the sinner's only hope. Unbelief is a great sin. The greater its power, the greater our guilt. As despair is unbelief consummated, it is superlative wickedness. If any man fears sin, let him chiefly fear this sin. It takes hold on destruction. No man can be justified or sanctified in whose heart this principle of pride, darkness, and stubbornness reigns. There may be a voluntary humility in despair, but that is only another name for pride. Despair also goes upon the ground that men are saved either by their own deservings, or because they have not greatly offended, and thus it excludes the salvation of the gospel, which is for the chief of sinners. And despair is full of stubbornness. What is a greater sin than to refuse to trust God when he bids us believe him; to decline to lean upon him when he extends to us his hand? We cannot have too low an opinion of ourselves, or too high an opinion of Christ. "It is the great design of the Scriptures to teach the best to despair of being self-saved; the worst not to despair of being saved by Christ, and to offer to all the help they want."

The foregoing are examples of the distresses and difficulties which often beset a soul in its endeavors to turn to the Lord. There are many cases like them. And there are others of an extraordinary kind, which cannot be anticipated. If any man is overcome by the adversary in these matters, the fault is his own. He has procured these things to himself. Such fruits never grow but in depraved hearts. For the direction of such as are truly desirous of being guided in the right way, the following suggestions may be profitable.

Beware of a spirit of impatience towards

God. With yourself you cannot be too much dissatisfied, until you believe in Christ and cease from sin. But with God and his ways you have no right to find fault. He is righteous altogether. Every sentiment of impatience towards him is highly criminal. During long years of rebellion, God waited on you for your return; and will you not let him judge the fittest time to grant you the light of his countenance and the joy of his salvation? "I waited patiently for the Lord; and he inclined unto me, and heard my cry." Psa. 40:1. God will not be dictated to. Impatience is both a sin and a hinderance. It speeds no deliverance. It must be laid aside.

Be not asking the advice of *many* in your sore perplexities. One *good* adviser is worth a thousand who know nothing thoroughly. And yet the most weak are often the most ready to proffer their services. The man of your counsel in all religious doubts and trials should be God's precious word. Human advisers are apt to say, "Lo, here is Christ;" and again, "Lo, there is Christ." But the Bible always speaks a uniform, consistent language. It always points to one star, that of Bethlehem; to one garden, that of Gethsemane; to one sacrifice, that of Calvary; to one sepulchre, that of Joseph of Arimathea.

Believe not that your convictions are too deep and too strong ever to leave you. They are perhaps not stronger than those of Felix when he trembled, of Herod when he heard John and did many things gladly, of Ahab when he humbled himself, or of king Saul when he lifted up his voice and wept. Conviction is not a saving grace. It is itself no pledge of salvation. It may leave one midway between carelessness and conversion, just as Lot's wife was left between Sodom and Zoar. If your convictions do not lead to Christ, and that speedily, you may become familiar with them, and their effect be lost upon you. Conviction is not conversion. Conviction can save no man.

Misconceive not the terms of salvation. On this point there is much danger. Be specially guarded that you do not attempt to substitute your own distress of mind for the sufferings of Christ. Sin is neither pardoned nor expelled by the anguish of any sinful worm. The more distressed men are, the stouter is their continued rebellion. Your own sufferings, in this world or the next, cannot save you.

No tears, no blood, no cross, no death, no intercession but those of Christ can avail for any. Never lose sight of the blessed truth, that salvation is wholly by grace, through faith in Christ Jesus.

Guard against false hopes. If the adversary sees you determined not to live without hope, he will earnestly endeavor to persuade you to build upon the sand; to lead you into mistakes respecting the nature of true conversion and the ground of justification. He is the arch deceiver. He is full of all subtlety. If it were possible, he would deceive the very elect. A sinner under conviction is in great danger of being more anxious to be comforted than to be converted. The world is full of popular errors on this subject. Nor can any man be too careful in counting the cost, in looking well to the foundations, in testing his own exercises by Scripture. Sometimes anxious souls are told that they must believe. When they ask, What must we believe? they are told that they must believe that their sins are pardoned and their souls converted. If some to whom such counsels are given should adopt them, they would believe a lie. We must believe the gospel; then we shall be saved. But to believe that we are interested in the salvation of Christ is a very different thing. The truth to be believed is, that Christ is able and willing to save our souls from sin and death—not that he has already done it. On this subject the Bible is explicit. It always holds up Christ, and not ourselves, nor our pardon, nor our conversion, as the object of saving faith. "Believe on the *Lord Jesus Christ*, and thou shalt be saved." Acts 16:31.

Be not led into the discussion of dark, abstruse, and therefore useless questions; and enter into no heated discussion of any subject. Such an exercise is well suited to put a stumbling-block in the way to heaven. If any endeavor to divert your mind to a matter of no importance, or to undue interest about any thing not essential to salvation, withdraw from such. Your great business is reconciliation with God. Whatever hinders this is hostile to your best interests. Stifle not convictions; grieve not the Spirit by going eagerly after a thing of little or no importance.

Keep constantly in mind that no pains, no distress, no tears, no prayers will be of any avail, unless we are soundly converted, being turned from darkness to light, from sin to holiness.

> "Our nature 's totally depraved,
> The heart a sink of sin;
> Without a change we can't be saved;
> We must be born again."

How much or how little you may feel, whether you have many or few thoughts, whether you are happy or miserable, in hope or despair, in carelessness or under conviction, will avail nothing, if you live and die without genuine holiness. But this cannot be obtained without a renewal of our whole nature. Holy views, holy frames of mind, holy tempers, holy affections, and holy purposes must take the place of our spiritual ignorance, our wicked prejudices, our carnal affections, our sinful plans, or we cannot go to the Father. Oh that men everywhere would cry mightily, "Create in me a clean heart, O God, and renew a right spirit within me."

Let all men know that, until they surrender themselves into the hands of the Saviour, they are throwing away all their opportunities. Christ is full of kindness and tenderness. None is so pitiful as he. Look at his sorrow as he beheld the city of his enemies and murderers. "When he was come near, he beheld the city, and wept over it." Luke 19:41. History tells us that Marcellus wept over Syracuse, Scipio over Carthage, and Titus over Jerusalem some forty years after Jesus entered it in the triumph decreed to him in prophecy. But all these wept over those whose blood they were about to shed. Jesus wept over those who were about to shed his blood. Cannot you trust your soul with a Saviour whose compassions are so free, so large, so divine? Behold him on the cross, lingering, bleeding, dying for the sins of men, and say if you are justified in longer resisting his claims and his charms. John says, "We love him, because he first loved us." 1 John 4:19. What could be more proper? Surely such love as his should beget love in us. That Jesus who wept over Jerusalem will surely have compassion on souls who weep for their sins, and forsake them, and flee to atoning blood for pardon, and to Christ's glorious righteousness for acceptance. Oh that men would believe and live. Through Christ there is hope. By him all our sins may be buried in the depths of the sea. By him the darkness flees away. Through his mediation we are brought to sing the song of Moses and the Lamb.

Finally, let no man take the word of any uninspired man as of binding force in any matter of religion. If such a course is dangerous in doctrinal religion, it is no less so in experimental and practical piety. If any thing that has been said shall guide or comfort any soul, to God be all the praise and glory. Meantime, "Out of the spoils won in battles have I dedicated these things to maintain the house of the Lord." 1 Chron. 26:27.

# CHAPTER VIII.

## SPIRITUAL DARKNESS.

In practical religion there is no greater mistake than the persuasion that if we are pleased with ourselves, God is also pleased with us. Pride, vain-glory, and self-complacency blind, bewilder, and intoxicate. In no form or degree do they make us meet for the inheritance of the saints in light. On the other hand, shame for our own vileness, sorrow for our shortcomings, self-loathing for undeniable turpitude of soul are profitable. Yea, "it is better to go to the house of mourning than to the house of feasting; for by the sadness of the countenance the heart is made better."

In this life God's people may expect much weeping and mourning. Waters of a full cup are wrung out to them. But the word of God puts limits to the griefs of the godly: "Weeping may endure for a night, but joy cometh in the morning;" "Blessed are they that mourn; for they shall be comforted;" "Ye now have sorrow; but I will see you again, and your heart shall rejoice." Psa. 30 : 5; Matt. 5 : 4;

John 16 : 22. Though the righteous shall not weep always, yet they may weep bitterly. The bare shedding of tears is not the only kind of weeping, nor the uttering of sighs the only mourning. Many who shed no tears and utter no sighs or groans, feel more deeply and painfully than those who hold out the usual signals of distress. There are states of mind far beyond the power of tears to relieve, far beyond the utterance of groans to alleviate. There is no pain of mind like that "dry sorrow, which drinketh up the blood and spirits."

Moreover, tears are often shed and sorrow often felt which God abhors. Tears of anger, of jealousy, of wounded pride, of detected wickedness, are all abominable to God. Jonah displeased the Lord by all his grief about his gourd. Amaziah was grieved for the hundred talents of silver, but God took no account of that.

Each one can determine the character of his sorrow, if he will but observe whether it improves his heart and temper, and whether it weans him from the world. That sorrow of the world which works death is always to be repented of.

One class of evils bringing sorrow to the

righteous is made up of the common calamities of life, such as sickness, poverty, the failure of hope, the want of friends, the want of means, the want of success, the death of friends, and the change of friends into enemies.

Another class of evils over which good men weep, are such as the sins of the times, ignorance, profaneness, lewdness, drunkenness, covetousness, lukewarmness, heresies, contentions, whisperings, and revilings. When God's cause languishes, the righteous must be sad. When iniquity abounds, he whose love waxes not cold must be grieved. When the foot of pride is on the neck of the saints, there will be mourning. David cried, "Let the wickedness of the wicked come to an end." Psa. 7:9. "Rivers of waters run down mine eyes, because men keep not thy law." Psa. 119:136. "Horror hath taken hold upon me, because of the wicked that forsake thy law." Psa. 119:53. So strong was this feeling in the mind of Paul, that he said to the Thessalonians, "Now we live, if ye stand fast in the Lord." 1 Thess. 3:8. This was equivalent to saying, If all things go on well in the church, I shall rise superior to all other trials; but if the church wanders into error and folly, my heart will die within me. So highly does God prize such dispositions, that when he was about terribly to punish Israel of old, he sent an angel with an ink-horn by his side through the midst of the city, to set a mark upon the foreheads of the men that did sigh and cry for all the abominations that were done in Jerusalem. Ezek. 9 : 4.

Other evils over which good men weep are found in themselves, such as error, ignorance, prejudice, pride, self-righteousness, worldliness, levity, uncharitable tempers and dispositions, censoriousness, envy, sinful anger, hatred, a proneness to remember wrongs, to indulge complaints, and to forget mercies. There is no plague like the plague of an evil heart. There is no misery like the wretchedness of conscious vileness. There are no sighs so long and so deep-drawn as those caused by indwelling sin. Job said, "I abhor myself, and repent in dust and ashes." David said, "Mine iniquities have taken hold upon me, so that I am not able to look up; they are more than the hairs of my head; therefore my heart faileth me." Isaiah said, "Woe is me, for I am undone; because I am a man of unclean lips, and I dwell in the midst of a people of unclean lips." And Paul said, "O wretched man that I am! who shall deliver me from the body of this death?"

Besides these things, God's people are subject to seasons of great spiritual darkness, which cause them long and loud and bitter weeping. These times of darkness and depression are more or less lasting and afflicting, according to the wisdom of Him who knows when, how, and how far his chosen servants need suffering.

These seasons of darkness sometimes come on very suddenly, but more commonly they are gradual in their approaches. There is first the little cloud. This spreads and thickens, till the whole heavens become black and angry. As in the natural world the elements of storm are often gathering when we perceive them not, so in the spiritual world, sins are often separating between us and God, and we know not our sad estate. Many think all is well, until to their surprise their day is turned into night, and their mirth into heaviness. Then to their grief they find their enemies upon them, and themselves shorn of the locks of their strength. Any sin may lead the mind to deep depression—may shroud it in terrible darkness.

This darkness consists of several things. Commonly it is attended with a loss of comfortable evidence of personal piety. Hope grows dim. Marks of piety become obscured. The troubled soul feels unable to claim the promises. It has some perception of their sweetness and faithfulness, but says they are not for me. Then thoughts about the mercy of God yield no comfort, for the soul says, I have abused all his kindness. I have rendered myself abominable by my base ingratitude. Reflections on past seasons of joyful experience but render the present trial the more painful. They show what has been lost. Or perhaps all former comforts are counted delusions. Once the man thought he never could question God's love to him; but now he is ready to turn away from all that is cheering, and look only on the gloomy side of his religious state.

Reading the Bible rather depresses than refreshes him; for although glorious things are there spoken of God's people, yet he discredits his claims to discipleship. Finding that in some things he has been sadly deficient in godly sincerity, he is much inclined to pronounce himself in all things hypocritical. The view he takes of his sins is, that they are so fearfully aggravated that they cannot be forgiven, even through the redemption that is in Christ. He does not see how one who loves God can be guilty of so heinous offences. Tears are his meat day and night. As with a sword in his bones, his enemies reproach him; while they say daily unto him, Where is thy God? Hope seems ready utterly to forsake him, and terrible darkness to take its place. His soul is cast down and disquieted within him. It is with feebleness that he utters the self-exhortation, "O my soul, . . . hope thou in God; for I shall yet praise him for the help of his countenance." He can no more confidently say, "The Lord will command his loving-kindness in the daytime, and in the night his song shall be with me." He is dejected, despondent, discouraged. He needs a guide, a friend, a counsellor, a comforter.

Many fears now torment him. He remembers God, and is troubled. Every divine perfection is contemplated with dread. God's truth, and mercy, and power, and holiness, and justice, and majesty become sources of terror. The King eternal, immortal, and invisible becomes the dreadful God. The love of Christ itself increases apprehensions lest the slighting of his mercies should hasten everlasting damnation. Fears of having grieved and vexed, and even quenched the Holy Spirit, so that he is turned to be an enemy, have now a sad prevalence. The threatenings of Scripture against such as have sinned against much light and many warnings spread dismay through his soul. Even the promises and invitations of Scripture, because they have been slighted, produce alarm rather than hope and peace.

In this state of mind, he is terrified at the thought of coming to the Lord's supper. To him it is indeed "the dreadful table of the Lord." In contemplating it, he sees far more of Sinai than of Calvary. Fierce flames shoot out where once he saw but the bright beams of unparalleled love and mercy, truth and faithfulness. Even the gospel becomes to him a dispensation of terror, a ministration of wrath.

Singing the songs of Zion is to such a one an unusual exercise. It brings no pleasure, unless it is of a mournful kind. Plaintive hymns and tunes best suit this state of depression. Sometimes they bring the relief of tears. And this is often considerable. Though we may weep without having our hardness of heart really cured, yet to one thus exercised it is a luxury to be able to have any evidence that all sense and feeling are not clean gone. And yet connected prayer is hardly undertaken, or if attempted, is found impossible. Instead of regular prayer to God, the heart ventures only to express wishes, but not accompanied by much hope that they will be gratified. If he asks any thing of God, he seems to himself to have little or no faith either in God's ability or willingness to grant his petitions.

Satan will now probably roar like a lion over his prey. He may suggest to the soul that God is its irreconcilable enemy, that Christ will surely deny it at last, and that the Holy Ghost is fighting against it. He says, "Your prayers are sin, your efforts are vain, your case is desperate, Christ has been rejected, the day of grace is past, salvation is impossible, heaven is lost, hell must be your portion." He thrusts a thousand fiery darts at the soul. He labors to arouse to the utmost some unsubdued lust, or suggests blasphemous thoughts, tempting the soul to curse God, or bid defiance to his wrath. Such thoughts are shocking; but the more they are resisted merely in human strength, the more powerful they may become.

All the while the soul is like the troubled sea, which cannot rest, whose waters cast up mire and dirt. His bones wax old through his roaring. He is consumed by the terrors of the Almighty. He finds no access to the mercy-seat, no cordial to revive his drooping spirit. Sometimes apprehensions of certain and speedy wrath become firm and fixed. At times it seems as if the pains of hell have already got hold upon him. The arrows of the Almighty stick fast in him. Something so much like despair that you can hardly tell the difference possesses him, and he will hardly allow that he is making any effort to flee from the wrath to come. He thinks, and perhaps speaks familiarly, of reprobation and hell. Sometimes the adversary pours in his horrid temptations in an almost perpetual stream. He suggests the great crime of self-murder, and assigns as a reason, that longer continuance will but aggravate a condemnation already felt to be exceedingly terrible.

Sometimes one whose heart is thus smitten and withered like grass hears the gospel preached publicly or privately, and for a season seems relieved, at least partially; but often this deliverance is only temporary, and the mind is apt to sink down again into gloom and wretchedness. To such a soul nothing is charming. Nature, in her gayest hues and dress, seems covered with a pall of sadness. The blue heavens wither. The green mountains look hoary. Even the flowers look drab. Well might he now sing,

"Sweet prospects, sweet birds, and sweet flowers,
Have lost all their sweetness with me;
The midsummer sun shines but dim,
The fields strive in vain to look gay."

Sleep departs, or is broken by frightful dreams. He forgets to eat his bread. Psa. 102 : 3.

Probably in the midst of all this suffering, when he most needs the sympathies of God's people, they will seem cold and distant; or perhaps they will judge him harshly, and regard his present distress as the fruit of some special sin. Perhaps trumpet-tongued slander will open wide her mouth, and proclaim falsehoods concerning him. Or perhaps sickness, or death, or pecuniary distress will invade his habitation; and thus he has sorrow upon sorrow. If God's word gives any relief in this state of mind, it is only those parts of it which describe his present state or express his present feelings. The complaints of Job or the mourning prayers of David show him that others before him have been in deep water, and so he sees that possibly he may yet escape; but "a horror of great darkness has fallen upon" him. "The spirit of a man sustaineth his infirmity; but a wounded spirit who can bear?" His soul sinks, and it seems as if all was lost. He may have days or weeks or months of apparently tideless, waveless, shoreless, fathomless woe.

But when God's purposes are accomplished, then comes relief. This may approach suddenly, but more commonly it comes gradually. Sometimes sudden and transient joy is given to prevent despair, before a settled calmness and quiet of soul is obtained. Generally the first step towards a return of joy is an increase of hope. Paul directs that we should take for a helmet the hope of salvation. We are saved by hope. Hope excites to action; and to the no little comfort of this distressed soul, he finds that with God's help he can do something.

He can resist the devil, and cause him to flee. The sword of the Spirit is God's word, and Satan finds its edge too keen for him.

When this man finds he can stop the mouth of the old lion, or discovers that he is a chained enemy, and that there is One stronger and mightier than the prince of the power of the air, he is very glad, and lays about him lustily.

This encourages hope, and faith begins again to lay hold of the promises. Confidence in God—in his power, wisdom, truth, and mercy—reassures the soul. The tongue of the dumb is loosed. The silent man begins to pray. The mourning soul begins to sing of mercies. Portions of Scripture begin to be brought home to the heart with heavenly sweetness. His views of the Saviour become refreshing and ravishing. He sees God in Christ, reconciling the world to himself. He glories in the cross of Christ. He esteems all things but loss, for the excellency of the knowledge of Christ Jesus his Lord. The Holy Ghost dwells in him, takes of the things of Christ, and shows them unto him. The Sanctifier becomes the Comforter. He now takes root downward, a sure pledge that he will yet bear fruit upward.

No precept of God's word is too strict for him. No promise is without its sweetness. No hours are so pleasant as those spent in devotion. He can now say in truth, "I had rather be a door-keeper—perform the humblest service—in the house of my God than to dwell in the tents of wickedness." His prejudices against men subside, his enmities are all buried, his heart-burnings give place to a spirit of love which embraces all mankind. He has a special delight in all God's people. He now knows that he has passed from death unto life, because he loves the brethren. His heart is full of gratitude. His mouth is full of praise. His thoughts burn within him. They are of salvation. Gladly does he offer all to Him who has brought him up out of the horrible pit and the miry clay, and set his feet upon a rock.

Now his meditation of God is sweet. And although sin is still at work, it no longer prevails against him. He looks forward with confident expectation to the period not distant, when he shall be done with temptation for ever, behold Christ in the fulness of his glory at God's right hand, and take up his abode on the banks of the river of life. He now takes just and profitable views of the nearness of eternity, of the shortness of time, of the worthlessness of things that perish, and of the priceless value of heavenly things.

And now the bent of the soul is towards God. The believer discovers the end of the Lord in his late trials. He sees how they were designed to prepare him for more abundant supplies of grace, strength, and enjoyment. He is therefore ready to say, "It is good for me that I have been afflicted." He is now like a child weaned of his mother. He is filled with the peaceable fruit of righteousness.

Such a view of one's experience is instructive. It teaches many lessons. It specially warns us to beware of the beginnings of sin. Neglect of duty, levity of mind, low views of God, a fretful temper, deceit, a want of the spirit of forgiveness, or any other sin, may plunge us into darkness. Fear of man is a great foe to grace. "He has begun to be a bad man, who fears to be a good man." We cannot be too vigilant over our own hearts. We cannot too tenderly love our Master and his people. We cannot be too zealous in the Lord's cause. "Sin's joys are but night dreams."

If at any time we should be overtaken with darkness, let us make diligent search for the cause. If moral, it will be found in that sin which we find ourselves averse to thinking of, or disinclined to hear faithfully reproved.

In times of darkness we should be very diligent in reading the Scriptures. Possibly we may have slighted some portion of God's word, while it contains the very truths whose cleansing, comforting power is most needed in our case. Especially labor to know the full import of those portions of Scripture which treat of experimental religion. The heavens themselves shall pass away, but God's word is for ever stable.

"The seas shall waste, the skies in smoke decay,
Rocks fall to dust, and mountains melt away;
But fixed *his word,* his saving power remains,
Thy realm for ever lasts; thy own Messiah reigns."

In darkness and perplexity consult, if you can, an *experienced* minister or Christian. Do not count them enemies if they probe your wounds and deal faithfully with you. Those who do but prophesy smooth things, will be found unprofitable in the end. The advice of weak, ignorant, or partial persons is apt to be injurious. Consult not those who are not fit to be advisers.

Labor to obtain clear views of the freeness and sufficiency of the salvation that is in Christ Jesus. Remember how in millions of cases where sin abounded, grace hath much more abounded. "Nothing can satisfy an offended conscience but that which satisfies an offended God," said Henry. Whereupon Adam said, "And well may that which satisfied an offended God pacify an offended conscience." Well did Cromwell in a letter to a friend say, "Salute your dear wife from me. Bid her beware of a bondage spirit. Fear is the natural issue of such a spirit; the antidote is love. The voice of fear is, 'If I had done this, if I had done that, how well it had been with me.' Love argueth in this wise; 'What a Christ have I; what a Father in and through him; what a name hath my Father, 'merciful, gracious, long-suffering, abundant in goodness and truth; forgiving iniquity, transgression, and sin.' What a nature hath my Father. He is love; free in it, unchangeable, infinite. What a covenant between him and Christ, for all the seed, for every one; wherein he undertakes all, and the poor soul nothing.' The new covenant is *grace*, to or upon the soul to which it is receptive." Your salvation depends not on your comfortable or uncomfortable frames, but on the grace and power of God. Remember the word, the oath, the covenant of God. Fight against despair. It is a great sin as well as a great misery.

Be conscientious in the performance of every duty. "He that loses his conscience, has nothing left worth keeping." It would be no token for good to have your affliction pass away while you are indulging in either sins of omission or of commission. "If you would not have affliction visit you twice, listen at once to what it teaches." God will never desert one who keeps a conscience void of offence. He may be weak as water, but God will gird him with strength. Leighton says, "When we consider how we are in ourselves, yea, the very strongest of us, and how assaulted, we may justly wonder that we can continue one day in a state of grace; but when we look on the strength by which we are guarded, the power of God, then we see the reason of our stability to the end; for Omnipotency supports us, and the everlasting arms are under us." A good old English bishop had for his motto, "Serve God, and be cheerful."

Beware of unnecessary expressions of your feelings in the presence of wicked men, lest they stumble at your temptations; or in the presence of weak brethren, lest you offend against the generation of God's children. Some men do not know that "a diamond with some flaws is still more precious than a pebble that has none." David kept his mouth with a bridle while the wicked was before him. He held his peace even from good. Do not wound Christ in the house of his friends by any exposure of your trials which will not be understood by others. Rather bear your sorrows in secret.

In your darkness call to mind the years of the right hand of the Most High, when the candle of the Lord shone upon you. Former joyful experiences of our Father's love are not so to be relied on as to make us careless about our present state. Neither are they to be forgotten. In meeting Goliath, David encouraged himself by calling to mind God's goodness on former occasions of great peril: "The Lord that delivered me out of the paw of the lion, and out of the paw of the bear, he will deliver me out of the hand of this Philistine." 1 Sam. 17:37.

When your darkness begins to be removed, do not rest satisfied with small attainments. Some good men think that one of the errors of our day is preaching a low experience. However this may be, let us beware of resting in few and small victories. "Open thy mouth wide, and I will fill it," says God.

One of the best ways to dispel fears for our personal safety is to labor for the salvation of others. Professed Christians often get into a morbid state of mind about their religious prospects. They are afraid they shall not be saved. Perhaps they will not be. If that is their chief anxiety, they can hardly expect comfort. It is selfish always to be thinking of their own future happiness, and in their terrible fears they are paying the just penalty of their low aims. But let them go out of themselves, and try to secure the salvation of others, and their fears are gone. Then they are doing God's work, and they have no doubt of his love.

Restored to spiritual comfort, beware of sin in every shape. Especially beware of spiritual pride and carnal security. In recounting God's dealings with you, praise not yourself, but glorify God. Extol his free, sovereign grace.

Let all God's people remember that soon all their sorrows will be gone, and the days of their mourning ended.

How different the character, experience,

and destiny of the righteous from those of the wicked. *Here* the righteous mourn; but they *shall be* comforted. *Here* the wicked have their good things; but they *shall be* tormented. At death the sorrows of the righteous end for ever, and eternal joy begins. At death the joys of the wicked terminate, and eternal sorrow begins. The righteous cry to God daily even in prosperity. The wicked commonly do not begin to pray till God has ceased to hear.

## CHAPTER IX.

### BACKSLIDING.

"A PERSON who suspected that a minister of his acquaintance was not truly orthodox, went to him and said, 'Sir, I am told that you are against the perseverance of the saints.' 'Not I, indeed,' answered he; 'it is the perseverance of sinners that I oppose.' The other replied, 'But that is not a satisfactory answer, sir. Do you think that a child of God cannot fall very low, and yet be restored?' The minister answered, 'I think it will be very dangerous to make the experiment.'" Whether the minister was orthodox or not, it is certain that his sentiments, so far as expressed, were quite consistent with the Bible. He who is determined to see how far he may decline in religion and yet be restored, will lose his soul. "The soul that doeth aught presumptuously shall surely be cut off." He that regards sin with so little abhorrence as willingly to commit it, cannot be walking in the way of life. He who allowedly and habitually departs from

God, proves that sin reigns in his mortal body, and that he is the slave of corruption.

The declensions of good and bad men are unlike in several particulars. When the wicked depart from God, they cry, "Peace and safety." When the righteous no longer maintain a close walk with God, they say, Oh that it were with us as in months past. In their wanderings, the wicked call themselves happy. Having forsaken God, the righteous lose enjoyment, and are filled with sadness. The wicked backslide perpetually. Jer. 8:5. The righteous err from God's ways but for a time. The wicked are bent to backsliding. Hosea 11:7. The righteous are betrayed into sin. The wicked are as the sow wallowing in the mire. It is their nature to work iniquity. The righteous are as the cleanly sheep. If they are in the slough, it is their calamity. "Whosoever is born of God doth not commit sin; for his seed remaineth in him; and he cannot sin, because he is born of God." The wicked fill up their sin always. They sleep not except they have done some mischief. They dig into hell. The righteous is not so. Even when he sleepeth, his heart waketh. When he falleth, he shall rise again. When he sitteth in darkness, the Lord shall be a light unto him. A just man falleth seven times, and riseth up again. All his backslidings are healed.

The danger of declension is very great. Many think not so. Their words and lives prove that they think it a small matter to offend God and grieve his Spirit. They are cold and heartless in his service. Their fear of offending God is a weak principle. It controls them not. It has not the force of law. We are always in danger when we have slight thoughts of the evil of sin, and have not our loins girt about. To depart from God is to seek darkness.

Let us then inquire who are backsliders. This is a point of high importance. Like all matters of practical religion, it demands candor, seriousness, and discrimination. He who wishes to deceive himself can commonly do so.

It is no conclusive evidence that one is not a backslider, that he is not himself convinced of the fact. A truly pious man in a state of declension usually has some fears respecting himself; but many grievously depart from God without being fully convinced of their error. It is a sad truth, that all sin blinds the mind and hardens the heart. It is very difficult to convince any man of his guilt. We have an account of a primitive church that was in a sad declension, neither cold nor hot, and ready to be spewed out; and yet, far from having any just sense of her state, she said, "I am rich, and increased with goods, and have need of nothing;" and knew not that she was wretched, and miserable, and poor, and blind, and naked. Rev. 3:16, 17.

Many are kept from owning their backslidings, because they are mercifully restrained from open sins. Had they publicly fallen into overt iniquity, they would blush, and be ashamed; they would bewail their wickedness before God and men. But as yet all is secret. They are merely backsliders in heart. No man knows of their spiritual wickedness. No man can accuse them of living in coldness or in iniquity. Hence they conclude that all is well. But they are mistaken. It may all come to the knowledge of men in a short time. It was so with David. To him God said, "Thou didst it secretly; but I will do this thing before all Israel, and before the sun." 2 Sam. 12:12.

It should also be stated that it is easy to

backslide from God. We go astray from the womb, speaking lies. It is as natural for us to do wrong as for the sparks to ascend. In our voyage heavenward, wind and tide are both against us. If we do nothing to overcome their action, they will carry us away. We can go to hell without intending to do so, without putting forth any efforts to that effect. But to go to heaven requires prayer, self-denial, vigilance, violence, running, wrestling, fighting.

All serious declension in religion begins in negligence of closet duties. These are, meditation, self-examination, reading the Scriptures, praise, and prayer. A close walk with God insures regularity and alacrity in performing these duties. But an indisposition for them is one of the first signs that spiritual health is failing. This symptom should produce alarm. Sometimes it does ; and then the enemy gains no permanent advantage. But often the soul is made quite at ease, is thrown quite off its guard, and allows the public duties of religion to supersede the secret. A true Christian can hardly live without any secret prayer ; but he may be in such a state as sadly to slight the means of personal communion with God. Trains of pious meditation may be few. The Scriptures may cease to be to the soul the lively oracles, honey and the honey-comb. Self-examination may prove a hard task, and a revealer of unlooked-for wickedness. Praise and thanksgiving may become strange things, and He who gave songs in the night may leave the soul to sighings and tossings. Then prayer will be regarded rather as an exaction to be granted than as a privilege to be enjoyed. When piety flourished in the soul, it was not enough to perform closet duties statedly and formally. Without having set a particular time for them, the soul would occasionally pursue its pious reflections, its self-examinations, its earnest inquiries, its grateful trains of thought. It would sing some notes of praise. It would cry out after God, even when removed from the usual place and circumstances of devotion. Yes, in the midst of worldly business, devout aspirations would ascend to the Father of mercies; the events of providence successively occurring would be piously contemplated; the tear of penitence would often trickle down, and hope would rouse the soul to great animation.

But when such a one backslides, religion

is gradually excluded from a place in the common affairs of life. Its duties are shoved into a corner or removed from hourly attention. Then one will go from his closet, quieting his conscience with the reflection that he has spent some time in the set observance of secret duties, and now he feels more free to welcome the affairs of the world. He follows the Lord, but not fully nor heartily. Here the sad work of declension begins. Sin advances apace. Thraldom and bewilderment commence. The soul is already in a net. Blessed is he who now takes the alarm, returns to duty and to the Saviour, and is restored to peace, a good conscience, and the light of God's countenance. Sometimes this is done. In every case it should be attempted. But often sin gains strength. The backslider proceeds to greater lengths.

The next step is the neglect of family and social religion. This may not soon be taken; but it is well-nigh impossible to be cold and formal in the closet, and lively and punctual in the social duties of devotion. Hypocrisy may go very far, but rarely as far as this. Men are affected by temptations to slight or omit family worship or social prayer, according to the state of their hearts. To the lively, growing Christian the adversary comes, but has nothing in him. His allurements take not effect. But to the neglecter of his spiritual duties, the enemy approaches boldly. He finds his reasonings vainly resisted, and finally yielded to. The stones of the domestic altar begin to be loose and ready to tumble down, and the little praying circle is quite forsaken. How sad a state is this. How blind the mind becomes under the power of sin. None but God can effectually check this painful declension.

In this state, ere long one feels uneasy and guilty. Therefore, to quiet conscience and keep up appearances with himself, he may for a long time be unusually strict and punctual in some of the public duties of religion. So his seat will seldom be vacant in the more public worship of God. For like reason he will become quite zealous about some of the externals of religion. Or he may insist much on the system of doctrine which he has embraced, having learned the art of holding the truth in unrighteousness. Or he may talk of experimental religion, deceiving himself with the belief that if he talks on the subject it is a sign of some right feeling. He is now sadly blind to his own wretchedness. If he has gone thus far, it will probably not be long till he will be detained from the house of God by causes that once could have had no hindering effect. His zeal even for forms and externals will probably soon betray weakness, or fierceness, or a spirit of contention. His love for truth will be substituted by a desire for controversy. Practical and experimental religion will engage but few of his words or thoughts. His heart has gone after other things. Sometimes indeed one acquires the evil habit of speaking fluently of things not felt nor loved. In this case recovery is less and less to be expected. All insincerity is unfriendly to our recovering ourselves out of the snare of the devil.

Such a soul will find duties and ordinances unprofitable. He will go away from prayer, from reading, from preaching, and even from the Lord's table, and be no more holy, no more humble, no more watchful, no more spiritually minded, no more able to resist temptation than before. Sometimes he hopes that he is receiving profit; but his conduct soon shows that he is mistaken. His expectation deceives him. "He looks for judgment, but there is none; for salvation, but it is far off from him." Isa.

59:11. He says, "What profit is it that I have kept his ordinance, and that I have walked mournfully before the Lord?" Mal. 3:14. It is with him even "as when a hungry man dreameth, and behold, he eateth; but he awaketh, and his soul is empty: or as when a thirsty man dreameth, and behold, he drinketh; but he awaketh, and behold, he is faint, and his soul hath appetite." Isa. 29:8. Sometimes the ordinances are like the fruit which Milton's serpents ate. To the eye it was beautiful and inviting, but in the mouth it turned to ashes, was bitter, and increased thirst. Or they are like the book the prophet ate, sweet in the mouth, but bitter afterwards. So sin often imbitters the most precious privileges. Backsliders are made miserable by an approach to God. They are not prepared for it.

As piety thus dies in the soul, charity diminishes, and censoriousness takes its place. A backslider will be more than formerly disposed to doubt the good motives, the upright intentions, and sincere professions of others. He will not be slow in entertaining severe judgments of others. Sometimes he will express harsh opinions of his fellow-men. Attaching great value to any little shreds of piety still about himself, he expresses surprise that others have not his seeming virtues. He wonders how a Christian can act so and so, while he himself is doing worse. His heart does not lead him instantly and spontaneously to cast a cloak over the faults of others. This spirit marks also his treatment of sinners. Reproach rather than persuasion, contempt rather than affection, mark his conduct towards them that are without. It cannot now be said of him that he "thinketh no evil," and "is kind." He shows much of the temper of those who make a man an offender for a word.

Soon you may find him vain and trifling in his plans and conversation. He prefers vain company. He selects unprofitable reading. He seeks amusement, not profit. Things must be found to suit his taste. When lively in religion, his conversation was seasoned with salt; but now any thing rather than religion is congenial to his feelings. On that topic he is cold. On temporal things he speaks with zest and animation. He may not wholly forsake the society of spiritual Christians, but he will not always shun the fool and the scorner. Mere works of taste or fancy will very much supersede the sound and solid treatises on religion, which once feasted his soul. The Bible does not refresh his spirit as once it did. His pious friends are often alarmed at his state, and weep over it in secret; yet he often thinks this is the usual way to glory.

In this state he will often exhibit a painful degree of indifference to the honor of Christ. An apostasy which once would have cost him bitter tears, hardly awakens a transient pang. He may not grossly profane the name, the word, or the Sabbath of the Lord, but he is far less than formerly grieved at such sins in others. When he sees people sunk in sin, his spirit is not stirred within him. He is not grieved for the affliction of Joseph. He does not weep between the porch and the altar as he once did, crying, Spare thy people, O Lord.

Nor does he rejoice as formerly in hearing of the spread of truth, the conversion of sinners, the progress of the gospel. Once his soul was inflamed with love and leaped for joy when he heard of the revival of religion. President Edwards the elder says, that when he first obtained settled peace of conscience, he felt irrepressible desires for the salvation of the world, and had peculiar delight in hearing of the progress of religion in any part of the earth. This is common Christian experience. A lively Christian unites with angels in rejoicing over even *one* sinner that repenteth. But the backslider has little interest in such events. It is doubtful whether he loves himself or his Saviour the most. It grieves him more to hear himself reviled than to hear his Saviour blasphemed. It rejoices him more to hear himself praised than to hear his Saviour commended. Such things render it doubtful whether he ever knew the Lord—whether he ever was born again. And it is a bad sign if they do not shake his confidence in his own conversion.

These things lead to a great diminution of solid religious comfort. He has few songs of holy joy. His heart is too cold to relish religious duties. He looks on the past with no real pleasure. It reminds him of time wasted, of vows broken, of opportunities lost, of comforts decayed, of mercies slighted. Of the future he is much afraid. He remembers God, and is troubled. He is afraid of evil tidings. He is looking out for some sore chastisement.

His old besetting sins revive with great power. Levity takes the place of seriousness; fretfulness expels gentleness. Ambition begins to burn in the bosom where formerly dwelt lowliness and contentment. Covetousness resumes her iron despotism; or prodigality breaks out afresh. The heavenly racer takes up one by one the weights which he had formerly laid aside. He runs, but as uncertainly; he fights, but with great feebleness.

Those who have thus departed from God are left to see what they can do alone. God permits them to try their own power and resources. Of such the Comforter says, "I will go and return to my place, till they acknowledge their offence and seek my face; in their affliction they will seek me early." Hos. 5:15. Samson is now shorn of the locks of his strength. It will be well if he be not forced to make sport for the Philistines. How long one may remain in this state none can tell. To escape from such error and sinfulness is no easy thing. It pleased God at once to restore Peter after he had denied his Lord. But it seems to have been months before David shed for his crimes the tears of true repentance. It is no easy matter to escape from the snare of the devil when we have once been led captive by him at his will.

Yet to all God's people his promise stands

sure: "I will heal their backsliding." Hosea 14:4. In fulfilling his promise, God will choose his own time. He heals when and how he pleases. None can hasten, none can retard his work. The good Shepherd restoreth the soul of his servants, and does not leave them to perish in their errors. He commonly begins the healing process by convincing the soul of its sad departures from him. This is done by calling the mind to reflection on its own evil doings. Sometimes God sends Nathan the prophet with a pointed message, charging home guilt upon the transgressor. Sometimes he employs affliction to humble the soul at his footstool. "In their affliction they will seek me early." God is not confined to any class of means. The crowing of the cock brought home to Peter Christ's words of warning with as much power as any truth that ever reached man's heart. God sometimes uses the derision and persecution of the wicked to awaken his people out of sleep. The word of God is, to such, quick and powerful, and sharper than any two-edged sword. The Spirit reproves. He convinces of sin; he reveals the baseness of the heart; he makes one see his folly and ingratitude in departing from the living God.

Now is fulfilled that scripture: "The backslider in heart shall be filled with his own ways." Prov. 14:14. He forsook God, the fountain of living waters. This was his first error. The second was like unto it: he hewed out to himself broken cisterns, which could hold no water. God may now let loose his corruptions upon him, or send a messenger of Satan to buffet him. He is afflicted; he is tossed with tempest, and not comforted. He is so "ashamed that he cannot look up." He is convinced that he deserves rejection. God often seems to fulfil the threatening: "I will meet them as a bear that is bereaved of her whelps." Hos. 13:8. Instead of comforting, he speaks words of terror. The afflicted soul says, "Oh that I knew where I might find him! that I might come even to his seat! I would order my cause before him, and fill my mouth with arguments. . . . Behold, I go forward, but he is not there; and backward, but I cannot perceive him: on the left hand, where he doth work, but I cannot behold him: he hideth himself on the right hand, that I cannot see him." Job 23:3, 4, 8, 9. Sometimes despairing thoughts enter his mind, and he cries, "Why is my pain perpetual, and my wound incurable, which refuseth to be healed? Wilt thou be altogether unto me as a liar, and as waters that fail?" Jer. 15:18.

Sometimes he cannot see any thing good implanted in his heart by God's Spirit. He almost concludes that no real child of God would be left to fall so low as he has done. The promises do not comfort him, though the threatenings often terrify him. He feels the force and justice of the charge God brings against him: "Hast thou not procured this unto thyself, in that thou hast forsaken the Lord thy God? . . . Thine own wickedness shall correct thee, and thy backslidings shall reprove thee: know therefore and see that it is an evil thing and bitter, that thou hast forsaken the Lord thy God, and that my fear is not in thee." Jer. 2:17, 19. He now has continual sorrow. He drinks wormwood and gall. His conscience makes his soul like the troubled sea. None can tell his griefs. "The heart knoweth its own bitterness." It is said by some that David seems never to have fully recovered his joyousness after his backsliding. However this may be, we know how the arrows of the Almighty stuck fast in him, and his waves and his billows passed over him. The pangs of a backslider's recovery often exceed those of a first conversion.

Such views lead one to a hearty confession of sin. "I acknowledge my transgression, and my sin is ever before me." Psa. 51 : 3. This confession may be minute and particular. It will go back and deplore original sin. Psa. 51 : 5. It will humble itself for sins committed before conversion: "Remember not the sins of my youth, nor my transgressions." Psa. 25 : 7. But sins committed since a profession of religion justly seem to call for deep abasement. They are against vows and promises, illumination and ordinances—against all that is solemn in the public owning of Christ. The fountains of the great deep are broken up. Witnesses of one's sinfulness arise on all hands. The stone out of the wall cries, and the beam out of the timber answers it. Thus his confession is not vague and general, but definite and particular. He sees good cause in many a misdeed why God should contend against him. Sins against man are not forgotten; but sins against God are fearfully multiplied and aggravated. Sometimes it seems as if the soul was made to see all the evil that ever it did, and then it cries, "I am undone." "O wretched man that I am." "God be merciful to me a sinner." "Enter not into judgment with thy servant; for in thy sight shall no man living be justified." "If thou, Lord, shouldest mark iniquities, O Lord, who shall stand?" "I abhor myself, and repent in dust and ashes."

Sometimes a soul thus convicted is turbulent, and rages like a wild bull in the net. And now his bones wax old through his roaring all the day long. It is a great thing to have the heart subdued, and the soul made like a weaned child. When the soul is thus humbled, quiet, and submissive, when high looks are brought down and high thoughts abased, then God grants a spirit of true believing prayer and of strong crying. He says, "Take with you words, and turn to the Lord: say unto him, Take away all iniquity, and receive us graciously: so will we render the calves of our lips." Hos. 14:2. This spirit of prayer is sure to be followed by tokens for good. Itself is a blessed fruit of Christ's mediation. He that asketh receiveth.

And now the Lord appears. As the spouse found it good to be of a quiet, patient spirit, so does the soul; for the next thing is, "The voice of my Beloved! behold, he cometh, leaping upon the mountains, and skipping upon the hills." Song 2:7. He "cometh out of the wilderness like pillars of smoke, perfumed with myrrh and frankincense." Song 3:6. When, in the fulness of his love and kindness and power and condescension and faithfulness, Christ makes his appearance and shows himself gracious to the repentant soul, there is a wonderful change. He comes both gently and seasonably. "His going forth is prepared as the morning." Hos. 6:3. He bids the soul take courage. He forgives all its sins, casting them behind his back. He gives a check to corruption. He causes the tempter to depart. He pours light into the mind. He hushes the tumultuous waves of human passion. He quiets the troubles of the soul. He says, "Peace, be still;" and suddenly there is a great calm. Thus Jesus is "a horn of salvation for us, in the house of his servant David.... That we should be saved from our enemies, and from the hand of all that hate us.... That we, being delivered out of the hand of our enemies, might serve him without fear, in holiness and righteousness before him, all the days of our life." ... Thus he "gives knowledge of salvation unto his people, by the remission of their sins, through the tender mercy of our God; whereby the day-spring from on high hath visited us, to give light to them that sit in darkness and in the shadow of death, to guide our feet into the way of peace." Luke 1:69, etc.

To a soul thus exercised, Christ in all his offices is precious. Its language is, "Whom have I in heaven but thee? and there is none upon earth that I desire besides thee." "Set me as a seal upon thy heart, as a seal upon thine arm; for love is strong as death. Many waters cannot quench love, neither can the floods drown it; if a man would give all the substance of his house for love, it would be utterly contemned." Song 8:6, 7. In such a soul the purposes of obedience are humble, but firm. Faith gains many an important victory. Penitence loves to shed her secret tears. Hope looks up, and says, I shall soon be for ever with the Lord. The spirit of adoption says, That awful God, who shakes the heavens with his voice, is my kind and merciful Father. Aversion to sin is now strong. The soul says, "What shall I render unto the Lord for all his benefits?" Gratitude is ready to make any offering; it withholds nothing.

In one thus dealt with by the Lord are strikingly fulfilled these passages of Scripture: "I waited patiently for the Lord; and he inclined unto me, and heard my cry. He brought me up also out of a horrible pit, out of the miry clay, and set my feet upon a rock, and established my goings. And he hath put a new song in my mouth, even praise unto our God: many shall see it, and fear, and shall trust in the Lord." Psa. 40:1–3. Nor is the following language of the psalmist less applicable to his case: "I love the Lord, because he hath heard my voice and my supplications. Because he hath inclined his ear unto me, therefore will I call upon him as long as I live. The sorrows of death compassed me, and the pains of hell gat hold upon me: I found trouble and sorrow. Then called I upon the name of the Lord; O Lord, I beseech thee, deliver my soul. Gracious is the Lord, and righteous; yea, our God is merciful. The Lord preserveth the simple: I was brought low, and he helped me. Return unto thy rest, O my soul; for the Lord hath dealt bountifully with thee. For thou hast delivered my soul from death, mine eyes from tears, and my feet from falling. I will walk before the Lord in the land of the living." Psalm 116:1–9. Thus experience teaches the sense and sweetness of many a passage of Scripture formerly read without understanding. Indeed it is not uncommon for those thus recovered to think that this is their first conversion, and that never before did they know in their souls the joy of God's salvation. The change is great. The grace is great.

When God thus heals backsliders, he kindly adds these blessings: "I will love them freely; for mine anger is turned away from him. I will be as the dew unto Israel." That is, I will send daily gentle, refreshing influences upon him. "He shall grow as the lily, and cast forth his roots as Lebanon. His branches shall spread, and his beauty shall be as the olive-tree, and his smell as Lebanon. They that dwell under his shadow shall return; they shall revive as the corn, and grow as the vine: the scent thereof shall be as the wine of Lebanon. Ephraim shall say, What have I to do any more with idols? I have heard him, and observed him: I am like a green fir-tree. From me is thy fruit found." Hos. 14:4–8. All the figures in this passage may not be intelligible to some; but plain honest minds will not doubt that here are promised rich supplies of free grace, securing pardon of sin, the indwelling of the Holy Spirit, deep-rooted vigor, increase of grace and of fruitfulness, usefulness to those under his influence, a sweet savor of piety at all times, together with an utter renunciation of idols and of self-dependence.

And now are you a backslider? Are you cold, formal, or negligent in the secret duties of religion? Do you feel the uneasiness of guilt? Are you "afraid of evil tidings?" Do you live in constant apprehension of sore calamities? Are ordinances unprofitable to you? Are you in the constant exercise of charity, or do you indulge in a censorious spirit? Are you vain, light, trifling? Do you prefer the society of the devout? What books do you select? Are you alive to the honor of Christ? Do you *enjoy* religion? Let these solemn questions be asked frequently and answered honestly, as you shall give account to God.

If you have evidence that you are not a backslider, then give God the glory, and "be not high-minded, but fear." Nothing but amazing grace can have preserved you from the snare of the fowler. But if you find that the evidence shows you to be in a state of declension, then open your eyes to your real condition, judge yourself, confess your sins, and cleave to God. Hear the kind call: "Come, and let us return unto the Lord." Hos. 6 : 1. If you should not return and be healed, and if you should be called to die, how sad would be your departure out of this world. Your sun would go down behind a cloud, leaving others in doubt whether it was not gone down in eternal night.

And if your sanctification shall not advance faster than it has done since you first believed in Christ, how long will it be before you are prepared unto glory? At your present rate of growth in grace, would you be fit for heaven in a thousand years? And yet there is no one of us who shall live a thousand months. Many will not live a thousand weeks, yea, not a thousand days. Possibly some will not live a thousand seconds. Indifference to eternal things in so critical circumstances is wholly irreconcilable with wisdom.

## CHAPTER X.

### FAITH.

EVERYWHERE in the Scriptures great stress is laid on faith. In scores of passages its absolute necessity is explicitly declared. With the word of God Christian experience well agrees. The young convert had neither hope nor joy till he believed. His faith being weak, he manifests great instability. But as it increases, he grows stronger until he is undaunted, and cries, "Though he slay me, yet will I trust in him." Old Christians speak much of faith, and always love to have the truth concerning it clearly explained.

But what is the faith on which the Scriptures so much insist? This is a matter of chief importance. An error here will affect our whole religious life. Faith is either human or divine. In human faith we rely upon what *men* say. This we do by the constitution of our minds. Thus children rest upon what their parents tell them. Human faith is properly confined to things on which God has not spoken. Its basis is human testimony. Divine faith rests on the testimony of *God*. It concerns things which are revealed from heaven.

A historical faith is an intellectual assent to the truth of any thing recorded in history, sacred or profane. Thus we believe that Cæsar conquered Gaul, and that William of Normandy conquered Britain. But this belief has no effect in making us better or worse. Many thus believe that Moses, David, Paul, and Christ said and did all that is ascribed to them, yet this faith produces no change in their hearts. It is purely intellectual. Thus king Agrippa believed the prophets, as Paul declared. Acts 26 : 27.

The faith of miracles was a belief that God could and would work a miracle by one or for one. This faith has long since ceased to exist. Yet in the days of Christ and his apostles it was quite common. It had no saving power. Many thus believed and perished. Matt. 7 : 22, 23 ; 1 Cor. 13 : 2.

The faith of devils is mentioned by James 2 : 19 : "The devils also believe and tremble." This is a reluctant belief. It is forced upon them. It is not confined to fallen angels. *Men* often have a belief of divine things which makes them very apprehensive. Thus Felix trembled under the terrors of conscience produced by Paul's preaching. Thus sinners often die in despair, choked with divine terrors. This faith has no love, no real penitence, no submission, no humility in it. It works wrath, terror, and alienation from God.

A temporary faith is a transient persuasion that the things of revelation are true, important, and interesting. It seizes upon the temporal benefits of the gospel, and fills the imagination with very vivid conceptions of the preciousness of godliness, at least for this life. But it never truly engages the affections to divine things. A little tribulation or persecution kills it outright. Luke 8:13. It never changes the heart. It is not in its nature saving.

The faith of God's people relates to things past, present, and to come. It believes that God made the world. There is the past. It believes that God is. There is the present. It believes that there will be a day of judgment. There is the future. Nor are these and other revealed truths believed by different kinds of faith, but all by one and the same faith. As with the same visual organ we look to the east, to the west, to the north, and to the south, at objects far from us or near to us, so with the same eye of faith we look at things thousands of years past, or thousands of years to come, or things now existing in the unseen world. Of old for thousands of years the pious believed in a Saviour to come. In the days of his flesh, his disciples believed in a Saviour then come. For nearly two thousand years God's people have believed in a Saviour that has come. In all these cases the faith was the same in principle and in its effects also.

The Westminster Confession says, "The grace of faith, whereby the elect are enabled to believe to the saving of their souls, is the work of the Spirit of Christ in their hearts, and is ordinarily wrought by the ministry of the word, by which also, and by the administration of the sacraments, and prayer, it is increased and strengthened. By this faith a Christian believeth to be true whatsoever is revealed in the word for the authority of God himself speaking therein, and acteth differently upon that which each particular passage thereof containeth; yielding obedience to the commands, trembling at the threatenings, and embracing the promises of God for this life and that which is to come. But the principal acts of saving faith are accepting, receiving, and resting upon Christ for justification, sanctification, and eternal life, by virtue of the covenant of grace. This faith is different in degrees, weak or strong; may be often and many ways assailed and weakened, but gets the victory; growing up in many to the attainment of a full assurance through Christ, who is both the author and finisher of our faith."

A little consideration of this account of faith will show how full, complete, and scriptural it is. The first thing asserted is that saving faith is not of earthly, but of heavenly origin; that it is not of man, but of God. Faith is the gift of God. It is expressly called a "faith of the operation of God." "Unto you it is given on the behalf of Christ to believe on him." "God hath dealt to every man the measure of faith." When "Peter said, Thou art Christ, the Son of the living God, Jesus answered and said unto him, Blessed art thou, Simon Barjona; for flesh and blood hath not revealed it unto thee, but my Father which is in heaven." This faith is particularly ascribed to the Holy Ghost as its author. He produces it in the heart. So say the Scriptures. "The fruit of the Spirit is faith." "To another is given faith by the same Spirit." "We having the same Spirit of faith, also believe." The reason why saving faith endures, is because it is the incorruptible seed of God.

It is next said that in working this faith in us, God puts honor upon his word as the ordinary instrument. With this also the Scriptures well agree. "How shall they believe in him of whom they have not heard? and how shall they hear without a preacher?... So then, faith cometh by hearing, and hearing by the word of God." "It pleased God by the foolishness of preaching to save them that believe." This is the foundation of all our encouragement in proclaiming the gospel. That which is sown in the weakness of man is raised in the mighty energy of the Holy Ghost. No wonder that such happy results flow from proclaiming the gospel whenever God's Spirit attends it. It is thus the power of God unto salvation to every one that believeth. "God's gracious biddings are effectual enablings."

In like manner this faith is chiefly nourished by the ministry of the word and other ordinances, and by prayer. "Lord, increase our faith." The baptism of water is effectual when accompanied by the baptism of the Holy Ghost. The breaking of bread and drinking of wine are means of nourishment to all those who drink spiritually of the Rock which follows them, even Christ, and who by faith eat the true bread which cometh down from heaven, even the Son of God. All the saints desire the sincere milk of the word, that they may grow thereby.

True faith respects all God's word. It receives narratives, promises, threatenings, doctrines, precepts, warnings, encouragements, all as they were designed for its use. It obeys God's commands. They were given for that purpose. It is afraid of his threatenings. It trembles at his word. It relies upon the promises, both as they respect this life and the next. It takes warning from many parts of Scripture. It rejoices in solid scriptural encouragement. It relies upon God's word as testimony that is infallible. Whatever God speaks, faith believes. It receives all he has said. The word of God liveth and abideth for ever. So faith receives it as his word, and not as the word of man. His authority is perfect.

But saving faith has special reference to Christ. So the Scriptures often teach. "Who is he that overcometh the world, but he that believeth that Jesus is the Son of God?" "If we receive the witness of men, the witness of God is greater; for this is the witness of God, which he hath testified of his Son. He that believeth on the Son of God hath the witness in himself: he that believeth not God hath made him a liar, because he believeth not the record that God gave of his Son. And this is the record, that God hath given to us eternal life; and this life is in his Son." "Believe in the Lord Jesus Christ, and thou shalt be saved." "He that believeth on the Son hath everlasting life." "He that believeth on him is not condemned." In God's word the great theme is Christ Jesus. "To him give all the prophets witness." "The testimony of Jesus is the spirit of prophecy." If to deny the Father is fatal, so is it also to deny the Son. If to do despite to the Spirit of grace involves the loss of the soul, to reject Christ as the Saviour makes destruction inevitable. But to receive Christ, to rest upon him, to look to him, to come to him, to flee to him for refuge, to take him as our Sacrifice, as our Prophet, Priest, and King, and to do this heartily, is the great office of saving faith.

This faith is not of equal strength in all believers, nor in the same believer at all times. We read of "him that is weak in faith," of "little faith," and of "great faith." Faith grows by the divine blessing. The faith of some grows "exceedingly." Every true disciple says, "Lord, I believe; help thou my unbelief." It finally gains every needful victory. In some cases it is matured into full assurance. This is all through Christ, who begins, carries on, and perfects the work of faith in us by his Spirit and grace.

This whole view of faith is consistent with itself and with all the Scriptures. It explains many things which otherwise would seem to us enigmatical.

First, we see why faith always was and always will be necessary. "By faith Abel offered unto God a more excellent sacrifice than Cain." This was the religion of those early times. "When the Son of man cometh, shall he find faith on the earth?" This will be the religion of the latest times. The reason why no man was ever able or shall ever be able to please God without faith, is, that unbelief at every step sets aside all that God has said and done for man's salvation. He who would be saved in unbelief, would put perpetual contempt on all the arrangements of heaven for the recovery of lost men.

We also see how reasonable it is that faith should be required of us. "Have faith in God." "Believe in the Lord your God, so shall ye be established." "This is the work of God, that ye believe on him whom he hath sent." "Be not faithless, but believing." These are but specimens of the authoritative tones in which God speaks to us on this subject. He could not say less if he sought our good. To permit us to live in unbelief would be to license all sin.

We can also now understand why the minds of truly religious people are so ready to take up with God's offers of grace and mercy. Believing all God says, they of course receive as true all that he has alleged concerning their fallen and depraved condition. In other words, they find out that they are sinners, lost, guilty, vile, and helpless. To such the gospel is always good news. It is indeed life from the dead to a poor convinced sinner, to see the door of mercy wide open, and Christ standing ready to receive all that come to him.

It is also clear that our friends can do for

us nothing more kind than earnestly to pray that our faith may abound. As Paul says, "We pray always for you that our God would count you worthy of this calling, and fulfil all the good pleasure of his goodness, and the work of faith with power." Nor should we cease to implore the same blessing for ourselves. He who has right views in this matter will never lean on himself, nor trust in his own goodness, or wisdom, or power. Boston well says, "Faith goes out of itself for all its wants." Its trust in Another is at war with all self-reliance.

Thus faith always begets humility. It brings down the haughty to a sense of dependence. It takes away vain-glorious notions and boastings. Venn says, "Faith, though it be weak and imperfect, instead of exalting itself against the justice of God, and standing before him in the confidence of a lie, puts all from itself, and gives the whole glory of our salvation where it is due." So that as faith goes abroad in quest of supplies, so it goes forth of itself to bestow its honors. Its unceasing language is, "Not unto us, not unto us, but to thy name give glory."

We can also see the difference between *im-*

*plicit* and *explicit* faith. The former takes God at his word, obeys, and is at peace. The latter would have every thing explained, and all difficulties removed, before it would trust the promise or obey the command. Implicit faith first relies, then proves. Explicit faith would first prove, then trust. This made Bishop Hall say, "With men it is a good rule to try first, and then to trust; but with respect to God it is otherwise. I will first trust him as most wise, omnipotent, and merciful, and try him afterwards. It is as impossible for him to deceive me as not to be." "The school of God and nature require two contrary manners of proceeding. In the school of nature we must conceive, and then believe; in the school of God we must first believe, and then we shall conceive. He that believes no more than he conceives, can never be a Christian; nor he a philosopher that assents without reason. In nature's school we are taught to elicit the truth by logical discourse; but God cannot endure a logician. In his school, he is the best scholar that reasons least and assents most. In divine things, I will conceive what I can; the rest I will believe and admire. Not a curious head, but a believing and plain heart is accepted with God." The same is strongly expressed in other words by Goodwin: "Of all acts of faith, this of pure trust doth honor God most, and hath indeed more of faith in it: the purer the trust is, the greater the trust is; and the greater the trust is, the greater the faith is; and the greater the faith, the more honor comes to God." Mason also says, "Men would first see, and then believe; but they must first believe, and then see." Our Saviour said, "Thomas, because thou hast seen me, thou hast believed: blessed are they that have not seen, and yet have believed." Of course, implicit faith in *man*, or in any system of doctrines taught by men, is great folly. There we have a right to demand explanation, reasons, proof. But when God says a thing is so, the more simply, promptly, and firmly we believe what he says the better. It is the height of wisdom to receive every word of God as pure and true, asking no questions expressive of doubt or distrust.

And yet faith, even the simplest and strongest, is not irrational, nor foolish. No man acts so wisely as he who implicitly believes God. Abraham never showed that his faculties were so well regulated and orderly as when he went straight forward at God's bidding to sacrifice Isaac. He asked no reasons, he stated no difficulties; he simply did as he had been commanded, and staggered not through unbelief. The reason why faith is so wise is, because it reposes confidence in God, who cannot lie, cannot change, cannot fail, cannot be deceived, thwarted, or even perplexed; who sees the end from the beginning, who loves beyond all names of love known to mortals, or even to angels; a God and Saviour who never trampled on a broken heart, who never despised the cry of the humble, who never left the penitent to perish in their sins, and who will infallibly bring to eternal glory all who take refuge in atoning blood. Implicit faith in each Person and in all the teachings of the Godhead is the height of wisdom and virtue among men, though implicit faith in any other, even in an angel from heaven, would be folly. Jer. 17:5; Gal. 1:8.

The view already given of faith harmonizes well with the definitions given of it by all sound writers.

The following is a good definition: "Justifying faith is a saving grace wrought in the heart of a sinner by the Spirit and word of

God, whereby he, being convinced of his sin and misery, and of the disability in himself and all other creatures to recover him out of his lost condition, not only assenteth to the truth of the promise of the gospel, but receiveth and resteth upon Christ and his righteousness therein held forth for the pardon of sin, and for the accepting and accounting his person righteous in the sight of God for salvation."

Haldane says, "Justifying faith is the belief of the testimony of Christ, and trust in him who is the subject of that testimony. It is believing *with the heart.*"

Mason says, "Reliance is the essence of faith. Christ is the object, the word is the food, and obedience the proof; so that true faith is a depending on Christ for salvation, in a way of obedience, as he is offered in the gospel."

Dr. Archibald Alexander says, "A full persuasion of the truth revealed is faith in every case; but when the truth believed is a divine promise, this persuasion is of the nature of trust or confidence."

Dwight says, "The faith of the gospel is that emotion of the mind which is called trust or confidence, exercised towards the moral character of God, and particularly of the Saviour."

Charnock says, "Faith is a receiving the testimony of Christ in the certainty of it and in the extent of it—the testimony of God's promises to encourage us, of his precepts to direct us, of his threatenings to awe us and make us adhere faster to him; a resting in this testimony as certain, as the centre of our souls, the only foundation of our hopes. God is the ultimate object of faith, Christ the immediate object of faith. Christ gives the testimony; God is the subject of that testimony. When the witness Christ gives of the things he hath seen and heard, is received to be rested in as the ground of our hope and the rule of our walk, this is faith."

Dr. Hodge says, "Faith is not the mere assent of the mind to the truth of certain propositions. It is a cordial persuasion of the truth, founded on the experience of its power, or the spiritual perception of its nature, and on the divine testimony. Faith is therefore a moral exercise. Men believe with the heart in the ordinary scriptural meaning of that word; and no faith which does not proceed from the heart is connected with justification."

John Owen, speaking of the way of life by Christ Jesus, says, "That faith which works in the soul a gracious persuasion of the excellency of this way, by a sight of the glory, wisdom, power, grace, love, and goodness of God in it, so as to be satisfied with it as the best, the only way of coming unto God, with a renunciation of all other ways and means unto that end, will at all times evidence its nature and sincerity."

Without further comparing formal definitions on this subject, it may be said that sound writers fully agree with the Scriptures in representing faith as a simple act of the mind, in which both the understanding and will are united; that the light of knowledge goes before it so far as to reveal the mind of God, and so it is not blind and credulous, but sober, watchful, and intelligent; and that it is the fruit of warm affections, and so is not cold, speculative, and without practical effect. Dr. A. Alexander says, "Faith is one simple exercise of the mind, including, however, both the understanding and will." John Calvin says, "The seat of faith is not in the brain, but in the heart; not that I wish to enter into any dispute concerning the part of the body which is the seat of faith, but since the word *heart* generally means a serious, sincere, ardent affection, I am desirous to show the confidence of faith to be a firm, efficacious, and operative principle in all the emotions and feelings of the soul, not a mere naked notion of the head."

Nearly all sound and lucid writers are careful to express in so many words their view of faith, as being more than mere assent of the mind to the truth proposed. "With the heart man believeth unto righteousness, and with the mouth confession is made unto salvation." Rom. 10:10. Mason says, "Assurance sets the notion of faith too high, assent too low." John Newton says, "Assent may be the act of our natural reason; faith is the effect of immediate almighty power. Assent is often given where it has little or no influence upon the conduct. Faith is always efficacious."

The effects of saving faith are many and of great value. Indeed they are so important, that without them salvation in any of its benefits is impossible.

1. True faith is the instrument of a sinner's justification before God. So the Scriptures abundantly teach. "The just shall live by faith." "Abraham believed God, and it was

counted to him for righteousness." "Being justified by faith, we have peace with God through our Lord Jesus Christ." "Therefore we conclude that a man is justified by faith without the deeds of the law." "If righteousness come by the law, then is Christ dead in vain." Here is a grand result. Sin is forgiven and the sinner is accepted simply by believing on Him who is the end of the law for righteousness to every one that believeth. This is indeed a mystery and an offence to many. "Justification by sanctification is man's way to heaven, and he will make a little serve the turn. Sanctification by justification is God's, and he fills the soul with his own fulness." God's way is as mighty as it is wise. There is great historical verity in the statement of Sir James Mackintosh, that "the Calvinistic people of Scotland, Switzerland, and New England have been more moral than the same classes among other nations. Those who preached faith, or in other words, a pure mind, have always produced more popular virtue than those who preached good acts, or the mere regulation of outward works." Justification by faith alone is a doctrine highly promotive of holiness.

2. Adoption is also by faith. "To as many

as received him, to them gave he power to become the sons of God, even to as many as believed on his name." "Ye are all the sons of God by faith in Jesus Christ." What a wonderful effect is this: a child of the devil becomes a child of God, an heir of perdition is changed into an heir of glory, and all by reliance on the word of God, and by confidence in the person and merits of Jesus Christ. No wonder believers have ever celebrated the wonders of faith.

3. Besides obtaining justification and adoption, we also by faith are made partakers of the Holy Spirit to all the ends of illumination, sanctification, and encouragement in the Lord. Christ says, "He that believeth on me, out of him shall flow rivers of living water. This spake he of the Spirit, which they that believe on him should receive." There is no success, progress, or comfort in religion, but through this blessed Spirit. To receive him in his fulness of grace, is to secure the earnest of all good things, the pledge of heaven itself. "If any man have not the Spirit of Christ, he is none of his." But if a man have the Spirit of Christ, nothing can prove him a castaway, a reprobate, an enemy.

4. Saving faith is an infallible sign of regeneration. None ever thus believed but those who "were born, not of blood, nor of the will of the flesh, nor of the will of man, but of God." "Whosoever believeth that Jesus is the Christ, is born of God." Genuine faith being ours, our regeneration is no longer doubtful. Charnock says, "Faith is of absolute necessity to regeneration... Faith is a radical, vital grace; as blood in the veins is to the body, so is faith to the soul. No regeneration without the Spirit; and faith is the first grace the Spirit infuseth."

5. The powerful effect of true faith in purifying the heart is among its transcendent blessings. This chiefly makes the difference between it and the faith of devils. It awakens intense hatred of sin, eager longings after holiness, blessed hopes of attaining complete conformity to God, and a purpose to do right, whatever may be the result. There is no effectual purifying of the heart but by faith—by faith laying hold of Christ, and obeying the truth. Hooker well says, "To make a wicked and sinful man most holy through his believing, is more than to create a world of nothing."

6. Another effect of true faith is, to enkin-

dle the affections. "It works by love." It draws out the heart intensely after Christ. "To you that believe he is precious;" or, as it might be rendered, "preciousness." It indeed causes a wholesome fear of God; but its reigning power is not that of terror, but of love. This sways every thing, counts no sacrifice for Christ too great, and gladly yields all to him. "The love of Christ constraineth us."

7. Another effect of faith is, that it overcomes the world, and so is unlike every kind of dead faith. 1 John 5:4. To gain a victory over the world is more than philosophy ever did, more than unaided nature ever made a tolerable show of doing, more than ever was done but by one who had the faith of Jesus. The lust of the flesh, the lust of the eye, and the pride of life are too strong for any but the power of God working by the Spirit in the hearts of believers. Therefore, God saves no man but by working this faith in him. Thus we read, "As many as were ordained to eternal life believed." If God designs any saving good to you, the first infallible evidence of it will be, that he will work faith in you.

8. Faith is the great foster-parent of all that belongs to scriptural piety. It begets

true worship, godly fear, devout thanksgiving, genuine humility, Christian boldness, holy joy, evangelical repentance, enlarged liberality, fervent love, a pure conscience, a holy life, and final victory. Arrowsmith says, "Faith can support when nature shrinks; faith can call God Father when he frowns, and make some discovery of a sun through the darkest cloud." I had rather be able to walk in darkness, and have no light, and yet trust in the Lord, than to work miracles and subdue kingdoms. There are no offerings like those of faith. It makes no conditions. It makes no reserves. It cavils not. It falters not. It gazes upon the cross till the course of the new nature is set on fire with heavenly love. It best of all promotes its own interest by utterly forgetting itself, and so realizes what a class of writers have asserted, that "true greatness is unconscious." Like the æronaut, the believer rises by throwing over all that could weigh him down to earth. And as faith is self-renouncing, so it goes forth to glorify God. John Owen says, "It is the proper nature of faith to issue itself in the admiration of that which is infinite." It consents to be as nothing, that God may be all and in all. It excludes boasting. Rom. 3:27. It is as jealous for God's honor as it is for personal salvation. Like the sun in nature, so faith in the new nature serves and warms all around it and under its influence. It begets repentance. Jonah 3 : 5. It kindles love to an unseen Saviour. 1 Pet. 1 : 8. It begets forgiveness to enemies. Luke 17:3–5. It is the great means by which the God of hope fills his people with all joy and peace. Rom. 15 : 13. It gives all the stability we have. Rom. 11:20. It nourishes other graces, as did Joseph his brethren in Egypt. It ever claims and clings to a fulness in Christ. It makes the soul willing to wait a thousand years for an explanation of an act of providence. It is ever laying its crown at the feet of Immanuel, and giving God the glory. It puts things in their proper place. It abases the sinner in the dust. It sets God on the throne of universal dominion, and Christ upon the mercy-seat. It pronounces all God's ways just and equal. It consents to the law that it is holy, just, and good. It receives the gospel as glad tidings of great joy, and cries, "How beautiful upon the mountains are the feet of him that bringeth good tidings, that publisheth peace; that bringeth good tidings of good, that publisheth salvation, that saith unto Zion, Thy God reigneth." It welcomes, and does not pervert, the doctrine of a gratuitous salvation. It says of the Saviour, "Thou art the Christ, the Son of the living God." It cries, "God forbid that I should glory, save in the cross of our Lord Jesus Christ." Yea, it counts all things but loss for the excellency of the knowledge of God's dear Son.

No marvel that inspired writers so much celebrate a grace that brings such good to man and such glory to God. They call it "precious faith." They say it is common to all the people of God. They declare a man blessed who has even the least unfeigned faith. They say, "Faith is the substance of things hoped for, and the evidence of things not seen." That is, "it gives the object *hoped for* at some future period a present subsistence in the soul, as if already possessed." "Faith is also the evidence, the internal conviction, the demonstration of all unseen things." A believer acts as really upon the existence of things invisible, future, eternal, and hoped for, as he does upon his past experience or his intuitive perceptions. Even "the trial of your faith" is said to be "much more precious than of gold that perisheth, though it be tried with fire;" and shall "be found unto praise, and honor, and glory, at the appearing of Jesus Christ." When inspiration would hold up God's sovereignty to the admiration of all right-minded men, it says, "Hearken, my beloved brethren, hath not God chosen the poor of this world, rich in faith, and heirs of the kingdom which he hath promised to them that love him?" In short, a scheme of religion without faith would be as futile and powerless as a scheme of mercy without a Saviour.

It is indeed true that faith shall not, like love, last and flourish for ever; but like hope, it shall give place to a new state. Faith shall be changed into sight, and hope into enjoyment. In this sense, love is greater than either of these graces. 1 Cor. 13:13. But this is not to their discredit. In this life, they do what no other graces can accomplish. In particular, faith unites to Christ, lays hold of salvation, conquers every foe, brings every blessing into the soul, pronounces death abolished, crying, "Death is swallowed up in victory. O death, where is thy sting? O grave, where is thy victory? The sting of death is sin, and the strength of sin is the law; but thanks be to God, which giveth us the victory through our Lord Jesus Christ." Oh it is worth a lifetime of toil, suffering, and self-denial, to be able in the end to say with Paul, "I know whom I have believed; and am persuaded that he is able to keep that which I have committed to him against that day;" or, "I am now ready to be offered, and the time of my departure is at hand. I have fought a good fight, I have finished my course, I have kept the faith; henceforth there is laid up for me a crown of righteousness, which the Lord, the righteous Judge, shall give me at that day; and not to me only, but also unto all them that love his appearing." One of Halyburton's dying sayings was, "The little acquaintance I have had with God within these two days, has more than ten thousand times repaid the pains I have in all my life taken with religion. It is good to have God to go to when we are turning our 'face to the wall.' 'He is known for a refuge in the palaces of Zion; a very present help in trouble.'"

In applying this discussion to practical use, observe,

1. The life of a Christian is one of war. The powers of darkness and the powers of

light make his soul the arena of deadly strife, the battle-field where their legions contend for victory. There is nothing good but it has its opposite. Arrayed against God is Satan. If God has given his law, Satan also issues his precepts.

Many, very wicked, and false are the great principles, the common maxims of Satan's kingdom, endorsed by the lives of wicked men, and pleasing to the natural heart. Who can resist their power? No one who is left to his own strength. Without lively faith in God, every man will but serve the wicked one. Without faith in Christ, the love of sin cannot be overcome. In this war we shall utterly fail without faith in God, without the help that comes from God by faith in Christ Jesus. Bridge well says, "True, saving, justifying faith carries the soul through all difficulties, discouragements, and natural impossibilities, to Jesus Christ." Be not cast down because the war lasts long, or because the conflict is terrible. Fight on. Entangle not yourself with the things of this world. Be of good courage. Quit you like men. Be strong.

2. We see from this subject the wisdom of submitting all our sentiments and practices to

God's word in the spirit of docility. "Do not teach the Bible, but let the Bible teach you." Come not to the study of God's word as a judge or a critic, but as a child, a scholar, a criminal. The world is full of mournful cases of persons, who believed what was agreeable and rejected all else. The result has always been sad. Many examples might be given. An authoress somewhat celebrated, who had declared her preference for the god of Thomson's Seasons or of Hutchinson's Ethics over the God revealed to the patriarchs, in her old age thus wrote:

"What does life offer past eighty? For my own part, I only find that many things I knew, I have forgotten; many things I thought I knew, I find I knew nothing about; some things I know, I have found not worth knowing; and some things I would give—Oh, what would not one give?—to know, are beyond the reach of human ken. The powers of man strive—how vainly!—to penetrate the veil, to pierce the thick darkness which covers the future. Life seems of no value but for what lies beyond; and yet our views of the future are perhaps cheerful or gloomy, according to the weather or our nerves." Lo, this is the woman who preferred the God of nature to the God of grace; whose imagination ruled her creed; whose fancy governed her faith.

How strong is the contrast between such faith and such dark views of life and those of that eminent servant of God, Mrs. Hannah More, who at eighty says, "When and whither belong to him who governs both worlds. I have nothing to do but to trust. I bless God I enjoy great tranquillity of mind, and am willing to depart and be with Christ when it is his will; but I leave it in His hands who does all things well." Still later in life she exclaimed, "God of life and light, whom have I in heaven but thee? Happy, happy are those who are expecting to meet in a better world. The thought of that world lifts the mind above itself. O glorious grace! It is a glorious thing to die."

If you wish a useful life, a pleasant old age, a comfortable death, or a blissful immortality, believe God, trust to his grace, rely on his Son. Mingle not human and divine helps and hopes. Rely on God alone as your Father, on Christ alone as your Redeemer, on the Holy Ghost alone as your Comforter. Charnock says, "He that hath many things to trust to, is in suspense which he should take hold of; but when there is but one left, with what greediness will he clasp about that. God cuts down worldly props, that we might make him our stay." John Newton says, "Grace and faith can make the lowest state of life supportable, and make a dismission from the highest desirable." Yield your understanding to be taught of God; yield your heart to be purified and educated for God; yield your life a sacrifice to God. All this is your reasonable service. To do less is to rob God. Remember that nothing will stand the test of experience but that which will endure the trial of a fair comparison with Scripture. Always believe just what God has revealed for your salvation. If some things are not pleasant at first, they may still be useful through life, and in the end a fountain of joy.

3. It may be proper here to say that assurance, or freedom from all doubt, is not of the essence of faith. "There is as much difference between faith and assurance, as there is between the root and the fruit," says Mason. He who says that one without assurance has no faith, might as well say that an infant is not a human being. The greatest source of unhap-

piness to the pious is the weakness of their faith. It was sad to hear Jacob crying out, "All these things are against me." They were in fact all for him and for his family. Assurance may be lost. Genuine faith cannot. David lost his assurance, but he did not cease to be a believer. Assurance is a flower that opens with the sun and shuts at night. But faith grows and flourishes in cloudy weather, in the shade, and even in total darkness. Assurance indeed is the faith of God's people matured, full-grown, perfected. It is every way desirable and vastly consolatory, and certainly attainable. We should all seek it, pray and labor for it; and if we attain it, take good heed that we lose it not. We should never forget that assurance is as purely the gift of God as the least degree of faith. It is greatly to be lamented that the faith of so many seems sickly. Strong faith is one of the best gifts. Yet let none forget that little faith, when genuine, is pleasing to God, and unites to Christ. "Assuredly the least exercise of true faith in Christ constitutes a man his disciple," says Dr. Scott. To be able to come trembling and touch the hem of Christ's garment, as surely proves us in the covenant as to have a faith that will remove mountains. This view is the more important, as true believers are always modest, and have a low opinion of their own attainments in all respects. There is many a man who cannot deny that he has some faith, who yet regards himself as the least of all saints, the most faltering of all the true friends of God. This may be the case with the most eminent saints. Let us never teach nor embrace a doctrine which would fill such with sadness.

4. The great guilt and misery of the unconverted are found in their want of faith. Unbelief is their great sin. "This is the condemnation, that light is come into the world, and men have loved darkness rather than light." The Spirit convinces the world of sin chiefly in this, because men believe not in Christ. The unhappiness of a state of unbelief is also fearful. It leaves the soul without any resource in trouble, without God in the world.

Unbelief is the great parent and patron of other forms of wickedness. It fills the mind with wicked and violent prejudices, as in the case of the unbelieving Jews in the time of our Saviour, as in the case of unbelievers in our own day. It begets and nourishes a strong voluntary preference for the things of time above those of eternity, for the riches of earth above the unsearchable riches of Christ, for the honor that cometh from man above the honor that cometh from God only, for the pleasures of sin for a season above the pleasures for evermore at God's right hand. It nourishes above all things else pride of intellect, of family, of learning, of spirit, of manliness, of personal virtue. It begets sloth, dulness of apprehension, want of inquiry. It generates stubborn perversity. It makes men walk contrary to their strong convictions, their avowed principles. It mars or renounces all the duties of spiritual religion. It is revengeful, and will not forgive injuries. It is self-willed, and refuses to bow to the authority of God. It begets all feelings of disloyalty to God. It prevents all true spiritual worship. It annihilates the promises and abrogates the covenant of God in the case of all in whose hearts it has sway. It makes the death of Christ of none effect. It scornfully rejects the remedy provided for us in our ruined condition. It is no wonder that God has said, "He that believeth not shall be damned."

For men to profess to be peculiarly philosophical when they say that they believe what they see and no more, is very absurd. Apply this rule to the things of this world, and who can properly believe that there is or ever was any man, city, island, or country, except those which he has seen? When God testifies, unbelief is as unphilosophical as it is wicked. How absurd for a creature to make a point with the Creator; for a worm of the dust to revise the decisions of infinite wisdom; for a sinner to reject the Saviour because there are in the plan of salvation some things too deep to be sounded by the line of created intellect.

In human nature there can be nothing blacker than unbelief. It impeaches God's wisdom, power, goodness, justice, mercy, truth, and faithfulness. It holds up the God of truth as unworthy of credit. It makes him a liar. It charges him with perjury. It derides all his goodness and despises all his mercy. It makes light of the bloody sweat and dying agonies of his dear Son. It is a sin against the law, against the gospel, against the divine attributes, against every Person in the Godhead, against the highest testimonies, against our own best interests, against the only way of life and salvation. Without faith it is impossible to please God.

5. Let all labor for an increase of faith. Let them resort to all lawful endeavors for the growth of this principle. Venn says, "Solitude is a great cherisher of faith; were we more alone to pray and look back upon ourselves, not to find any good, but to observe more of the amazing blindness of heart, unbelief, selfishness, and vile idolatry, which so benumb our feelings of the love of Christ; were we to be more alone for these purposes, we should enjoy more of the presence and joy of God." The reading of good religious biography, and in particular of the sufferings of the martyrs, does, with the divine blessing, mightily strengthen the faith of God's people. For the same reason we should rejoice in all tribulation, because under God it strengthens the faith of all his people. Blessed is the man who by faith lays up a good foundation against the time to come.

6. We should especially so live and labor that we may die in faith. How blessed is he who is permitted to close his earthly existence in the confidence of that holy belief which disarms death of all stings and terrors. But this is not to be expected after a life of carelessness. Good old Willison gives "these advices"

to all who would be so happy as to die in faith: "1. Be careful to get faith beforehand; for death is a time to use faith, not to get it. They were foolish virgins who had their oil to buy when the bridegroom was close at hand. 2. Study to live every day in the exercise of faith, and be still improving, and making use of Christ in all his offices, and for all those ends and uses for which God hath given them to believers. 3. Frequently clear up your evidences for heaven, and beware of letting sin blot them to you. 4. Record and lay up the experiences of God's dealings with you, and be often reflecting upon them, that you may have them ready at hand in the hour of death. Lastly, meditate much on those promises which have been sweet and comfortable to you in the time of trials, and beg that the Lord may bring them to your remembrance when you come to die."

In short, a life of faith is the only sure pledge of a death of faith, and a death without faith is a death without hope.

> "Faith lights us through the dark to Deity;
> Faith builds a bridge across the gulf of death,
> To break the shock that nature cannot shun,
> And lands thought smoothly on the further shore."

# CHAPTER XI.

## REPENTANCE.

Repentance belongs exclusively to the religion of sinners. It has no place in the exercises of unfallen creatures. He who has never done a sinful act, nor had a sinful nature, needs neither forgiveness, conversion, nor repentance. Holy angels never repent. They have nothing to repent of. This is so clear that it is needless to argue the matter. But sinners need all these blessings. To them they are indispensable. The wickedness of the human heart makes it necessary. Under all dispensations, since our first parents were expelled the garden of Eden, God has insisted on repentance. Among the patriarchs, Job said, "I abhor myself, and repent in dust and ashes." Under the law David wrote the thirty-second and fifty-first psalms. John the Baptist cried, "Repent, for the kingdom of heaven is at hand." Christ's account of himself is that he "came to call sinners to repentance." Just before his ascension, Christ commanded "that repentance and remission of sins should be preached in his name, among all nations, beginning at Jerusalem." And the apostles taught the same doctrine, "testifying both to the Jews, and also to the Greeks, repentance towards God, and faith towards our Lord Jesus Christ." So that any system of religion among men which should not include repentance, would upon its very face be false. Matthew Henry says, "If the heart of man had continued upright and unstained, divine consolations might have been received without this painful operation preceding; but being sinful, it must first be pained before it can be laid at ease, must *labor* before it can be at rest. The sore must be searched, or it cannot be cured." "The doctrine of repentance is right gospel doctrine. Not only the austere Baptist, who was looked upon as a melancholy, morose man, but the sweet and gracious Jesus, whose lips dropped as a honey-comb, preached repentance; for it is an unspeakable privilege that room is left for repentance." This doctrine will not be amiss while the world stands.

Though repentance is an obvious and oft-commanded duty, yet it cannot be truly and acceptably performed except by the grace of God. It is a gift from heaven. Paul directs

Timothy in meekness to instruct those that oppose themselves, "if God peradventure will give them repentance to the acknowledging of the truth." Christ is exalted a Prince and a Saviour "to give repentance." So when the heathen were brought in, the church glorified God, saying, "Then hath God also to the Gentiles granted repentance unto life." All this is according to the tenor of the Old Testament promises. There God says he will do this work for us and in us. Listen to his gracious words: "A new heart also will I give you, and a new spirit will I put within you; and I will take away the stony heart out of your flesh, and I will give you a heart of flesh. And I will put my Spirit within you, and cause you to walk in my statutes, and ye shall keep my judgments, and do them." So that true repentance is a special mercy from God. He gives it. It comes from none other. It is impossible for poor fallen nature so far to recover herself by her own strength as truly to repent. The heart is wedded to its own ways, and justifies its own sinful courses with incurable obstinacy, until divine grace makes the change. No motives to good are strong enough to overcome depravity in the natural heart of man.

If ever we attain this grace, it must be through the great love of God to perishing men.

Yet repentance is most reasonable. No man acts wisely till he repents. When the prodigal came to himself, he went straightway to his father. It is so obviously proper that he who has done wrong should be heartily sorry for it, and never do so any more, that some infidels have asserted that repentance was sufficiently taught by natural religion without the Bible. But this is a mistake. The true doctrine of repentance is understood nowhere but in Christian countries, and not even there by infidels. Besides, that which is required of us may be very reasonable, and yet be very repugnant to men's hearts. When called to duties which we are reluctant to perform, we are easily persuaded that they are unreasonably exacted of us. It is therefore always helpful to us to have a command of God binding our consciences in any case. It is truly benevolent in God to speak to us so authoritatively in this matter. "God now commandeth all men everywhere to repent." The ground of the command is that all men everywhere are sinners. Our blessed Saviour was without sin, and of course he could not repent. With that solitary exception, since the fall there has not been found any just person who needed no repentance. And none are more to be pitied than those poor deluded men who see in their hearts and lives nothing to repent of.

But what is true repentance? This is a question of the highest importance. It deserves our closest attention. The following is probably as good a definition as has yet been given. "Repentance unto life is an evangelical grace, whereby a sinner, out of the sight and sense not only of the danger, but also of the filthiness and odiousness of his sins, as contrary to the holy nature and righteous law of God, and upon the apprehension of his mercy in Christ to such as are penitent, so grieves for and hates his sins as to turn from them all unto God, purposing and endeavoring to walk with him in all the ways of his commandments." That this definition is sound and scriptural will appear more and more clearly the more thoroughly it is examined. True repentance is sorrow for sin, ending in reformation. Mere regret is not repentance, neither is mere outward reformation. It is not an imitation of virtue, it is virtue itself. Hooker says, "Is it not clear that as an inordinate delight did first begin sin, so repentance must begin with a just sorrow, a sorrow of heart, and such a sorrow as rendeth the heart; neither a feigned nor a slight sorrow: not feigned, lest it increase sin; nor slight, lest the pleasures of sin overmatch it."

He who truly repents, is chiefly sorry for his *sins*. He whose repentance is spurious, is chiefly concerned for their *consequences*. The former chiefly regrets that he has *done evil;* the latter that he has *incurred* evil. One sorely laments that he *deserves* punishment; the other that he must *suffer* punishment. One approves of the law which condemns him; the other thinks he is hardly treated, and that the law is rigorous. To the sincere penitent sin appears exceeding sinful. To him who sorrows after a worldly sort, sin, in *some* form, appears pleasant. He regrets that it is forbidden. One says it is an evil and bitter thing to sin against God, even if no punishment followed. The other sees little evil in transgression if there were no painful consequences sure to follow. If there were no hell, the one would still wish to be delivered from sin. If there were no retribution, the other would sin with increased greediness. The true penitent is chiefly averse to sin as it is an offence against God. This embraces all sins of every description. But it has often been observed that two classes of sins seem to rest with great weight on the conscience of those whose repentance is of a godly sort. These are secret sins, and sins of omission. On the other hand, in a spurious repentance the mind is much inclined to dwell on open sins, and on sins of commission. The true penitent knows the plague of an evil heart and a fruitless life. The spurious penitent is not much troubled about the real state of heart, but grieves that appearances are so much against him.

David says, "Against thee, thee only have I sinned, and done this evil in thy sight." Whether we interpret these words to mean that he had sinned secretly as to men, but in plain view of God, or as expressing that God had been chiefly dishonored by his sins, will not in the end make any practical difference. Both are true. Horne and some others incline to the former view. But the majority of good writers seem to favor the latter interpretation. Bishop Hall says, "It is thy prohibition, O God, that can make a sin. I have sinned against men, but it is thy law that I have violated; in that is my offence." Bishop Patrick's paraphrase is, "Not because I stand in fear of punishment from men, who have no power over me, but because I am so obnoxious to thee, whose judgments I ought to dread the more the less I am liable to give an account of my actions unto others." Scott says, "David's crimes had deeply injured Bathsheba, Uriah, Joab, and the other accessaries to his murder.... Yet the chief malignity of his conduct consisted in this, that it was a complication of most daring rebellions against the great and glorious Governor of the world; contempt of his majesty, excellency, and righteous law.... This view seems to have possessed and overwhelmed his mind to such a degree as to make every other consideration appear comparatively as nothing." Matthew Henry adopts both views: "To God the affront is given, and he is the party wronged. It is his truth that by wilful sin we deny, his conduct that we despise, his command that we disobey, his promise that we distrust, his name that we dishonor, and it is with him that we deal deceitfully and disingenuously." But he adds, "That it was committed in God's sight. This not only proves it upon me, but renders it 'exceeding sinful.'" The greater the being sinned against, the greater is the sin. That in a very special and strong sense all sin is directed against God the Lawgiver, is clear from the nature of things, and from other parts of Scripture. Thus when murder is committed in a state, it is not chiefly the man who was killed nor his family, but the commonwealth, whose peace and dignity were infracted. Thus also the bloody persecutions against God's people are expressly said to have been against God. "He that toucheth you, toucheth the apple of his eye." "Saul, Saul, why persecutest thou ME?"

It is indeed true that oftentimes some one sin is very prominent in the thoughts of the genuine penitent. Peter wept bitterly for having denied his Lord. David says of the matter of Uriah, "My sin is ever before me." On these words Luther says, "That is, my sin plagues me, gives me no rest, no peace; whether I eat or drink, sleep or wake, I am always in terror of God's wrath and judgment." And how often and penitently does Paul refer to the great sin of his life, the murder of the saints. Biddulph says, "He singled it out as the grand evidence of the natural malignity of his heart.

Though pardoned, accepted, renewed, and joyful in the salvation of his Lord and Saviour, he carried to the block of martyrdom the remembrance of this sin." But though one sin may be first or most deeply impressed on the mind, yet in true repentance the mind does not rest there. The Samaritan woman was first convicted of living with a man who was not her husband. But soon she says that Christ had told her all things that ever she did. On the day of Pentecost, Peter labored to convict his hearers of the guilt of Christ's death. He was successful to a great extent. The result was their repentance for all sin, and their conversion unto God. "He that repents of sin as sin, does implicitly repent of all sin." So soon and so clearly as he discovers the sinful nature of any thing, he abhors it. A wicked thought, no less than a vile word or evil deed, is for a loathing to the true penitent. The promise runs, "They shall loathe themselves for the evils which they have committed in all their abominations." So that if there were no beings in the universe but God and the true penitent, he would have very much the same emotions of sorrow and humiliation that he has now. And if instead of countless offences he was conscious of comparatively few, the *nature* of his mental exercises would be the same as now. It is therefore true that he who ingenuously repents of sin, repents of all sin. To change one sin for another, even though it be less gross or more secret, is but disowning one enemy of God to form an alliance with another.

Nor is a true penitent afraid of humbling himself too much. He does not measure the degrees of his self-abasement before God. He would take the lowest place. He says, "Behold, I am vile; what shall I answer thee?" "O God, thou knowest my foolishness, and my sins are not hid from thee." "All our righteousnesses are as filthy rags." "If thou, Lord, shouldest mark iniquity, O Lord, who shall stand?" "Have mercy upon me, O God, according to thy loving-kindness; according unto the multitude of thy tender mercies, blot out my transgressions." It is not of the nature of genuine lowliness of heart before God to be nice and careful not to get too prostrate in the dust. Its great fear is, that it will after all be proud and self-sufficient.

The question is sometimes asked, whether every true penitent regards himself as the chief of sinners. If the question were of crimes against person or property, most penitents could easily find, in history or in the world, some who had excelled them in flagrant enormities. Nor is it possible for any but God absolutely and infallibly to say who is the greatest sinner that ever lived. But is it not true that every sinner who has truly repented, has seen more evil in his own heart and life than he ever saw in another? Comparing himself with the law, in its extent, holiness, and spirituality, taking a candid view of all that enters into a just estimate of his case, how can he but put his hand upon his mouth, and his mouth in the dust? Indeed, nothing but great self-ignorance enables any man to have a good opinion of himself. It is with good cause that God says, "Know every man the plague of his own heart." "Commune with your own heart upon your bed, and be still." As soon as David properly thought on his ways, he turned his feet unto God's testimonies. O come, ye proud ones, and cast yourselves at the footstool of God's mercy. "To be low, is the safest and comeliest posture for sinful creatures." True repentance has in it much profound humility.

True repentance has in it also much shame.

This relates not only to open and disreputable crimes, but also to secret sins, to vain thoughts and evil imaginations. "I blush to lift up my face to thee, my God." "Show the house of Israel that they may be ashamed for their iniquities." He who does not blush for his sins, has never been truly ashamed of them; has never really and heartily forsaken them. "The blush equally as the tear becomes every sinner. To look back on the past with shame, no less than with sorrow, becomes him. If he has no cause to be ashamed before men, yet he has great cause to be ashamed before God. If we need not blush for our treatment of our fellow-creatures, yet ought we not to blush for our treatment of our God and Saviour? All true penitents do blush as well as weep. They are ashamed as well as grieved for the things they have done." Nor does this shame cease with the hope of pardon, but is rather thereby increased. So God says, "I will establish unto thee an everlasting covenant. Then thou shalt remember thy ways, and be ashamed... And I will establish my covenant with thee; and thou shalt know that I am the Lord; that thou mayest remember, and be confounded, and never open thy mouth any more because of thy shame, when I am pacified towards thee for all that thou hast done, saith the Lord God." On this point, universal Christian experience fully accords with God's word. Paul never forgave himself for his cruel persecutions. Peter never ceased to be ashamed of his cowardly denial of his Lord. David never ceased to be ashamed of his base conduct.

This sorrow, humility, and shame are not merely for a wicked life, but for a sinful nature; not only for actual, but also for original sin. This point seems to be clearly settled in the case of David, who, having confessed his guiltiness for personal misconduct, traces all up to the fountain of native depravity. Listen to his words of anguish: "Behold, I was shapen in iniquity, and in sin did my mother conceive me." Not a spot is placed by inspired history on the character of David's father. He himself records more than once the excellency of his mother. He cannot therefore here intend to allege any thing against their moral character, except as all who are descended from our first parents are corrupt. Bishop Horne says, "No more can be intended here, than that a creature begotten by a sinner, and formed in the womb of a sinner, cannot be without that taint which is hereditary to every son and daughter of Adam and Eve." In fact, David in this psalm is occupied with his own case, and only as he saw truth suited to make him sorry, humble, and ashamed, had he any occasion even to allude to others. President Davies, treating of the nature of repentance, says, "David's repentance reached his heart. Hence, in his penitential psalm, he not only confesses his being guilty of the blood of Uriah, but that he was shapen in iniquity and conceived in sin, and earnestly prays, *Create in me a clean heart, O God, and renew a right spirit within me.*" Luther well says, "It is a great part of wisdom for one to know that there is nothing good in us, but vain sin—that we do not think and speak so triflingly of sin as those who say that it is nothing else than the thoughts, words, and deeds which are contrary to the law of God. But if thou wilt rightly point out, according to this psalm, what sin is, thou must say that all is sin which is born of father and mother, even before the time that man is of age to know what to do, speak, or think." Calvin also says, "Now David does not confess himself guilty merely of some one or more sins, as formerly, but he rises higher, that from his mother's womb he has brought forth nothing but sin, and by nature is wholly corrupt, and as it were immersed in sin. And certainly we have no solid convictions of sin, unless we are led to accuse our whole nature of corruption. Nay, each single transgression ought to lead us to this general knowledge, that nothing but corruption reigns in all parts of our soul." If these views are correct, then it is vain for men to pretend to genuine repentance who renounce the doctrine of native depravity, or original sin. This doctrine holds an important place in all true religious experience. "Though we cannot wash in original innocency, we must wash in ingenuous penitency." Rev. David Dickson therefore well says, "As original sin is common to all men by natural propagation, so is it not abolished out of the most holy in this life; and as it is found to show itself in the children of God by actual transgressions, so must the evil thereof be acknowledged by them; and that not to extenuate, but to aggravate their sin, as David showeth here."

A true penitent also reforms. A holy life is the invariable fruit of genuine repentance. "If I have done iniquity, I will do no more." Augustine says, "He truly repents of the sins he has committed who does not commit the sins he has repented of." When Ephraim sincerely repented, he utterly renounced idolatry, saying, "What have I to do any more with idols?" He does not really confess sin who does not forsake it. He who hates sin turns from it. It was not the habit of David's life to commit murder and adultery, though he *once* did both; nor of Peter to deny his Lord, and curse and swear, though he was once guilty of both these. A true penitent is not willing to be always sinning and repenting. We often read of "fruits meet for repentance," or "fruits worthy of repentance." Paul, having said that "godly sorrow worketh repentance not to be repented of; but the sorrow of the world worketh death," gives a very lively account of the effects of true repentance: "For behold this self-same thing, that ye sorrowed after a godly sort, what carefulness it wrought in you, yea, what clearing of yourselves, yea, what indignation, yea, what fear, yea, what vehement desire, yea, what zeal, yea, what revenge." Richard Baxter says, "True repentance is the very conversion of the soul from sin to God, and leaveth not any man in the power of sin. It is not for a man, when he hath had all the pleasure that sin will yield him, to wish then that he had not committed it, which he may do then at an easy rate, and yet to keep the rest that are still pleasant and profitable to his flesh. Like a man that casts away the bottle which he hath drunk empty, but keeps that which is full... If thou have true repentance, it hath so far turned thy heart from sin, that thou wouldst not commit it if it were to do again, though thou hadst all the same temptations; and it hath so far turned thy heart to God and holiness, that thou wouldest live a holy life if it were all to do again, though thou hadst the same temptations as afore." Mason says, "Repentance begins in the humiliation of the heart, and ends in the reformation of the life." All repentance is to be repented of, until it leads to holiness.

"Repentance is the heart's sorrow,
And a clear life ensuing."

Genuine repentance also draws its chief motives from the milder aspects of the divine character and the sweet influences of the cross. It is not the severity so much as the mercy of God that melts the heart. "The goodness of God leadeth thee to repentance." Rom. 2:14. It melts the heart when it sees God's kindness and its own baseness. None but a soul not touched by the finger of God can agree to be bad because God is good, or consent to a career of folly because the Lord is merciful. Repentance unto life invariably looks not merely at the goodness of God in creation and providence, but has a special regard to the work of redemption. "They shall look on Him whom they have pierced, and mourn and be in bitterness." This is specially stated to have been the ground of the repentance of the three thousand on the day of Pentecost. It is so still. Nothing breaks the heart like a sight of Christ crucified. This is obtained by faith only. There can be no evangelical repentance without saving faith. Indeed, "the true tears of repentance flow from the eye of faith." To "repent and believe the gospel" are not separate, though they are distinct duties. He who sincerely does one never omits the other. He who lacks one of these graces never attains the other. So that true repentance is always also connected with love. "Godly sorrow is the sorrow of love, the melting of the heart; love is the pain and pleasure of a melting heart." Right views of Christ and real love to him will make every man determine on the death of all his sins, and bring him in deep sorrow of heart to the feet of the Saviour. Such motives are of the right kind. They appeal to the higher principles of our renewed nature. If they are not effectual, nothing will melt us. Terror and wrath are in vain, if love move us not. It is all a delusion which supposes that strange and startling events are better suited to affect the human mind than the things of love. Yet this delusion in many is strong. It follows some to a death-bed, and even into hell. The rich man said, "If one went unto them from the dead, they will repent."

The kind of repentance above described is a saving grace. He who exercises it shall not perish. It produces joy, as in the case of the prodigal, and of the converts in Jerusalem and Samaria. "The same Jesus who turned the water into wine turns the waters of repentance into the wine of consolation." So that it is most true of *godly* sorrow, that "sorrow is better than laughter." "Blessed are they that mourn; for they shall be comforted." Thus saith the Lord, "I dwell with him that is of a contrite and humble spirit; to revive the spirit of the humble, and to revive the heart of the contrite ones."

The Scriptures speak of two kinds of repentance. Indeed, there are two very different words in the Greek Testament which are translated *repentance*. One means a change of mind thorough and entire, a turning away of the soul from sin and vanity to God and holiness. It is called "repentance to salvation." Elsewhere it is called "repentance unto life." This is the word used by John the Baptist, Matt. 3:2, and by Christ, Matt. 4:17, when they preached saying, "Repent, for the kingdom of heaven is at hand." They would have us make thorough work of it. This is the kind of repentance which is said to awaken joy in heaven. This is that repentance which Christ is exalted at the right hand of God to grant unto Israel. Indeed, generally where repentance in the New Testament is spoken of, either as a duty or as a saving grace, the word in the original is that the sense of which is given above.

The other word translated *repentance* means simply regret, or change of purpose. In this sense Herod repented, when he found that his rash and wicked oath would end in the beheading of John. He was sorry, but not after a godly sort. Yea, he was "very sorry," but his sorrow worked death both to John and himself: temporal death to the former, spiritual death to the latter. This word is found in some of its forms five times in the New Testament: Matt. 21:29, 32, and 27:3; 2 Cor. 7:8; Heb. 7:21. One of them is where Paul says, "Though I made you sorry with a letter, I do not repent, though I did repent;" that is, I do not regret it, though I did regret it. In Hebrews we read, "The Lord sware, and will not repent"—will not change his purpose—"Thou art a priest for ever after the order of Melchizedek." It is found in Matthew three times. It is said of the first son in the parable, that "afterwards he repented," changed his purpose, "and went." Chap. 21:29. So in the same chapter, verse 32: "The publicans and harlots believed John; and ye, when ye had seen it, repented not"—changed not your purpose, did not even regret the course you had taken—"that ye might believe Him." The other case is in Matt. 27:3–5: "Then Judas, which had betrayed him, when he saw that he was condemned, repented himself"—or simply repented, the word *himself* not being in the original—"and brought again the thirty pieces of silver to the chief priests and elders, saying, I have sinned in that I have betrayed innocent blood. And they said, What is that to us? See thou to that. And he cast down the pieces of silver in the temple, and departed, and went and hanged himself." Here it is stated that Judas regretted his conduct, had the sorrow which works death; but this was all.

As this case of Judas is very instructive in the nature of a spurious repentance, let us dwell on it a little. His regret was unfeigned. Higher proof of his being really sorry that he had betrayed Christ he could not give. Mere sincerity is not all that is required in religion generally, or in repentance in particular. There must be a change of heart as well as of purpose, a turning to God as well as sorrow. Nor is the strength of our emotions any test of their genuineness. It is no proof that your sorrow for sin is of a godly sort, that it is violent, and fills your soul with anguish. It is not probable that any man was ever more distressed than Judas. Quality rather than amount of feeling is to be sought. Nor is conviction of guilt proof that our repentance is genuine. Not only Judas, but Saul and many others have had as deep and distressing convictions as perhaps ever wrung the human heart; yet they still loved sin, and turned not to the Lord. Nor is a full, frank, and public statement of our wickedness in a particular affair any proof that we repent unto salvation. Judas went before the very men who had hired him to treason, and without any inducement from men, told them the whole matter and its wickedness. As to his confessing his offence before God, we have no information. The presumption is that he did not attempt it. There are deeds which drive the soul far from the mercy-seat, and destroy all heart for prayer. Yet Judas did all he could to prove to man that he condemned his act of treachery. To that deed two strong passions are commonly supposed to have contributed: first, covetousness. His conscience so far gained the victory over this vice, that he not only offered to pay back the money, but when it was refused, he threw it down in the temple and left it there. The second passion supposed by many to have led to Christ's betrayal by Judas was revenge, settled malice for what he felt to be a painful exposure of his character. Those who thus interpret his conduct found their opinion upon John 13:26–30. But Judas so far gave up his malice as publicly to declare that it had no justification.

"I have sinned in that I have betrayed the innocent blood." And to show how earnest he was in all this, how terrible his compunctious visitings were, and how fearfully he dreaded the longer contemplation of his sin, he actually took his own life, and rushed unbidden into the presence of God. Men may give their bodies to be burned, yet all will not avail without love to God, faith in Christ, and godly sorrow for sin. That Judas' repentance was not genuine is certain; for Christ said, "It had been good for that man if he had not been born."

The great defects of his repentance were these: 1. It seems to have been confined to thoughts about one or two sins, and did not extend to the sins of his life and heart, especially the wickedness of his nature. 2. Like Saul and others he said, "I have sinned;" but not like David, "I have sinned against the Lord." He seems to have had no great thoughts of God. 3. All the sorrow which he felt was upon principles of human nature common to all wicked men, and liable to be brought into operation at any time. He had not the Spirit. There was no spiritual discernment in all his exercises. 4. His repentance was without hope.

It had in it the sullenness of despair. The more he repented, the more wicked he was, until to his other offences he added the guilt of the worst kind of murder, even suicide. 5. So that his sorrow did not lead him towards God. He had no confidence in atoning blood, no reliance upon the mercy of God in Christ Jesus, none of that faith which led the dying thief to look to Christ and live. 6. It had no genuine humility in it. Judas died as proud as he had lived. 7. Like all cases of spurious repentance, this did not end in a reformation. It produced no fruits meet for repentance. It made the guilty man worse and worse at every step, until he "went to his own place." Were this case of Judas duly considered, wicked men would not with so much security and quiet of mind live on in their sins. There is something very fearful in the thought, that much which among men is highly esteemed is abomination in the sight of God, and that a repentance which goes no further than that of Judas but prepares a man for the prison of the damned.

Having spoken of confession of sin before men, it may be proper to preclude the possibility of mistake, by observing that those sins which are known to men, and thus injure the cause of God because they do a public harm, are to be publicly repented of and renounced; but of those which are private, Chrysostom lays down the true rule: "I wish thee not to bewray thyself publicly, nor accuse thyself before others. I wish thee to obey the prophet who saith, Disclose thy way unto the Lord; confess thy sins before him; tell thy sins to him, that he may blot them out. If thou be abashed to tell unto any other wherein thou hast offended, rehearse them every day between thee and thy soul. I wish thee not to confess them to thy fellow-servant, who may upbraid thee with them; tell them to God, who will cure them; there is no need for thee in the presence of witnesses to acknowledge them; let God alone see thee at thy confession. I pray and beseech you that you would more often than you do confess to God eternal, and reckoning up your trespasses, desire his pardon. I carry you not into a theatre or open court of many of your fellow-servants; I seek not to detect your crimes before men; disclose your conscience before God, unfold yourselves to him, lay open your wounds before him, the very best Physician, and seek of him salve for them."

Whether in those sins which injure men, and so admit of reparation, we are bound to make restitution, there seems to be no doubt. Lev. 6:2–5; Luke 19:1–10. The same is clear from Paul's epistle to Philemon.

Therefore be warned in time as to the following things:

1. See that your repentance is not that of the hypocrite or worldling. See that it goes beyond the repentance of fallen angels. Many repent of all their good resolutions and reformations so soon as the temptation offers. He that stole, and repented after his way, steals again. He that lied, and was caught in untruth, and so was ashamed, repeats the offence, but more cautiously than before. Let not your repentance be of this kind. It is a very important truth, that every spurious kind of repentance is soon known by the lack of fruits produced in the life. It is also true that there is much sorrow for sin that is not ingenuous and hearty. Many look upon repentance as an evil, necessary indeed, but still an evil. Such repentance as they have is probably of that kind. It does them no good. It works death. Beware especially of superficial views and experiences. Some seem to think themselves

well occupied in trying to prove that sin is not a very great evil, that the heart of man is not very far wrong. If such should succeed, they will but lay a foundation for the most serious mistakes in personal experience. "They that are whole need not a physician, but they that are sick." Avoid all men and books that make the impression that there is no need of a thorough change of principles and affections, or that it is easy for him that is accustomed to do evil to learn to do well. Never rely on a repentance that is partial—for some, but not for all sins; or a repentance that is temporary, and produces no permanent change of heart or life; a repentance that refuses to confess or repair a wrong done to man; a repentance that regards God's law as too strict, or seems reluctant to take a low place before God; a repentance that is offended with the exact rules of Scripture, or with proper distinctions and discriminations in judging of piety. Rest assured that such a state of mind will be of no avail. It is peculiarly strange that men will hold fast the price of iniquity, and yet hope that they have gracious affections. Ahab humbled himself mightily, he covered himself with sackcloth, but he was careful not to restore; indeed he seems never to have thought of restoring Naboth's vineyard; while Zaccheus seems never to have thought of any thing less than full restitution from the time that he first turned to the Lord.

The greatest defect, however, in the religious experience of many, is the want of proper tenderness of heart and of conscience based upon clear evangelical views. Repentance without any regard to the cross of Christ is as worthless as a faith that knows not the Saviour. If you would have a vital warmth in your repentance, it must be obtained from Christ crucified. In every sense he is our life. See to it, as you value the favor of God, that you often visit Gethsemane and Calvary, the cross and the sepulchre of Jesus.

2. Be careful not to deny the grace of God shown you in softening your heart, and cherish all those sentiments which either belong to true repentance or may lead to it. Especially labor to acquire clear views of the number and aggravations of your sins against God. Be not deterred from comparing your heart with the divine law. It is a great mercy when God grants us so much repentance as to lead us to acknowledge that we are sinners and need his

mercy. The prodigal had really made some progress towards recovery when he was heartily willing to say, "Father, I have sinned against heaven and before thee, and am no more worthy to be called thy son. Make me as one of thy hired servants." A small degree of genuine repentance may lead to more, and so to life. Remember of whom it was said, "A bruised reed shall he not break, and the smoking flax shall he not quench: he shall bring forth judgment unto truth." If the Saviour seems to be passing in the way near you, be encouraged to cry to him to undertake your case. Readily give up all for his favor. It is better than life. Forsake all that you have, and be his disciple. "Strive to enter in at the strait gate; for many shall seek to enter in, and shall not be able." "If thy right hand offend thee, cut it off; for it is profitable for thee to enter into life maimed or halt, rather" than with all thy members "to be cast into hell-fire." Rest assured that God will favorably regard even the beginnings of genuine godly sorrow. "He looketh upon men, and if any say, I have sinned, I have perverted that which is *right*, and it profiteth me not; he shall deliver his soul from going down into the pit, and his life shall see the light." "He that covereth his sins shall not prosper; but he that confesseth and forsaketh his sins shall find mercy." Oh that all would turn to the Lord Jesus, and with many tears give all to him. He came to bind up the broken-hearted, to comfort all that mourn, to give unto them beauty for ashes, the oil of joy for mourning, and the garment of praise for the spirit of heaviness. One genuine tear of penitence avails more in salvation than all the costly gifts that ever were made. Take heed that you fall not under any delusion of the wicked one, whereby you would be rendered dull and sluggish in this work. Labor for the meat that endureth unto life eternal. Work out your salvation with fear and trembling. Often and solemnly review your life. Compare your ways with the rules by which you will be judged in the last day. Get a clear insight into the nature of sin, into the multitude of your own offences, and into the blessed scheme of mercy by which the vilest may be saved. If there be a spark of good within you, it is a token of more good. Be careful not to extinguish it. Rather raise it into a flame. Neglect no means of deepening your serious impressions. Judge not your self unworthy of everlasting life by slighting the calls of mercy. Think of your own guilt and misery; think of God's love and mercy, especially in the gift of his dear Son, and lift up your voice and cry mightily to the Lord, till he come near and bid the waters of true repentance to flow in abundance. Of one thing we may be assured, and that is, our repentance will never be too deep. We cannot hate sin too much. We cannot turn from it too determinately or too speedily.

3. There is no substitute for repentance. It is the best offering a sinner can make. "Rend your hearts, and not your garments." "The sacrifices of God are a broken spirit: a broken and a contrite heart, O God, thou wilt not despise." Nothing will do but this, and this will do well. The only alternative is repentance or perdition. "Except ye repent, ye shall all likewise perish." "Repent and turn from all your transgressions; so iniquity shall not be your ruin." "Next to innocence, repentance is the greatest honor." Although repentance is no satisfaction for sin, yet it is so necessary that we look in vain for salvation without it. "Repent and be converted, that your sins may be blotted out." And "as there

is no sin so small but it deserves damnation, so," blessed be the name of the Lord, "there is no sin so great that it can bring damnation upon those who truly repent." Listen to God's voice addressed to men far, very far gone in sin: "Wash you, make you clean: put away the evil of your doings from before mine eyes; cease to do evil; learn to do well: seek judgment, relieve the oppressed, judge the fatherless, plead for the widow. Come now, and let us reason together, saith the Lord: though your sins be as scarlet, they shall be as white as snow; though they be red like crimson, they shall be as wool." "Let the wicked forsake his way, and the unrighteous man his thoughts: and let him return unto the Lord, and he will have mercy upon him, and to our God, for he will abundantly pardon." More gracious words were never uttered. Nothing can be kinder than God's urgent calls to repent. The Lord has very graciously spared you to this hour. This shows his readiness to save. Peter says that we greatly err when we ascribe God's patience and forbearance to any slackness in his character, any feebleness in his purposes. But he is "long-suffering to us-ward, not willing that any should perish, but that all should come to repentance." According to God's word, an impenitent heart is a sign of all that is evil. Yes, wicked man, "after thy hardness and impenitent heart," thou "treasurest up wrath against the day of wrath, and revelation of the righteous judgment of God." Indeed, the great complaint of God against men is that they remain unaffected: "I hearkened and heard, but they spake not aright: no man repented him of his wickedness, saying, What have I done? every man turned to his course, as the horse rusheth into the battle. Yea, the stork in the heavens knoweth her appointed times; and the turtle, and the crane, and the swallow, observe the time of their coming; but my people know not the judgment of the Lord." Jer. 8:6, 7. And whenever a sinner truly repents, how surely and how speedily is he forgiven. "I said, I will confess my transgressions unto the Lord, and thou forgavest the iniquity of my sin." There is no lack of mercy with our God. His arms are wide open, and his heart is full of tenderness to all who will return unto him. Every offer of mercy, every call of the gospel, every affliction of life, every reproof of conscience, every sermon, and every sacrament are so many loud and earnest calls to repentance. God may not require of you to be a preacher, but upon pain of damnation he demands that you be a penitent. Nothing is more presumptuous or vain than a hope of salvation in impenitency. God has given solemn warning, "lest there should be among you a root that beareth gall and wormwood; and it come to pass, when he heareth the words of this curse, that he bless himself in his heart, saying, I shall have peace, though I walk in the imagination of my heart, to add drunkenness to thirst: the Lord will not spare him, but then the anger of the Lord and his jealousy shall smoke against that man, and all the curses that are written in this book shall lie upon him." Deut. 29 : 18–20.

4. But when shall I repent? After all, here is the point where failure is most common. Multitudes would be greatly offended if told that they will die without repentance, and yet they persist in neglecting it. As to the time of repentance, no wise man will dare to say a word different from the truths of the Bible. There God says, "To-day if ye will hear his voice, harden not your heart." "Behold, now is the accepted time; behold, now is the day of salvation." Genuine repentance

cannot be too soon. "God has made promises *to* late repentance; but where has he made a promise *of* late repentance?" Saving repentance is always well-timed; it is not put off till the fixedness of an eternal destiny has made sorrow hopeless. True repentance commonly begins its work early in life—always in time. Eternity is for retribution, not for turning to God. None but the presumptuous defer this work till the last. "The repentance of a dying man often dies with him," says Augustine. "If we put off our repentance to another day, we have a day more to repent of, and a day less to repent in." Ambrose, speaking of a death-bed repentance, says, "I will counsel no man to trust to it, because I am loath to deceive any man, seeing I know not what to think of it. Shall I judge such a one a castaway? Neither will I declare him safe. All I am able to say is, let his state be left to the will and pleasure of Almighty God. Wilt thou therefore be delivered of all doubt? Repent while yet thou art healthy and strong. If thou defer it till time give no longer possibility of sinning, thou canst not be thought to have quit sin, but sin has rather quit thee." Oh that men were wise! Oh that they would consider! Oh that they would lay to heart the things which belong to their peace, before they are for ever hid from their eyes! "You cannot repent too soon. There is no day like today. Yesterday is gone; to-morrow is God's, not yours. Oh think how sad it will be to have your evidences to seek when your cause is to be tried; to have your oil to buy when you should need it to burn." If ever there was a wise rule, it is this: "Whatsoever thy hand findeth to do, do it with thy might." Perhaps you think that repentance is in your own power without God's help, and that you can turn to the Lord at any time. But do not deceive yourself. It was Christ who said, "Without me ye can do nothing." Repentance is the gift of God; and are you taking the right course to secure his gift when you are wilfully abusing his mercies and his grace? It is a solemn thought too, that we have the best reason for believing that of all those called to repentance, but few at any time obey and turn to God. Besides, none but a madman would willingly pursue a course which he knows must end in misery temporal or eternal. To expect that the pains or terrors of death will beget true repentance in your case is superlative folly.

They never have had that effect in any case. The sorrows of the damned are still more terrible, but even they are neither purifying nor atoning. Many in every age are much troubled with fears and terrors, especially in sickness; but do you not see how, upon recovery, they return like the dog to his vomit, or the sow that was washed to her wallowing in the mire? If you cannot be won by kindness, the terrors of the Lord will never make a good man of you.

One of the most afflicting thoughts respecting a death-bed repentance, is that it is impossible for any man to prove that it was genuine, and the soul enters eternity, to say the least, with an untried preparation. Beware lest by trifling with your soul's affairs, you at last die in utter despair. I have read of a sick man who was exhorted to repent. He said he would not yet; for, if he should recover, his companions would make merry at his expense. But growing worse, his friends again urged him to repent. His reply was, "It is too late, for now I am judged and condemned." Oh turn to the Lord. "Wilt thou not be made clean? When shall it once be?"

## CHAPTER XII.

### HUMILITY.

We rise in glory as we sink in pride;
Where boasting ends, there dignity begins.

THE word translated *humility* in the New Testament occurs seven times. It is once rendered lowliness, once lowliness of mind, once humbleness of mind, and twice by the simple word humility. In Col. 2:18, 23, it is used either for a feigned humility or for a degrading subjection of mind, such as all will-worship begets and fosters. The heathen, not having any virtue corresponding to Christian humility, had no word to express such a quality of the mind; and when the New Testament writers gave us their thoughts, they adopted the language of the age, and so use in a good sense words which among the heathen often had a very different sense. "The philosophers thought humility to be the opposite of magnanimity." It is one of the peculiar glories of Christianity that it teaches unfeigned humility, and yet so as to elevate and dignify all who practise it.

Humility is lowliness of mind, the opposite of pride and arrogance. It belongs to the essence of experimental religion. Bates calls it "the peculiar grace of Christians, the parent and nurse of other graces, that preserves in us the light of faith and the heat of love; that procures modesty in prosperity and patience in adversity; that is the root of gratitude and obedience, and is so lovely in God's eyes, that he 'giveth grace to the humble.'" A lowly spirit is the opposite of a lofty one. True humility is an inward grace based on a view of our own guilt, weakness, vileness, ignorance, and poverty, as compared with the infinite excellence and glory of God. It is one of the most lovely of all the traits of a child of God. It is opposed to all ostentation. It not only hides the other graces of the Christian from the gaze of self-admiration, but it hides itself also. Its aim is not to be thought humble, but to be humble. The good man loves to lie low, and cares not to have it known. In the eyes of others this virtue is willing to take a low place, but claims no merit on that account.

The Bible says, "*Be clothed with humility.*" Have no secret or single way of display. Be not humble merely respecting some things, and proud or self-conceited about others. Let the robe of lowliness of mind, like the ample folds of a cloak, cover up all else; and be not afraid of thus suffering loss. Humility will not disfigure, but adorn you. As Rebecca was not the less lovely, but the more so, when she took a veil and covered her beauty and all her jewels; so the child of God is peculiarly beautified when arrayed in humbleness of mind. Of the wicked it is said, "Pride compasseth them about as a chain," Psa. 73:6; but the righteous are "clothed with humility." Rowland Hill says, "I could say a thousand things concerning this next to celestial valley of humiliation. The air is so salubrious, the ground is so fertile, the fruit so wholesome; while from the branches of every tree the voice of prayer and praise are heard in delightful concert with each other. While living in this valley, no weapon that is formed against us shall prosper, as all the fiery darts of the devil are sure to pass over our heads, since the enemy of souls cannot shoot *low* enough to reach us to our hurt."

To prevent mistake, it is right to say that humility has a sacred regard to truth. Its judgments are formed on that sure foundation and by that unerring standard. God requires of us not meanness, but humility; not degradation, but a judgment and sense of ourselves according to truth. We are not at liberty to think of ourselves more lowly or more highly than the truth requires. We are required to think soberly of ourselves. It is certain that all sober thoughts of ourselves will give us a very low place. A high estimate of ourselves is never according to truth.

Neither does humility consist in decrying pride in general, nor in speaking against the haughtiness of some of our neighbors, nor in seeking intercourse with low people for selfish ends, nor in covering one's self with rags or rough garments, nor in affecting unusual manners, nor in those self-restraints which are intended to win the good opinion of others respecting our humility, nor in confessing sins which we do not forsake, nor in a servile disposition or manner towards men, nor in proudly maintaining the humbling doctrines of the gospel.

Even the semblance of humility is often thought advantageous by designing men. Lord Bacon says, "Envy, which is the canker of honor, is best extinguished by declaring a man's self in his ends rather to seek merit than fame; and by attributing a man's successes rather to divine providence and felicity, than to his own virtue or policy." The cunning know that the best way to secure is to seem to shun applause.

Where the mind is assured that the humility of another is unfeigned, it easily confides, and loves to show affection. We love to express admiration where we suppose we are not flattering. Virtuous minds love not to give unreasonable commendation, though they delight in uttering salutary encouragement. This is so true that, even where the grace of God has not renewed the heart, but there is merely a natural diffidence, we esteem it amiable. It is with pleasure we read that Saul, when he heard of his being chosen king, went and hid himself among the stuff. Our feelings towards him entirely change when he becomes ambitious and cruel and self-confident by the use of power, and by dazzling prospects for himself and his family. No small part of the enthusiasm of the people in regard to some public men is chiefly owing to the belief that they will not be spoiled by public attention. The charm of their character is in their modesty. Honors are often lavished on such, and as often withheld from men of an opposite character. Mankind meet not the demands of the bailiff or tax-gatherer with more surliness than they do the *claims* of men to distinction. To be proud and to be popular is not given to men. In any virtue, the reality is better than the semblance. It is so in humility. Nature is commonly stronger than art, and will finally show itself. In one sense, it is easier to be good than to seem to be good. It is less trouble to act out an ingenuous nature than it is to conceal an evil nature under any disguise.

The commendations bestowed on this virtue are high and numerous. Our Saviour said, "Whosoever shall exalt himself shall be abased; and he that shall humble himself shall be exalted." Matt. 23 : 12. In a note on this passage, Dr. Doddridge says, "Christ seems, by the frequent repetition of this *maxim*, to intimate that he intended it not only for those who were to be *teachers* of others, but for *all his disciples* without exception. And it is well worthy of our observation that no one sentence of *our Lord's* is so frequently repeated as this, which occurs at least *ten times* in the *evangelists.*" He then refers to Matt. 18: 4; 20: 26,

27; 23:10, 11; Mark 9:35; 10:43, 44; Luke 14:11; 18:14; 22:26; John 13:14.

When we examine other parts of God's word, we find they speak the same language. This will appear more fully presently. Soon after the death of the last apostle, we find Christian writers dwelling with great urgency upon this virtue. Jerome says, "With God nothing stands higher than humility." Augustine, speaking of pride, says, "That which first overcame man is the last thing which man overcomes." When Demosthenes was asked what was the first thing in a good orator, he said, Delivery; and the second, he replied, Delivery; and the third, he still answered, Delivery. So says Chrysostom, "If I be asked what is the first thing that makes a Christian, I answer, Humility; and the second, Humility; and the third, Humility."

Later writers of eminence speak the same language. Venn says, "As soon as pride is humbled enough not to enter into controversy with God about the justice of his own declarations, every man confesses himself a guilty sinner, in danger of eternal ruin."

Manton says, "The nettle mounteth on

high, while the violet shrouds itself under its own leaves, and is chiefly found out by its fragrancy. Let Christians be satisfied with the honor that cometh from God only."

Bates says, "Humility is the most precious ornament in God's sight; and to be approved by the divine mind and accepted by the divine will is the highest honor, the most worthy of our ambition. Humility is like the precious balm that, mixed with other liquors, sinks to the bottom; but then it is visible and most amiable in the sight of God."

Evans says, "Those who are destitute of humility, whatever profession they have made of Christianity, have in truth the rudiments of it yet to learn. If they have been soaring upward to heaven itself in the sublimest speculations, if they have built up their hopes to the greatest height on other grounds, without laying this at the foundation, they must be content to come down again to learn this lesson, which enters into the elements of Christ's religion. A proud Christian is a contradictory character; as much so as it would be to say, a wicked saint. The whole gospel, in its precepts, its great example, its glorious prospects, tends to humble the pride of man; and therefore, whoever will come after Christ must in this respect deny himself."

Dr. Gill says, "Generally speaking, those that have the most grace and the greatest gifts, and are of the greatest usefulness, are the most humble, and think the most meanly of themselves. So those boughs and branches of trees which are most richly laden with fruit bend downwards and hang lowest."

Dr. Watts says, "Saints increase in humility as they draw nearer to heaven. 'Unworthy to be called an apostle,' said Paul concerning himself some years after his conversion. As he advanced still further in years, he cried out, 'Less than the least of all saints.' A little before his martyrdom, his cry is, 'the chief of sinners.'"

Mason says, "God had rather see his children humble for sin than proud of grace... Neither all the devils in hell nor all the temptations of the world can hurt that man who keeps himself humble and depending on Christ... As the first step heavenward is humility, so the first step hellward is pride."

The Persian proverb is, "A man passes for a sage when he seeks for wisdom; but if he thinks he has found it, he is a fool."

John Angell James says, "Humility is the certain fruit of a heart wherein true religion is duly cultivated, and is most conspicuous in those whose lives are adorned with the most exemplary piety."

As nothing so well explains and enforces one's meaning as examples, a few are here given to hold forth both the nature and beauty of humility. The first is that of President Edwards the elder. On receiving information of his election to the presidency of Princeton college, he thus wrote to the trustees: "I am not a little surprised on receiving the unexpected notice of your having made choice of me to succeed the late President Burr as the head of Nassau Hall. I am much in doubt whether I am called to undertake the business which you have done me the unmerited honor to choose me for... The chief difficulties in my mind in the way of accepting this important and arduous office are, first, my own defects unfitting me for such an undertaking, many of which are generally known, besides others of which my own heart is conscious. I have a constitution in many respects unhappy, attended with flaccid solids, vapid, sizy, and scarce fluids, and a low tide of spirits, often occasioning a kind of childish weakness and contemptibleness of speech, presence, and demeanor, with a disagreeable dulness and stiffness much unfitting me for conversation, but more especially for the government of the college. This makes me shrink at the thought of taking upon me in the decline of life such a new and great business, attended with such a multiplicity of cares, and requiring such a degree of activity, alertness, and spirit of government, especially as succeeding one so remarkably well qualified in these respects, giving occasion to every one to remark the difference. I am also deficient in some parts of learning, particularly in algebra and the higher parts of mathematics, and in the Greek classics, my Greek learning having been chiefly in the New Testament." Thus spoke the greatest divine of New England and the greatest metaphysician of his century. How many with a hundredth part of his attainments in any respect would never have had nor have suggested the slightest difficulty.

Hear too the Rev. Samuel Davies, who, as he was recovering from a dangerous illness, wrote, "I am rising up with a desire to recommend Christ better to my fellow-sinners than I have done; but alas, I hardly hope to accomplish it. He has done a great deal more by me already than I ever expected, and infinitely more than I deserved. But he never intended me for great things. He has beings both of my own and of superior orders, that can perform him more worthy service. Oh, if I might but untie the latchet of his shoes, or draw water for the service of his sanctuary, it is enough for me."

Take another case. The Rev. John Livingston was one of the wonderful men of Scotland, and the ancestor of the family of the same name so widely and so favorably known in America. When a licentiate, he preached June 21, 1630, on a Monday after a communion, in the churchyard of the kirk of Schotts, with an effect so remarkable as to have been celebrated ever since. John Brown of Haddington says, that under this one sermon "five hundred were converted to Christ." Many others have pointed to that day as closely resembling the day of Pentecost. Livingston's own account of it is simple and modest. He says, "The night before, I had been with some Christians *who spent the night in prayer and conference.* When I was alone in the fields about eight or nine o'clock in the morning, before we were to go to sermon, there came such a misgiving spirit upon me, considering my unworthiness and weakness, and the expectation of the people, that I was consulting with myself to have stolen away somewhere, and declined that day's preaching; but then I thought I durst not so far distrust God, and so went to sermon, and got good assistance about an hour and a half upon the points which I had meditated on, Ezek. 36: 25, 26. And in the end, offering to close with some words of exhortation, I was led on about an hour's time in a strain of exhortation and warning with such liberty and melting of heart as I never had the like in public in all my lifetime." Such is the humble statement of the great man who preached the most remarkable sermon which has been delivered for perhaps fifteen hundred years.

When Moses came down from the mount, "he wist not that his face shone." I once heard a man boasting that he and his coadjutors were Smithfield men. He forgot that the Smithfield men of a former century never knew that they were such until they went home to God. They were humble men, and greatly distrusted themselves to the last. They had contemporaries who thought themselves ready to die in the cause of Christ; but as prison and death stared them in the face, they turned Papists.

In the New Testament we have several pleasing examples of humility. Thus in the gospel which bears his name, Matthew does not tell us that he was rich and made a great feast for Christ. We learn that fact from another evangelist. Matthew simply tells us what occurred when Jesus sat at meat, without hinting who gave the entertainment. When the apostolic authority of Paul was questioned, and for the truth's sake he was compelled to defend it, he seems really pained by being led to speak of himself so much, and calls it folly, but says it was necessary. True humility is opposed both to egotism and ostentation. It is also opposed to all self-conceit before God or man. Look too at the woman of Canaan. How illustriously did she prove that true humility is not easily offended.

Humility, when genuine, runs through all the deportment. It is an ingredient of the character. It influences both public and private behavior. But there are special occasions when it displays itself in a very unmistakable manner. One of these is, when reproof is administered. Its language ever is, "Let the righteous smite me; it shall be a kindness; and let him reprove me; it shall be an excellent oil, which shall not break my head." Psa. 141:5. When reproved, the truly humble do not fall into a rage, nor hate the man who has shown fidelity in warning them of their fault or danger. Again, some of the duties of life are honorable. Offices are to be filled, courtesies are to be shown, deference is to be manifested. The truly humble man is not at a loss at such times. Paul directs that in such cases we should "in honor prefer one another." Rom. 12:10. Elsewhere he says, "Let nothing be done through strife or vain-glory; but in lowliness of mind let each esteem other better than themselves." Phil. 2:3. The humble man is not offended with such rules. The apostle Peter in like manner says, "Likewise, ye younger, submit yourselves unto the elder. Yea, all of you be subject one to another, and be clothed with humility; for God resisteth the proud, but giveth grace to the humble."

Nor is the humble man pleased with flattery. It may be adroitly administered; but he knows that any lifting up of his soul is not for his good. He is not one of those silly ones who relies upon the praises of men. He cares not to have them. Nor is he much affected by their slanderous accusations. With him it is a rule, "by well-doing to put to silence the ignorance of foolish men," and so to live that he who "is of the contrary part may be ashamed, having no evil thing to say" of him. An humble walk is the best defence against the charge of pride.

The conduct of the humble man in times of sore judgments is also noticeable. Instead of resorting to doubtful expedients, he casts his care upon the Lord. Of this we have two noted examples in the history of David. When driven from Jerusalem, and cursed by Shimei, he refused to avenge the insult offered him, or to permit Abishai to do it. He left it all to God. So when for numbering the people God was angry, and sent Gad to David, and Gad said, "Shall seven years of famine come unto thee in thy land? or wilt thou flee three months before thine enemies, while they pursue thee? or that there be three days' pestilence in thy land? Now advise, and see what answer I shall return to him that sent me. And David said unto Gad, I am in a great strait; let us now fall into the hand of the Lord; for his mercies are great; and let me not fall into the hand of man." How wise this choice. Humility loves to depend on *God*, even when his fatherly displeasure is expressed against us. Famine and war make men brutal to those around them. When the palmer-worm and the locust and the caterpillar and the canker-worm, strong and without number, waste the pleasant fields; when the heavens glow like heated brass, and the earth is like iron, and drought cuts off "the meat before our eyes, and the seed is rotten under the clods, and the garners are laid desolate, and the beasts groan, and the herds of cattle are perplexed because they find no pasture, and the rivers are dried up, and fire devours the pasture in the wilderness," then oftentimes fathers have no pity and mothers become monsters. War too is full of brutal outrages, committed especially by the cowardly. It is full of spectacles of misery and slaughter, and carries with it awful terror. "Every battle is with confused noise, and garments rolled in blood." Isaiah 9:5. Then at least

"There is no flesh in man's obdurate heart;
It does not feel for man."

The humble prefers the hand of God to that of his enemies. He falls into Jehovah's arms. He humbles himself under God's mighty hand. His strength is to sit still. Instead of saying, What have I ever done to deserve such strokes? he rather says, What have I not done?

The humble also abase themselves much when God grants them great prosperity in their plans. His mercy humbles them. Thus David was greatly affected at his success in collecting treasure for building the temple, and said, "Who am I, and what is my people, that we should be able to offer so willingly after this sort? for all things come of thee, and of thine own have we given thee." 1 Chron. 29:14. So Paul, being led to say in a necessary defence, "I labored more abundantly than they all," instead of being lifted up by it, immediately adds, "Yet not I, but the grace of God that was in me."

In like manner the humble carry themselves softly and lowly when God comes down in anger to afflict their enemies or the foes of his church. They know the meaning of that injunction, "Rejoice not when thine enemy falleth, and let not thy heart be glad when he stumbleth; lest the Lord see it, and it displease him, and he turn away his wrath from him. Fret not thyself because of evil men, neither be thou envious at the wicked." Prov. 24:17–19.

The ordinances of God's house, the emblems of his love, the light of his countenance, the presence of his Spirit, all have a blessed effect on the humble in making him bow in deeper lowliness before God.

On three very different classes of matters we are called to humility.

1. The first comprehends our beauty, strength, rank, success, power, wealth. For these things we are indebted to God. He is their author. His mercy, not our wisdom, secured them to us. His kindness granted us comeliness, health, activity, reputable parentage, and all these things. Yet how many are swollen with pride by the possession of even one of these things. Nay, fine clothing and costly jewels puff up many. How seasonable is the warning of God: "Let not the wise man glory in his wisdom, neither let the mighty man glory in his might, let not the rich man

glory in his riches: but let him that glorieth, glory in this, that he understandeth and knoweth me, that I am the Lord, which exercise loving-kindness, judgment, and righteousness in the earth." Jer. 9:23, 24. Others have toiled as hard, studied as carefully, risen as early, sat up as late, eaten only the bread of carefulness, and yet have not gained our measure of success. Oh that men would remember that "promotion cometh neither from the east, nor from the west, nor from the south; but God is Judge of all. He raiseth up one and putteth down another." Between men's best and last efforts and success, there is always a chasm which none but God can bridge over. So that the honor of all is due to him. No man is the more base for being poor, nor is any one more noble for being rich. No man deserves well because he has been successful. "The race is not to the swift, nor the battle to the strong."

2. A second class of matters respecting which we should be humble, comprehends mental qualities, such as memory, imagination, judgment, wit, logical power, learning, and skill as writers or speakers. In a free government the tenor of public sentiment opposes the

coarser displays of pride on account of birth, rank, or fortune; but then intellectual superiority has unwonted power. Intellect is indeed never to be despised. It is right that mental strength should have more influence than mental imbecility. Nor does God's word encourage feebleness of intellect. On the contrary, wherever it goes, it says, "In understanding be ye men." But it does forbid us to be proud of any mind we have. It also warns us not to boast ourselves of a false gift, lest we be like clouds and wind without rain. How amazingly contented are the masses of men with their quantum of intellect. Some indeed complain of bad memory, but very few of bad judgment. In a world full of ignorance we have swarms of teachers and few scholars; hosts of instructors and but few learners, few readers, few inquirers. This is positive proof that there is great lack of sobriety in the estimates men form of themselves.

It is a universal law that genuine modesty and humility are essential to any great mental attainments. Lord Bacon says, "The access to the kingdom of man, which is founded on the sciences, resembles that to the kingdom of heaven, where no admission is conceded except to children." Sir Isaac Newton said of himself nothing more flattering than this: "He who comes after me may by diligence know something." Near the close of his life he said, "I stand on the shore of the ocean of knowledge, and all I have been able to do was to pick up a few pebbles." This was in human science. In the history of the church, Paul was preëminent for gigantic powers and depth of knowledge; yet how lowly was he. Listen to him: "Now we see through a glass darkly;" "Now we know in part;" "Not as though I had already attained, either were already perfect; . . . forgetting those things which are behind, I press towards the mark for the prize of the high calling of God in Christ Jesus."

In studying God's word, how little humility is there, and consequently how little success. John Newton says, "Those who seek not assistance from God, can find it nowhere else: for 'every good gift and every perfect gift is from above, and cometh down from the Father of lights,' who hath said, 'If any man lack wisdom, let him ask of God.' A critical knowledge of the original languages, a skill in the customs and manners of the ancients, an acquaintance with the Greek and Roman classics, a perusal of councils, fathers, scholiasts, and commentators, a readiness in the subtleties of logical disputation—these, in their proper place and subserviency, may be of considerable use to clear, illustrate, or enforce the doctrines of Scripture; but unless they are governed by a temper of humility and prayer; unless the man that possesses them accounts them altogether as nothing, without the assistance of the Spirit of God, which is promised to guide believers into all truth; unless he seeks and prays for this guidance no less earnestly than those who understand nothing but their mother tongue; I make no scruple to affirm, that all his *apparatus* of knowledge only tends to lead him so much the further astray; and that a plain, honest ploughman, who reads no book but his Bible, and has no teacher but the God to whom he prays in secret, stands abundantly fairer for the attainment of true skill in divinity."

Charnock says, "If grace be given to the humble, the grace of the best knowledge is not excluded from God's liberality. We gain it sooner by an humble contemplation than by proud wranglings. As to obey God we must deny our wills, so to know him we must deny our reasonings; will must submit to precept, and reason to revelation. Agur acknowledged himself *brutish*, who came behind none of his age, unless Solomon, in understanding. Prov. 30 : 2. The humble person will soon be a scholar in this learning, when a Pharisee shall remain as ignorant as he is proud. God reveals himself to *babes*. Matt. 11 : 25. *The meek will he teach his way*. Psa. 25 : 9. As *God knows the proud afar off*, Psa. 138 : 6, so doth the proud man know God afar off. . . . A proud scholar and a dove-like teacher can never accord."

In full agreement with these sentiments, the Scriptures declare, "If any man think that he knoweth any thing, he knoweth nothing yet as he ought to know." How timely are such warnings as these: "Be not wise in thine own eyes;" "Be ye not wise in your own conceits;" "Seest thou a man wise in his own conceit? there is more hope of a fool than of him;" "Woe unto them that are wise in their own eyes, and prudent in their own conceit." Yet to how many might the irony of Job be applied: "No doubt but ye are the people, and wisdom will die with you." How many profess to see into things which they have never studied. "The sluggard is wiser in his own conceit than seven men that can render a reason." Very few men are willing to know their own ignorance. But for their self-conceit, armed with malignity, the learned scribes and doctors of our Saviour's day might have become apostles in knowledge. One has said that "hell may be full of learned scribes and subtile disputers, of eloquent orators and profound philosophers, who, when they knew God, glorified him not as God, but became vain in their imaginations, and their foolish heart was darkened." "The world by wisdom knew not God." The human heart perverts unsanctified knowledge to the blinding of the mind in the things of God. Hence astronomers and anatomists have not unfrequently been materialists and atheists. Some wonder that two sciences of so elevated and instructive a character should lead to such results. They do not thus affect the humble. But the proud pervert every thing. Accordingly it is as true of some moderns as of some ancients, that "seeking to become wise, they became fools." This self-conceit makes men averse to receiving counsel from men or reproof from God. It makes them violent and dogged in their temper. It makes them rash, reckless, officious, insolent, and censorious. The Bible doctrine is, "If any man among you seemeth to be wise in this world, let him become a fool, that he may be wise." Here God clearly teaches that humility is an ingredient of docility. To sit at the feet of Jesus is essential to our solid learning. Will you thus humble yourself? Is any duty more reasonable?

3. In all ages, true piety has borne the same marks. In like manner sin exhibits the same tempers and tendencies from age to age. Self-esteem and self-justification belong to the unregenerate heart. This is its habitual and prevailing state. Some go so far as to claim absolute exemption from all sin. They have sometimes been so left to themselves and given up to believe a lie as to declare that for many months, and even years, they have not been chargeable with one sinful thought, word, or deed. The language of Scripture to such persons is very direct and pungent: "If we say that we have no sin, we deceive ourselves, and the truth is not in us." A conscience not seared as with a hot iron must feel the force of such a declaration. The Old Testament speaks the same language: "There is not a just man upon earth, that doeth good, and sinneth not." Eccl.

7:20. Though you may be far from asserting that you are perfect, yet if you have never been taught of God, nor humbled at the foot of the cross, you have an extravagantly good opinion of yourself. The Bible says, "There is a generation that are pure in their own eyes, yet is not washed from their filthiness." Judaical pharisaism, with its broad phylacteries and street-corner devotions and idle ceremonies, you may not practise; but are you not in spirit a Pharisee? Is not the earth full of those who "trust in themselves that they are righteous, and despise others?" of those who say, "Stand by thyself, come not near me, I am holier than thou?" How little is thought of the precious blood and righteousness of Jesus Christ! Traill says, "All zealous, devout people in a natural religion are enemies to the gospel. By natural religion, I mean that which is the product of the remnant of God's image in fallen man, a little improved by the light of God's word. All such cannot endure to hear that God's law must be perfectly fulfilled in every tittle of it, or no man can be saved by doing: that they must all perish for ever who have not the righteousness of a Man who never sinned; who is also 'God over all, blessed for ever,' to shelter and cover them from the anger of a holy God, and to render them accepted of him: that his righteousness is put on by the grace of God, and a man must take himself to it, and receive it as a naked, blushing sinner: that no man can do any thing that is good till gospel grace renew him, and make him first a good man. This they never will receive; but do still think a man may grow good by doing good."

Alas for men! Few of them feel themselves so dreadfully diseased and ruined by sin as to betake themselves to that fountain of which the pool of Bethesda was but a type. Honesty, truth, and love require every messenger of God to declare to his hearers that they are transgressors of the best, the wisest, the most benevolent code of laws ever enacted. By this code, all are sinners, shut up to guilt and wrath, prisoners to eternal justice. No man can answer for one of a thousand of his transgressions. It is solely of God's mercies that we are not all consumed. We have all sinned and come short of the glory of God. If we had any sense, we should each cry, "Enter not into judgment with thy servant, for in thy sight shall no man living be justified."

Surely no room is left us for boasting.

"We are unprofitable servants." "Who can say, I have made my heart clean; I am pure from my sin?" The best men that this world has ever seen have cried out like Paul, "I am carnal, sold under sin;" or like Josiah, "Woe is me, for I am a man of unclean lips;" or like the publican, "God be merciful to me a sinner." How then dare any of us lift up our heads in arrogance, and like those in whose skirts blood was found say, "I am innocent?" Jer. 2:35; or like the woman of infamy, "who wipeth her mouth and saith, I have done no wickedness?" Prov. 30:20; or like fraudulent Ephraim, with the balances of deceit in his hands, "In all my labors they shall find none iniquity in me that were sin?" Hos. 12:8.

He who lacks humility on the score of his personal sinfulness, precludes the possibility of improvement in his spiritual state. "Before honor is humility." "God resisteth the proud, but giveth grace unto the humble." Men must either part with their pride and good opinion of themselves, or they must part with hope and a blessed eternity. Will you cast yourself at the feet of sovereign mercy? You must either take your place in the dust before God, or be cast down to hell.

Nor does any grace carry with it richer advantages than humility. It is above most things a means and a guaranty of a peaceful and peaceable life. "Only by pride cometh contention." Prov. 13:10. "He that is of a proud heart stirreth up strife." Prov. 28:25. Humility casts its care upon the Lord, knowing that he careth for us, 1 Pet. 5:7; and so leaves in his hands those things which disquiet the lives of so many. It is also the great means and guaranty of avoiding self-deception. If ever men are puffed up with delusive notions respecting their virtues or powers, the Scripture gives the reason: "The pride of thy heart hath deceived thee." Obad. 3. Humility is also the great means and pledge of a tender heart. The way that Nebuchadnezzar became such a monster of wickedness was, that his "heart was lifted up and hardened in pride." Dan. 5:20. By humility men avoid much and terrible mortification, and final ruin; for "when pride cometh, then cometh shame." Prov. 11:2. "Pride goeth before destruction, and a haughty spirit before a fall." Prov. 16:18. "Before destruction, the heart of man is haughty." Prov. 18:12. Newton says, "A spirit of humiliation is both the strength and beauty of our profession. A broken and contrite spirit is pleasing to the Lord; he has promised to dwell with those who have it; and experience shows that the exercise of all our graces is in proportion to the humbling sense we have of the depravity of our nature... If we could receive and habitually maintain a right judgment of ourselves by what is plainly maintained in Scripture, it would probably save us many a mournful hour; but experience is the Lord's school, and they who are taught by him usually learn that they have no wisdom by the mistakes they make, and that they have no strength by the slips and falls they meet with."

John Owen says, "In *humility* alone there is safety. 'His soul, which is lifted up, is not upright in him,' Hab. 2:4; for he draws back from God, and God hath no pleasure in him, as the apostle expounds these words. Heb. 10:38."

Everywhere the Scriptures represent humility as the road to honor. This is the doctrine of both Testaments. "Before honor is humility." Prov. 15:33, and 18:12. "By humility and the fear of the Lord are riches, and honor, and life." Prov. 22:4. "He that humbleth himself shall be exalted." Luke 14:11. Not only does honor come after humility, but ultimately it is in proportion to it. Thus it was with Joseph. Thus it was with JESUS, of whom Joseph was but a type. Humility is also the best evidence of piety. Without it all other evidences are useless. A good writer says, "The Christian's temper Godward is evidenced by *humility*. He has received from Gethsemane and Golgotha such a sense of the evil of sin and of the holiness of God, combined with his matchless love to sinners, as has deeply penetrated his heart." Here too is the great secret of improvement. Would you gain strength? know your weakness. Would you gain wisdom? know your folly. Seneca said, "I suppose many would attain to wisdom, if they did not suppose they had already attained to it." If you would be more like God, know how little you are yet like him.

Humility is also the way to communion with God. "Thus saith the high and lofty One that inhabiteth eternity, whose name is Holy: I dwell in the high and holy place, with him also that is of a contrite and humble spirit, to revive the spirit of the humble, and to revive the heart of the contrite ones." Isaiah 57:15. And so it appears that humility is essential to salvation. The Scriptures not only teach this incidentally, but explicitly. "When men are cast down, then thou shalt say, There is lifting up; and he shall save the humble person." Job 22 : 29. "Though the Lord be high, yet hath he respect unto the lowly; but the proud he knoweth afar off." Psa. 138 : 6.

If you would cultivate humility, you must acquire self-knowledge; you must practise self-inspection; you must be willing to know the worst of your own case; you must settle it in your heart that humility is a great good; you must compare yourself with those who have been brighter examples of virtue than yourself, and especially with our great exemplar Jesus Christ; you must think much of your indebtedness to God's grace—for what hast thou that thou hast not received?—you must reflect on the odiousness of a religious character which is destitute of this essential qualification; you must get clear views of the law, its extent, spirituality, and strictness; you must get clear views of God. This was what brought Job into the dust: "I have heard of thee by the hearing of the ear; but now mine eye seeth thee; wherefore I abhor myself, and repent in dust and ashes." Job 42 : 5, 6.

Would you obtain humility? Ask for it. Never adopt the belief that you can work this or any other grace in your heart without the help of God's Spirit. It was a good prayer of a saint of former days: "O thou who only knowest what I would do if I had health, ease, and abundance, do thou in thy wisdom and mercy so proportion thy gifts and restraints as thou knowest best for my soul. If I be not humbled enough, let me wait; and so order all my condition that I may want any thing save thyself." Pray for humility, and when the answer comes, be not angry that God has abased you, but trust him with all your heart.

Take root downwards, and then you shall bear fruit upwards. If there be no deepness of earth, things will not grow. If the foundation be laid on the surface, the house will not stand. With the lowly is wisdom. Their peace is settled. Their salvation is certain.

This discussion leads to these observations:

1. No man is ultimately the loser by any virtue whatever. Nothing is so self-renouncing as humility, yet nothing in the end leads to such riches and honors and glories. A grace may provoke the contempt, the envy, or the rage of men; yet what of that? The con-

tempt of man is not to be compared with the derision of God. And the worst that malice can inflict is to torture and kill the body. It is not position, but worth, that deserves esteem. "A diamond fallen into a dunghill is not the less precious; and the dust, raised by high winds to heaven, is not the less vile." It is always wise, it is always profitable to practise every Christian virtue. If present loss comes to us in the path of duty, the end will be eternal gain.

2. The truly godly need not fear that their pious labors and sufferings will be overlooked. They shall all be found unto praise and honor and glory at the appearing of Jesus Christ. Their humility may very properly lead them to put a low estimate upon all they do. But God will not forget their labors of love. "The good works of some are manifest beforehand; and they that are otherwise cannot be hid."

3. The praise that cometh from man is as nothing compared with the praise that cometh from God only. The barbarous people who without evidence pronounced Paul a murderer, as suddenly and blindly declared him to be a god. If you could get all men to praise you to-day, they would probably execrate you to-

morrow. But when God pronounces a man blessed, there is permanency, there is durability in it. "The gifts and calling of God are without repentance."

4. This subject furnishes a good test of doctrinal statements. Does a doctrine flatter, or does it stain the pride and glory of man? The answer to this question, fairly made, will be a safe guide to a decision on any views in religion which we may have. If in the science of astronomy the earth be considered as the centre, and the sun be made to revolve around it, we have one system, a system full of error. At every succeeding step and with every growing conception, we get further and further from the truth. So in religion. If one feels himself to be the centre of worth and importance, and looks on others as ministering to him, then we have one form of religion, one code of practice which fully coincide with the sentiments and demeanor of Pharisees and fallen angels. But if a man in his mind and heart puts Jehovah on the throne, and himself in the dust, then we have another and a very different system of religious belief and practice. In all this is order, concord, the right of divine law, and a solid basis for peace and obedience. This is

one ingredient of heavenly bliss. There the will of the King, eternal, immortal, and invisible, is received with shouts of joy. It was an attempt to introduce a different state of things that constituted the rebellion which broke out in heaven, and led the Eternal to build his prison-house Tophet, that was ordained of old. Reject all teachings that flatter the pride of man. A doctrine which makes you greater than the least of God's mercies is not from heaven.

5. This subject affords a guide in the performance of religious duties. As far as their nature will allow, they should be modest and retiring. "Take heed that ye do not your alms before men, to be seen of them: otherwise ye have no reward of your Father which is in heaven. Therefore, when thou doest thine alms, do not sound a trumpet before thee, as the hypocrites do, in the synagogues, and in the streets, that they may have glory of men. Verily I say unto you, They have their reward. But when thou doest thine alms, let not thy left hand know what thy right hand doeth; that thine alms may be in secret: and thy Father which seeth in secret, himself shall reward thee openly. And when thou prayest,

thou shalt not be as the hypocrites are: for they love to pray standing in the synagogues, and in the corners of the streets, that they may be seen of men. Verily I say unto you, They have their reward. But thou, when thou prayest, enter into thy closet, and when thou hast shut thy door, pray to thy Father which is in secret; and thy Father which seeth in secret shall reward thee openly." Matt. 6:1–6. Here are the very words of the Son of God, delivered in his first set discourse to his disciples. Let them never be forgotten.

## CHAPTER XIII.

### THE FEAR OF GOD.

God's word clearly teaches that there is a fear connate with true religion. Once the Scriptures assert that "the fear of the Lord is the beginning of knowledge," Prov. 1 : 7; and twice they say that "the fear of the Lord is the beginning of wisdom." Psa. 111 : 10, and Prov. 9 : 10. There is no higher wisdom than to fear God, as there is no true wisdom till he is feared. This is both alpha and omega in wisdom. "The very first, and indeed the principal thing, to be instilled into all men's minds, is a religious sense of the divine Majesty, and an awful regard towards him." With the foregoing well agrees the prophet Isaiah: "The fear of the Lord is his treasure." Isa. 33 : 6.

It is the more important to dwell upon this grace, as it seems not to be much spoken of. Very seldom is it a subject of pulpit discourse; rarely do we find it treated of at length in modern books; yet the Bible is full of it. Not only the Old Testament, but the New also, insists upon reverence and godly fear as essential ingredients of Christian character. Perhaps one reason why so little is said of it is, that many minds are confused respecting its qualities. It will therefore be wise to seek to understand its nature, and the difference between it and all those kinds of fear which are spurious.

Godly fear does not at all consist in servility and guilty dismay, nor in mere dread and terror. This kind of fear is neither holy nor useful. Indeed it sadly perverts men, and fits them for a life of sin. "Fear, if it have not the light of a true understanding concerning God wherewith to be moderated, breedeth superstition," says Hooker.

Godly fear consists with love. This is so true, that the more we fear God, the more we love him; and the more we love him, the more do we fear him. It is not a destroyer, but a regulator of other graces. Without it faith might become presumptuous, hope might lose its sobriety, love might degenerate into fondness or familiarity, and joy might become giddy. But where the heart is full of godly fear, all these unhappy results are avoided. So far from agitating, it calms and quiets the mind. It seems to give both gravity and cheerfulness. It moderates without depressing; it animates without intoxicating. It is good ballast to the ship in her passage through tempestuous seas.

This fear is a fruit of God's bounty. It is gracious. "Let us have *grace*, whereby we may serve God acceptably, with reverence and godly fear." Without an interest in God's favor, we can never make so excellent an attainment. It is a saving grace. It is declared to be a part of true religion in all dispensations. "They shall fear thee as long as the sun and moon endure, throughout all generations." Psa. 72 : 5. So that religion without love is not more spurious than religion without fear. One of the most striking features of synagogue worship for centuries past has been an evident want of profound reverence for God in the entire manner of conducting the religious services of the Jews.

The basis of this fear is found in the nature, word, and works of God. Jehovah is "the great and dreadful God." We must gain a knowledge of him. "As the justice of God and his anger must be apprehended before he can be feared slavishly, so the majesty of God and his goodness must be understood before he can be feared filially. Who can stand in awe of a majesty he is ignorant of? Men, knowing not God's nature, have often presumed so much upon his mercy, that they have been destroyed by his justice." Any right thoughts of God's amazing purity of nature will surely beget a pious fear of him. Because he is "glorious in holiness," he is "fearful in praises." "As the approach of a grave and serious man makes children hasten their trifles out of the way; so would the consideration of this attribute make us cast away our idols, and our ridiculous thoughts and designs." And not only God's majesty and holiness, but also his love and mercy beget a great fear of him. So says the Psalmist, "There is forgiveness with thee, that thou mayest be feared." Psa. 130:4. So says Paul, "We receiving a kingdom, let us have grace, whereby we may serve God acceptably with reverence and godly fear." Heb. 12:28. The same is true of God's power and government. "Thou art great, and thy name is great in might; who would not fear thee, O King of nations?" Jer. 10:6, 7. Jesus Christ told us to fear him who had power to cast into hell. Luke 12:5.

In like manner, to fear and tremble at God's word is an effect produced on the heart of all the pious. So the Scriptures teach; so God's people experience. And how often does God awaken sentiments of fear, not only by exhibitions of his wrath and displays of his power, but by marvellous acts of his grace and mercy towards the rebellious and perishing. Psa. 40:3; Acts 2:43.

There are some remarkable examples of the fear of God recorded in Scripture. One is that of Moses, mentioned in Heb. 12:21, where it is said that the giving of the law on mount Sinai produced the deepest awe and even terror. "So terrible was the sight, that Moses said, I exceedingly fear and quake." A similar record is made by Isaiah: "In the year that king Uzziah died, I saw also the Lord sitting upon a throne, high and lifted up, and his train filled the temple. Above it stood the seraphim: each one had six wings; with twain he covered his face, and with twain he covered his feet, and with twain he did fly. And one cried unto another, and said, Holy, holy, holy is the Lord of hosts: the whole earth is full of his glory. And the posts of the door moved at the voice of him that cried, and the house was filled with smoke. Then said I, Woe is me! for I am undone; because I am a man of unclean lips, and I dwell in the midst of a people of unclean lips: for mine eyes have seen the King, the Lord of hosts." Isa. 6:1–5.

A still more remarkable effect, if possible, was produced on the prophet Habakkuk by an unusual display of God's glory. The song reads thus: "God came from Teman, and the Holy One from mount Paran. His glory covered the heavens, and the earth was full of his praise. And his brightness was as the light; he had horns coming out of his hand: and there was the hiding of his power. Before him went the pestilence, and burning coals went forth at his feet. He stood, and measured the earth: he beheld, and drove asunder the nations; and the everlasting mountains were scattered, the perpetual hills did bow: his ways are everlasting. I saw the tents of Cushan in affliction: and the curtains of the land of Midian did tremble. Was the Lord displeased against the rivers? was thine anger against the rivers? was thy wrath against the sea, that thou didst ride upon thy horses, and thy chariots of salvation? Thy bow was made quite naked, according to the oaths of the tribes, even thy word. Thou didst cleave the earth with rivers. The mountains saw thee, and they trembled: the overflowing of the water passed by: the deep uttered his voice, and lifted up his hands on high. The sun and moon stood still in their habitation: at the light of thine arrows they went, and at the shining of thy glittering spear. Thou didst march through the land in indignation, thou didst thresh the heathen in anger. Thou wentest forth for the salvation of thy people, even for salvation with thine anointed; thou woundedst the head out of the house of the wicked, by discovering the foundation unto the neck. Thou didst strike through with his staves the head of his villages: they came out as a whirlwind to scatter me: their rejoicing was as to devour the poor secretly. Thou didst walk through the sea with thy horses, through the heap of great waters. When I heard, my belly trembled; my lips quivered at the voice: rottenness entered into my bones, and I trembled in myself, that I might rest in the day of trouble." Habakkuk 3:3–16.

A reason given by Paul for serving God with reverence and godly fear is, that he "is a consuming fire." Heb. 12:28, 29. A very high degree of holy fear is therefore well founded. There is cause for adoring reverence for the heavenly Majesty.

Although there is not much said in modern writers respecting the fear of God, yet it is different with those who lived long ago. Thus says Bishop Hall, "There is a fear without diffidence, and a trembling that may consist with joy. Trembling is an effect of fear, but the fear which we must cherish is reverential, not slavish, not distrustful. . . . I will so distrust myself, that I may be steadfastly confident in the God of my salvation. I will so tremble before the glorious majesty of my God, that I may not abate aught of the joy of his never-failing mercy." So also Bishop Hopkins on the first commandment says, "Certainly we cannot have the Lord for our God unless we supremely fear and reverence him. Yea, as the love, so the fear of God is made the sum of all the commandments, and indeed the substance of all religion; for, although it be but one particular branch and member of that worship and service which we owe to God, yet it is such a remarkable one, and hath such a mighty influence upon all the rest, that oftentimes in Scripture it is put for the whole." How clearly too does John Bunyan describe this virtue in his account of Mr. Fearing. As he says, "No fears, no grace. Though there is not always grace where there is the fear of hell, yet to be sure there is no grace where there is no fear of God."

Where this fear of God is genuine, it is not an occasional exercise, but an abiding principle. "Be thou in the fear of the Lord all the day long." Prov. 23 : 17. "Happy is the man that feareth always." Prov. 28 : 14. "Rejoice with trembling." Psa. 2:11. "Pass the time of your sojourning here in fear." 1 Pet. 1:17. We are to "perfect holiness in the fear of God." 2 Cor. 7:1. We are to work out our "salvation with fear and trembling." Phil. 2:12. When the Holy Spirit rested on Christ, it "made him of quick understanding in the fear of the Lord." Isa. 11:2, 3. So that it is clear that there is, there can be no genuine piety without the fear of God.

Some one may ask how these views agree with the statement of John, that "there is no fear in love; but perfect love casteth out fear, because fear hath torment. He that feareth is not made perfect in love." 1 John 4:18.

The proper answer is, that John is here speaking of servile fear, which, as he says, "hath torment;" whereas we are speaking of a fear which has no torment. John Newton says, "The Lord bids me 'fear not;' and at the same time he says, 'Happy is the man that feareth always.' How to fear and not to fear at the same time is, I believe, one branch of that secret of the Lord which none can understand but by the teaching of his Spirit. When I think of my heart, of the world, of the powers of darkness, what cause of continual fear! I am on an enemy's ground, and cannot move a step but some snare is spread for my feet. But when I think of the person, grace, power, care, and faithfulness of my Saviour, why may I not say, I will trust and not be afraid, for the Lord of hosts is with us, the God of Jacob is our refuge. I wish to be delivered from anxious and unbelieving fear, which weakens the hands and disquiets the heart. I wish to increase in a humble jealousy and distrust of myself and of every thing about me." Charnock says, "Men are apt to fear a just recompense for an injury done to another, that he will do him one ill turn for another; and fear is the mother of hatred. God being man's superior, and wronged by him, there follows necessarily a slavish fear of him and his power; and such a fear makes wrathful and imbittered thoughts of God, while he considers God armed with an unconquerable and irresistible power to punish him." But the fear which arises from just views of the whole of God's character produces very different effects, and is in fact very different in its nature.

The benefits of godly fear are many and of great value. It is the best preservative against sinful and dangerous alliances with the wicked. "Say ye not, A confederacy, to all them to whom this people shall say, A confederacy; neither fear ye their fear, nor be afraid. Sanctify the Lord of hosts himself; and let him be your fear, and let him be your dread." Isa. 8:12, 13. How many wicked alliances are formed; and for no other reason than that men are led into them through a want of sterling religious principle. The consequence is, misery for ever. From how many distressing entanglements men would be rescued by the fear of the Lord.

It also drives away that fear of man which bringeth a snare. Christ says, "Be not afraid of them that kill the body, and after that have no more that they can do. But I will forewarn you whom ye shall fear: Fear Him, which, after he hath killed, hath power to cast into hell; yea, I say unto you, Fear him." Luke 12:4, 5. Christ himself proposes the fear of God as the great remedy for the fear of man. Nor is there any other that is found adequate. But this is enough. How justly does God rebuke that fear of man: "Who art thou, that thou shouldest be afraid of a man that shall die, and of the son of man which shall be made as grass; and forgettest the Lord thy Maker, that hath stretched forth the heavens, and laid the foundations of the earth; and hast feared continually every day because of the fury of the oppressor?" Isa. 51:12, 13. It is not possible for us to fear God too much, or man too little. And so surely as we have just conceptions of the eternal power and majesty of God, we shall have no tormenting fear of the puny arm of mortals.

The fear of the Lord inspires confidence and boldness in a righteous cause. That this is experienced by all God's people, has been illustrated in a thousand striking cases in history, and is clearly declared in Scripture. "In the fear of the Lord is strong confidence, and his children shall have a place of refuge." Prov. 14:26.

The fear of God is the great preservative against sin. Than this, nothing could be more important. "Keep thyself out of sin, and fear nothing." If we can resist all temptations to sin, and be pure from iniquity, nothing can harm us. This may be done by a proper fear of God. "The fear of the Lord is a fountain of life, to depart from the snares of death." Prov. 14:27. The care of good men in all ages has been against sin. And as their spiritual enemies are very many and insidious, they have learned to be much afraid of that which in others awakens no apprehension. They are cautious about little sins, and their cry is, "Take us the foxes, the little foxes that spoil the vines; for our vines have tender grapes." Song 2:15. In ancient vineyards a tower was erected, and a watch set there for birds, foxes, and thieves, the three great enemies of the vintage. Birds always, and thieves sometimes, approached vineyards in the day-time; but foxes commonly came at night. Larger foxes preyed much on poultry and on smaller animals, but the young foxes that ventured abroad resorted much to the vineyards.

This they did both day and night. They were numerous, cunning, greedy, and destructive. If there were many of them, they ruined the vintage. They did their work slyly. Great vigilance was therefore requisite. Some suppose that in the passage just quoted, "tender grapes" represent young converts. The truth is that all Christians, and especially those who have but little knowledge of the deceitfulness of sin and of the doctrines of Scripture, should be ever on their guard.

But why should we give good heed to little things in the Christian life? It is a fair question; let it be answered. Many things which seem to us little are followed by the greatest consequences. One spark of fire has kindled a flame that burnt a city. A word has often shaped the course of an empire, or determined the destiny of a soul. Till we see the end of a thing, we cannot tell whether it is to be great or small in its effects. On earth we see the end of nothing in moral causes. They are mighty. They take hold on eternity. Their sweep is everlasting. Their effects are much more certain than those of natural causes. They work incessantly. Our greatest rivers have their rise in little springs whose streams are often buried under leaves and shrubs. The causes now at work in forming men's character seem contemptible to many. But a leak, though not larger than a rye straw, will sooner or later sink a ship. The smallest opening made by a mole in the bank of a canal will of itself grow to a waste of all its waters. One weak link in a chain-cable causes the vessel to drift on the rocks. One of the most heroic deeds ever performed was suggested by the perseverance of the ant. A little white powder or a drop of some poisons is fatal to human life. A scratch has brought on inflammation that ended in death. A glance of the eye has led to crimes that will not be forgotten while eternity endures. A sentence has subverted the labors and schemes of a lifetime.

The greater part of human life is made up of acts that do not seem great in themselves, but the whole series completes the character. What is lighter than a word? Yet for every idle word that men shall speak they shall give account to God. What is quicker than thought? Yet as a man thinketh in his heart, so is he. As "sands form the mountains and minutes make the year," and as syllables compose the web of the greatest speeches, so many comparatively trivial acts determine the character. One harsh word now, another an hour hence, and so on, will prove a man a churl. A few irreverent words scattered along through a day mark a man as profane. One stealthy act of pilfering proves a man a thief. He who would not be convicted of grand larceny, must avoid petty larceny. He who would not defile his soul with perjury, must eschew lying. He who would not be found a liar, must beware of equivocation. The sum of human character is made up of many apparently small things. Every great stream is fed by many lesser ones.

But what are the "little foxes?" One says they are worldly thoughts. This is true. Another says they are wrong opinions. This is as true. Another, no less wisely, says they are our hidden corruptions, our sinful appetites and passions, that destroy our graces and comforts, quash good motions, and crush good beginnings. When men fear not little sins, they will soon fall into presumptuous iniquities. When they are not conscientious about minor duties, they will soon fail in weightier matters. He who cannot walk well, cannot run well. Envy is the forerunner of murder, and naturally leads to it. Covetousness is the fountain of all theft. As a grain of sand will fret a sound eye and make it weep, so the least sin perceived will tenderly affect a good conscience. We must take and destroy these little foxes by a right use of the word of God. It is clear. It is pure. By it are all God's servants warned. We must watch day and night. We must pray frequently and fervently. We must have the Holy Ghost dwelling in us. We must make constant application to the blood of cleansing. Above all, we must be in the fear of the Lord all the day long. Blessed is the man who avoids little sins and minds little duties; in the great steps of life he shall not be covered with dishonor. His heart is right. God is with him. Christ will never forsake him. "The fear of the Lord is clean, enduring for ever."

Another benefit flowing from the fear of the Lord is freedom from worldly anxiety. In the passage quoted from Habakkuk we saw how wonderfully the fear of God took possession of the prophet. In the words immediately following he gives us that triumphant song: "Although the fig-tree shall not blossom, neither shall fruit be in the vines; the labor of the olive shall fail, and the fields shall yield no meat; the flock shall be cut off from the fold, and there shall be no herd in the stalls: yet I will rejoice in the Lord, I will joy in the God of my salvation. The Lord God is my strength, and he will make my feet like hinds' feet, and he will make me to walk upon my high places." Hab. 3:17–19. Thus the greatest degree of holy trembling was followed by the highest degree of freedom from carking care about temporal affairs. All this is according to the promise, "The fear of the Lord tendeth to life: and he that hath it shall abide satisfied; he shall not be visited with evil." Prov. 19:23.

The fear of God also quiets the afflicted soul, and hushes all its agitations on the bosom of the Eternal. Thus David speaks: "O God, thou hast cast us off, thou hast scattered us, thou hast been displeased; O turn thyself to us again. Thou hast made the earth to tremble; thou hast broken it: heal the breaches thereof; for it shaketh. Thou hast showed thy people hard things: thou hast made us to drink the wine of astonishment." In the midst of all this distress and perplexity, what shall be done? Who has courage and strength?

The very next words are, "Thou hast given a banner to them that fear thee, that it may be displayed because of the truth." Psa. 60:1–4.

The fear of the Lord also leads to communion with God. This is abundantly taught in Scripture. "The secret of the Lord is with them that fear him; and he will show them his covenant." Psa. 25:14. Again, "The Lord taketh pleasure in them that fear him, in those that hope in his mercy." Psa. 147:11.

The cultivation of the fear of the Lord is the best means we can use to promote and retain revivals of genuine religion. Thus Luke, describing the state of the early church, says, "Then had the churches rest throughout all Judea and Galilee and Samaria, and were edified; and walking in the fear of the Lord, and in the comfort of the Holy Ghost, were multiplied." Acts 9:31.

On the other hand, if religion be not revived, if the love of many wax cold, and wickedness abound, here is the way to avoid guilt and to please God. The prophet Malachi lived in times of unusual and dreadful apostasy and sin, when men called the proud happy, when they that wrought wickedness were set up, when they that tempted God were even delivered. Yet he says, "Then they that feared the Lord spake often one to another; and the Lord hearkened, and heard it, and a book of remembrance was written before him for them that feared the Lord, and that thought upon his name. And they shall be mine, saith the Lord of hosts, in that day when I make up my jewels; and I will spare them as a man spareth his own son that serveth him." Mal. 3:16, 17.

In fine, without the fear of the Lord no service is acceptable, however decent, however costly, however painful. But with the fear of God, any commanded service is pleasing to God, however poor our offering may otherwise be. "Let us hear the conclusion of the whole matter: Fear God and keep his commandments, for this is the whole duty of man." Eccl. 12:13.

## CHAPTER XIV.

### HOPE.

WITH some it is common to speak slightingly of hope. Surely such do not draw their views from the word of God, nor from the experience of his people. These well agree in giving it a high place among the Christian graces, and in declaring its excellence and usefulness. "We are saved by hope." We are rescued from the fell influences of despair, we are aroused and animated in our whole course, and are finally made victorious by the power of hope. This is one of the great bands which holds together the church of God. As "there is one body and one Spirit, . . . . one Lord, one faith, one baptism, one God and Father of all," so also "ye are called in one hope of your calling."

Hope consists of desire and expectation. It is the opposite of fear, which is composed of aversion and expectation. Richard Baxter says, "Hope is nothing but a desirous expectation." It is also the opposite of despair, which, though it desires, does not expect.

When we regard any thing as impossible, we cannot hope for it, although we may greatly wish for it. As to the general nature of hope there is no dispute.

The hope of the Christian is a longing expectation of all good things both for this and the next world. It embraces all the mercy, truth, love, and faithfulness promised in Scripture. It lays hold of the perfections and government of God as the sure foundation of its expectations. It has special reference to the person, offices, and exaltation of the Lord Jesus Christ. In Scripture the word not only means the sentiment already described, but sometimes it is used for the thing hoped for. Thus Paul speaks to the Colossians of "the hope which was laid up for" them in heaven, where he plainly designates the good things hoped for. The hope of a Christian relates to the whole of what is promised in God's word. There grace is promised. And on every child of God comes the blessing: "Behold, the eye of the Lord is upon them that fear him, upon them that hope in his mercy." In like manner hope finds aliment in all the divine perfections. It looks for them to be continually exercised for its good. Thus it expects bread and water, raiment and shelter, guidance and protection during life, with a blessed victory in death. It goes further. Each Christian can say as Paul, "I have hope towards God . . . . that there shall be a resurrection of the dead, both of the just and of the unjust." Yea, more, he is always "looking for that blessed hope, and the glorious appearing of our God and Saviour Jesus Christ." Yea, more, the souls of believers are sustained "in hope of eternal life, which God, that cannot lie, promised before the world began."

The living agent, who is at once the author and object of pious hope, is God himself. Accordingly pious men cry out, "Why art thou cast down, O my soul? and why art thou disquieted within me? hope thou in God: for I shall yet praise him for the help of his countenance." One of the dearest names by which God is known to his people is that of "The Hope of Israel, the Saviour thereof in the time of trouble." To the end of time "the Lord will be the hope of his people, and the strength of the" true Israel. There is none like him. He is "the God of hope."

All genuine Christian hope is a fruit of the mercy of God to sinners. It comes from heaven, and not from men. Vain, carnal hopes spring up spontaneously in the human soul. But truly pious hopes have a heavenly origin. Therefore when Paul would have the Romans abound in this grace, he prayed, "Now the God of hope fill you with all joy and peace in believing, that ye may abound in hope, through the power of the Holy Ghost." Rom. 15 : 13. God "hath given us everlasting consolation and good hope through grace." 2 Thess. 2 : 16. This is the first great difference between a true and a false hope in religion. The former is from above; the latter is from beneath. One is God-inspired; the other has Satan for its author.

The second mark of true religious hope is, that it is no vain persuasion, no idle dream, but a sure expectation. It rests upon an immovable foundation, God's unchanging word and oath and covenant. "We through the Spirit wait for the hope of righteousness by faith." We shall not be disappointed. This "hope we have as an anchor of the soul, both sure and steadfast, and which entereth into that within the veil." His word is pledged in every form. "I will be a God to thee;" "I will never leave thee, nor forsake thee;" "Because I live, ye shall live also;" "Them that sleep in Jesus will God bring with him." These are but samples of his word. To these he has added his oath: "I have sworn that I would not be wroth with thee: for the mountains shall depart, and the hills be removed; but my kindness shall not depart from thee, neither shall the covenant of my peace be removed, saith the Lord that hath mercy on thee." Isa. 54 : 9, 10. Here we have his covenant as well as his oath. Indeed it is a covenant established upon promises and oaths. Elsewhere God says, "I will make a new covenant with the house of Israel; not according to the covenant I made with their fathers, which my covenant they brake, although I was a husband unto them." Jer. 31:31, 32. Behold here are the sure mercies of David. God bids us rest our all on him, and take his veracity for the basis of all our hopes. The wicked have no such foundation for their delusive expectations. Their hopes are all like a dream when one awaketh. They vanish before the realities of life, before any right test of truth. But the hope of the righteous endureth. It is the anchor, the sheet-anchor. It holds all steady, and enables the soul to outride the storms of sorrow which God permits to beat upon it. Behold here the excellent use of Scripture. "For whatsoever things were written aforetime were written for our learning, that we through patience and comfort of the Scriptures might have hope." Rom. 15 : 4. Therefore a favorite form of prayer is that of pleading the promises: "Remember the word unto thy servant, upon which thou hast caused me to hope." Psa. 119 : 49. This blessed hope, more than most things, makes Christians helpers of each other's faith and joy. "They that fear thee will be glad when they see me; because I have hoped in thy word." Psa. 119 : 74.

A third difference between a true and false hope is, that the former is the fruit of the mediation of Christ, and has special regard to him as a Redeemer; while the latter quite neglects his finished work. Many hope for impunity, and yet despise gospel grace. But a truly good hope always has a chief reliance upon Christ. Therefore Paul says of our Lord Jesus Christ, that he "is our hope." 1 Tim. 1 : 1. If you ever have a genuine "hope of glory," it must spring from "Christ in you." Col. 1 : 27. Legal hope is just the opposite of evangelical. The former springs from supposed personal obedience to the law; the latter relies upon Christ's obedience unto death. These two cannot agree. You must look to Christ exclusively, or not at all. If this be so, some may ask, What is the difference between faith and hope? To this question the answer is, that though they are distinct, yet they are cognate exercises of the mind. Haldane says, "By faith we believe the promises made to us by God; by hope we expect to receive the good things which God has promised; so that faith hath properly for its object the promise, and hope hath for its object the things promised and the execution of the promise. Faith regards its object as present, but hope regards it as future. Faith precedes hope, and is its foundation. We hope for eternal life, because we believe the promises which God has made respecting it; and if we believe these promises, we must expect their effect." Leighton says, "The difference of these two graces, *faith* and *hope*, is so small, that the one is often taken for the other in Scripture; it is but a different aspect of the same confidence, *faith* apprehending the infallible truth of those divine promises of which *hope* doth assuredly expect the accomplishment, and that is their truth; so that this immediately results from the other. This is the anchor fixed within the veil which keeps the soul firm against all the tossings on these swelling seas, and the winds and tempests that arise upon them. The firmest thing in this inferior world is a believing soul." But like faith, hope admits of degrees, varying from a faint expectation, Psa. 42 : 5, to a "full assurance." Heb. 6 : 11. Like faith, it always keeps Christ in view. Like faith, also, it will last until death, and then give place to enjoyment; "for what a man hath, why doth he yet hope for?" Let us therefore "hold fast the confidence, and the rejoicing of the hope firm unto the end." Heb. 3 : 6. "Wherefore gird up the loins of your mind, be sober, and hope to the end for the grace that is to be brought unto you at the revelation of Jesus Christ." 1 Pet. 1 : 13.

A fourth difference between a true and false hope in religion is, that the former is operative, and produces powerful, happy effects; while the latter is inoperative and dead. The hope of the Christian is expressly said to be "lively." 1 Pet. 1 : 3. It has life in itself, and communicates animation to the soul. It arouses, awakens, and gives vigor to the mind.

It produces the grandest effects, making the people of God triumphant over all their foes and fears, and bearing them up when all appearances are discouraging. But a dead hope is without any abiding effect. It does no good in the day of trial.

A fifth difference between a true and a false hope is, that the former leads to holiness, while the latter begets carelessness. Of genuine Christian hope it is said, that "every man that hath this hope in him purifieth himself, even as Christ is pure." 1 John 3 : 3. The stronger it is, the greater is the soul's aversion to evil. But the hope of the deluded makes him reckless. To him sin is a trifle, and holiness a thing of naught. This indeed is the great difference between all genuine and all spurious hopes. If any of our religious affections or mental exercises do not tend to holiness, we may surely know that they are not of God.

A sixth difference is, that a spurious hope gives no support when we most need help; but a genuine hope bears up our souls above all our foes. Leighton says, "Hope is the great stock of believers. It is that which upholds them under all the faintings and sorrows of their mind in this life, and in their going 'through the valley and shadow of death.' It is the 'helmet of their salvation,' which, while they are looking over to eternity, beyond this present time, covers and keeps men head-safe amid all the darts that fly around them."

According to God's word, genuine Christian hope has many and important *uses*. It does great things for the soul.

1. It makes us patient in tribulation. "If we hope for that we see not, then do we with patience wait for it." Accordingly Paul alike commends in the Thessalonians "the work of faith, and labor of love, and patience of hope in our Lord Jesus Christ." 1 Thess. 1:3. To this happy effect of this grace Jeremiah refers when he says, "It is good that a man should both hope and quietly wait for the salvation of the Lord. It is good for a man that he bear the yoke in his youth. He sitteth alone, and keepeth silence, because he hath borne it upon him. He putteth his mouth in the dust; if so be there may be hope." Lam. 3:26–29. All Scripture and all experience show, that through much tribulation we must enter the kingdom of God. We can purchase no exemption. Pa-

tience must have her perfect work. Patience is fed by hope. It is thus we are supported in trials. What but this can give strength in the day of trouble? The church of God has often waded through rivers of blood; she has often been bound in affliction and iron; the fiercest onsets ever made upon her have often threatened something still worse; yet hope has begotten patience, a patience that could not be worn out. Despondency is unquiet, dissatisfied, and full of pain; but hope cries, "Be thou faithful unto death, and Christ will give thee a crown of life."

2. Hope also gives courage in facing danger, and fortitude in enduring pain. "Hope maketh not ashamed; because the love of God is shed abroad in our hearts by the Holy Ghost which is given unto us." Rom. 5:5. Unless we have "for a helmet, the hope of salvation," 1 Thess. 5:8, we shall but play the coward in the day of battle. Here is the great difference between the real child of God and the self-deceiver. The former has an expectation of future glory which makes present ignominy to be esteemed as nothing. The latter has perhaps some vague hope of future good, but he has never relinquished his hold of present

good. So when he finds he must let go either the present or the future, he always cleaves to the present, vainly purposing hereafter to seize upon the things to come. Every man who knows any thing at all of his own heart, is painfully convinced of his sad timidity and wicked shame as to all that is good, until God by his grace gives him the hope of the gospel. Indeed, such is the fearful sway of shame over many minds, that some persons have seemed to think *that* almost the only hinderance to men's salvation. Our blessed Saviour was not beating the air nor giving a vain warning when he said, "Whosoever therefore shall be ashamed of me and of my words in this adulterous and sinful generation; of him also shall the Son of man be ashamed when he cometh in the glory of his Father, with the holy angels." Mark 8:38. You will never be able to overcome your natural shame of religion but by a "good hope through grace."

3. The great animating principle in labor is hope. This encourages the mariner, the husbandman, and every industrial class. This is no less the animating principle in labors for the spread of the gospel, the good of men, and the glory of God. Thus Paul argued: "It is writ-

ten in the law of Moses, Thou shalt not muzzle the mouth of the ox, that treadeth out the corn. Doth God care for oxen? Or saith he it altogether for our sakes? For our sakes, no doubt, this is written: that he that plougheth should plough in hope; and that he that thresheth in hope should be partaker of his hope." 1 Cor. 9:9, 10. What would the apostles have effected but for a hope that entered within the veil? They had regard to the recompense of the reward in a future life. God never puts and keeps his people at work for him without adequate motives, without influences suited to their nature as men.

4. Christian hope is the great nourisher of Christian joy. "We rejoice in hope of the glory of God." Rom. 5:2. Our present circumstances have in them much to make us sad and desponding. But hope looks to the future, when the glory of God shall be revealed in us. So steadfastly does hope take hold on what is future, that both Haldane and Hodge propose to read the first clause of Rom. 8:24, "We are saved *in* hope;" meaning thereby that we are saved in prospect, in expectation. No Christian in this life is in full possession of all the blessings of salvation. He has indeed

foretastes, earnests, pledges of good things to come, but not the very things themselves. Yet his title to eternal life is good, is perfect. Nothing could be more so. In due time deliverance shall come in all its fulness. As "rejoicing in hope" is a duty, Rom. 12:12, so it is a great privilege. Charnock says, "Desired happiness affects the soul; much more expected happiness. Joy is the natural issue of a well-grounded hope. A tottering expectation will engender but a tottering delight; such a delight will madmen have, which is rather to be pitied than desired. But if an imaginary hope can affect the heart with some real joy, much more a hope settled upon a sure bottom, and raised upon a good foundation; there may be joy in a title as well as in possession."

5. It is Christian hope that makes death easy and comfortable. God's people know that their flesh shall rest in hope. They know who it is that has said, "Thy dead men shall live; together with my dead body shall they arise. Awake and sing, ye that dwell in dust: for thy dew is as the dew of herbs, and the earth shall cast out the dead." Isa. 26:19. Job disarmed death of all his terrors by being able to lay hold on this very truth. So did

Paul also, and so have thousands of the humble people of God.

In short, we may well unite with Owen in saying that "hope is a glorious grace, whereunto blessed effects are ascribed in the Scripture, and an effectual operation unto the supportment and consolation of believers. By it we are purified, sanctified, and saved. . . . . Where Christ evidenceth his presence with us, he gives us an infallible hope of glory; he gives us an assured pledge of it, and works our souls into an expectation of it. Hope in general is but an uncertain expectation of a future good which we desire. But as it is a gospel grace, all uncertainty is removed from it which would hinder us of the advantage intended in it. It is an earnest expectation proceeding from faith, trust, and confidence, accompanied with longing desires of enjoyment. . . . The height of the actings of all grace issues in a well-grounded hope; nor can it rise any higher." Rom. 5 : 4, 5.

So that if what has been said be true, there is no force whatever in the infidel objection respecting the want of certainty as to eternal things. They are as certain as the existence and perfections of God—as certain as eternal truth and justice can make them. If our hope is weak, it is yet sure. What there is of it will never be disappointed. Nay, its largest expectations will be infinitely more than realized. God will do exceeding abundantly above all that we ask or think. Our hope is uncertain in no other sense than that it lays but feeble hold of things which it ought to seize with the utmost tenacity. Therefore to say that the Christian's hope is full of uncertainty is an untruth, unless men simply mean to say that the virtuous principle, even in good men, is weak. This all good men confess and bewail.

Nor do wicked angels and men offer us any thing worth our attention when they invite us to forego spiritual for carnal hopes, to give up the next world and lay fast hold of this. For what is this mortal life without the hope of the gospel? Is any thing more uncertain? What is more delusive than worldly hopes? The conqueror of yesterday is the prisoner of to-day; the rich man of to-day is the beggar of to-morrow. Pleasures bring pains; honors provoke envy; and what is more malicious or mischievous than that? Riches vex us while we have them, and may leave us any moment. He who forsakes heavenly for earthly hopes, prefers the chaff to the wheat; he snuffs the wind, and delivers himself over to vanity.

Christians should therefore labor to be rid of all sinful despondency. True, our frames change, but God's nature and counsels are immutable. Our salvation is made sure, not by our strength, but by the strength of God; not by our goodness, but by the merits of the Redeemer; not by our wisdom, but by the wisdom of God. God sometimes withdraws, that we may learn our utter helplessness. John Newton says, "If I may speak my own experience, I find that to keep my eye simply upon Christ as my *peace* and my *life*, is by far the hardest part of my calling. Through mercy he enables me to avoid what is wrong in the sight of men; but it seems easier to deny self in a thousand instances of outward conduct than in its ceaseless endeavors to act as a principle of righteousness and power." Yet to yield in this point is ultimately to sink into despondency. All good and lively and enduring hope springs from the cross alone. "Let Israel hope in the Lord: for with the Lord there is mercy, and with him is plenteous redemption." Psa. 130:7.

And how rich an inheritance have all the

saints in God. He is their hope and their portion, their refuge and the rock of their inheritance. Bishop Hall said, "O my God, I shall not be worthy of my eyes if I think I can employ them better than in looking up to thy heaven; and I shall not be worthy to look up to heaven if I suffer my eyes to rest there, and not look through heaven to thee, the almighty Maker and Ruler of it, who dwellest there in all glory and majesty; and if, seeing thee, I do not always adore thee, and find my soul taken up with awful and admiring thoughts concerning thee. . . . While others look at the motions, let me look at the Mover, and adore that infinite power and wisdom which preserve those numberless and immense bodies in such perfect regularity." While others grow wiser, let us grow more holy. While they trust in the creature, and make flesh their arm, let us set our faith and hope in God. Let us think upon his name. If we are really his, we shall ever be with him. You cannot dwell too much on future glory. Nor can you overestimate the value of your future inheritance. It is worth ten thousand worlds. It is worth a thousand times more than any man ever endured for it. Men of the world often congratulate each other on their prospects. But Christians may well give each other joy in view of their bright future, their sure and certain hopes. "Hope, like a star in the firmament, shines the brighter as the shadows of sorrow darken. A new view opens to us. We live in the prospect of another and a happier world," says Dr. John James. A poet well describes this grace when he says,

"Hope, like a cordial, innocent though strong,
Man's heart at once inspirits and serenes,
Nor makes him pay his wisdom for his joys."

How dismal are the prospects of the poor guilty sinner! Scripture describes such as "without Christ, being aliens from the commonwealth of Israel, and strangers from the covenants of promise, having no hope, and without God in the world." Eph. 2:12. Could more dreadful destitution exist? The question has sometimes been raised, What will be the ingredients of future misery? No man may be able to give a full answer. But it is certain that a poor soul, as destitute as sinners are here, and then shut out from all that now renders existence tolerable, must be dreadfully and eternally undone. "The day cometh"— Oh how soon it will be here!—which "shall burn as an oven, and all the proud, yea, and all that do wickedly, shall be stubble, and the day that cometh shall burn them up, saith the Lord of hosts, that it shall leave them neither root nor branch." And as the wicked die without hope, without Christ, without God, so shall they continue without them for ever.

Unconverted sinner, ask thy soul a few questions of great weight.

1. What shall it profit a man, if he gain the whole world and lose his own soul?

2. Did ever any harden himself against the Lord, and prosper?

3. Can thy hands be strong, or thy heart endure, when he shall deal with thee?

4. What wilt thou answer when he shall punish thee?

5. How can you escape, if you neglect so great salvation?

## CHAPTER XV.

### LOVE TO GOD.

THAT love to God is a pressing duty is manifest from all the Scriptures. By Moses God said, "Thou shalt love the Lord thy God with all thy heart, and with all thy soul, and with all thy might." Deut. 6 : 5. "And now, Israel, what doth the Lord thy God require of thee, but to fear the Lord thy God, to walk in all his ways, and to love him, and to serve the Lord thy God with all thy heart and with all thy soul?" Deut. 10 : 12. "Thou shalt love the Lord thy God, and keep his charge, and his statutes, and his judgments, and his commandments, alway." Deut. 11 : 1. "It shall come to pass, if ye shall hearken diligently unto my commandments which I command you this day, to love the Lord your God, and to serve him with all your heart and with all your soul, that I will give you the rain of your land in his due season." Deut. 11 : 13. "If ye shall diligently keep all these commandments which I command you, to do them, to love the Lord your God, to walk in all his ways, and to cleave unto him; then will the Lord drive out all these nations from before you." Deut. 11 : 22. "If thou shalt keep all these commandments to do them, which I command thee this day, to love the Lord thy God, and to walk ever in his ways; then shalt thou add three cities more for thee." Deut. 19 : 9. "The Lord thy God will circumcise thy heart, and the heart of thy seed, to love the Lord thy God with all thy heart, and with all thy soul, that thou mayest live." Deut. 30 : 6. Again, "Know therefore that the Lord thy God, he is God, the faithful God, which keepeth covenant and mercy with them that love him and keep his commandments to a thousand generations." Deut. 7 : 9. The same duty is clearly and repeatedly urged in other parts of the same book.

Thus it appears that in his early revelations, love to God was greatly insisted on as a high duty; that its nature was well explained; that men were taught that it well agreed with fear; that it always produced the fruit of obedience; that great blessings, temporal and spiritual, were connected with it; and that it was one of the promises of the covenant that God would implant this grace in the hearts of his people.

When our Saviour came, he dwelt much on the love of God, declared it the greatest and first duty of men, essential to true religion, and incapable of being substituted by outward observances. His apostles taught the same doctrine.

It may be well to observe that love to God includes the three Persons of the Trinity. Love to the Father is not different from love to the Son or to the Holy Spirit. In each case it is the same. He who loves him that begat, also loves him that was begotten of him. He who loves the Son loves the Father, for he and the Father are one. One person of the Trinity is no less lovely than another. All the persons of the Godhead are the same in substance and in attributes, though having different offices in man's salvation. Love to either person is love to God. Love to God is love to all the persons of the Godhead. Let this view be retained in mind. It will prevent many painful and perplexing doubts respecting our duty. He who honors the Son, honors the Father and the Spirit. He who loves the Spirit is sure to love the Father and the Son.

It should be stated that love to God is sometimes spoken of in Scripture as properly expressive of an affection of the mind, and sometimes it is used figuratively as a fit term to designate the whole of religion, or all the fruits of genuine love to God. In most cases there is little difficulty in learning the precise sense in which it is to be taken. Nor is *this* variation in the sense of a term confined to the word *love*, nor to the modes of speaking adopted by the inspired writers. Several of the Christian graces are spoken of in the same way in Scripture. And in all the best writers of our language a part is often put for the whole.

It is also proper to say that the phrase, *the love of God*, as used in Scripture, has two senses. Sometimes it expresses our love to God. Thus our Saviour said, "Woe unto you, Pharisees! for ye tithe mint and rue and all manner of herbs, and pass over judgment and the love of God." Luke 11 : 42. Again, "I know you, that ye have not the love of God in you." John 5 : 42. In like manner Paul says, "Hope maketh not ashamed; because the love of God is shed abroad in our hearts by the Holy Ghost which is given unto us." Rom. 5 : 5. John also says, "This is the love of God, that we keep his commandments." 1 John 5 : 3.

In like manner Jude says, "Keep yourselves in the love of God." Jude 21. In all these and many other places, by "the love of God," is to be understood love to God.

But in the following texts, "the love of God" means God's love to us. "Nor height, nor depth, nor any other creature, shall be able to separate us from the love of God, which is in Christ Jesus our Lord." Rom. 8 : 39. "God commendeth his love toward us, in that, while we were yet sinners, Christ died for us." Rom. 5 : 8. The same sense attaches to the phrase elsewhere. But this variation produces no confusion. The import in any one passage of Scripture is clear. We have just the same form of speech when we discourse of the love of a father or mother, where we may either intend the love of a parent to a child, or that of a child to a parent.

Love to God is commonly spoken of under three distinctions.

1. There is the love of gratitude. As ingratitude is one of the basest vices, embracing almost all others, so gratitude is one of the noblest virtues, and is never found but with many others in its train. The judgment of mankind fully sustains this view. A cele-

brated writer says, "He that calls a man ungrateful, sums up all the evil that a man can be guilty of." Yet how common is this vice. Seneca says, "If it were actionable, there would not be courts enough in the whole world to try the cases in." On the other hand, gratitude is a noble virtue. It carries much that is just and amiable with it. A deaf mute is said to have defined it to be "the memory of the heart." It is wonderful that some *refining* philosophers and divines, who have been thought very fond of distinctions, even where there was no difference, have not been able to discriminate between love to the gift and love to the giver, and so have made gratitude a sordid affection. This is the more marvellous in theologians, as the Bible always speaks well of gratitude to God. If this be not so, we have no safe rule for interpreting such texts as the following: "We love him, because he first loved us." "I love the Lord because he hath heard my voice and my supplications. Because he hath inclined his ear unto me, therefore will I call upon him as long as I live." "Her sins, which are many, are forgiven; for she loved much: but to whom little is forgiven, the same loveth little." He who loves God as

David, Mary, and John, has the genuine affection demanded by the word of God. There is on earth no love to God without warm and lively gratitude. The unconverted rejoice in the gifts of God, and often pervert them to their carnal gratifications. Such have no genuine holy gratitude. They even despise his chief gifts, his unspeakable gift, his Son, and his precious gift of the Spirit. Holy gratitude would never leave men to such daring wickedness. It would mightily draw them to God. Alas for us: "We inscribe our afflictions upon a rock, and the characters remain; we write our mercies in the sand of the sea-shore, and the first wave of trouble washes them out."*

2. There is the love of complacency. This consists in delight in the character of him whom we love. The entire nature and perfections of God are amiable and admirable. Mere power, separated from wisdom and goodness, is not amiable, though it may be wonderful. But we never separate God's attributes, though we distinguish between them. Infinite power, guided by infinite love and infinite skill, is a rock of delight. That was a great revelation to the patriarch, "I am the Almighty God." In it

* Jay.

the saints have ever since rejoiced. To a wicked man the omniscience of God is a source of terror and aversion. To him who loves God it is a fountain of delight. He heartily invokes the scrutiny of him who knows all hearts. He cries, "Search me, O God, and know my heart: try me, and know my thoughts, and see if there be any wicked way in me." So that those who love God delight even in his natural attributes. Without these he would be no God to them. Yet the moral perfections of God are special objects of direct complacency. All the saints delight in that proclamation which Jehovah made of himself to Moses: "The Lord, the Lord God, merciful and gracious, long-suffering and abundant in goodness and truth, keeping mercy for thousands, forgiving iniquity and transgression and sin, and that will by no means clear the guilty." No regenerate person would think the character here drawn improved by the omission of a single trait. All is lovely. This love of complacency in God is mighty in its power. Show me a child of God, and I will show you one who loves to sing, "Whom have I in heaven but thee? and there is none upon earth that I desire besides thee." The highest point of holy delight in the character of God is reached when his glorious attributes are seen harmoniously uniting in the production of some vast and happy result. This is a chief part of our pleasure in contemplating the plan of salvation. There mercy and truth, righteousness and peace, wisdom and power, goodness and severity, wrath and love, strangely and illustriously meet and embrace each other. They unitedly produce glory to God in the highest, and at the same time peace on earth, good-will to men. This scheme will form a perpetual study to men and angels. I am not surprised that angels desire to look into it. I wonder not that heaven is filled with thundering hallelujahs to God and the Lamb for ever and ever. In this plan of mercy, as in a lens, all the rays of the divine glory meet. Yet their brightness may be endured. The flesh of the Son of God is a veil which hinders the radiance from being intolerable. Yet on earth he was seen "full of grace and truth." "The fulness of the Godhead" dwelt in him bodily. The great attraction of the moral law is, that it is a copy of God's character. The great source of pious delight in Scripture is, that it is the word of God. Creation and providence are never so exalted themes of delightful contemplation as when we most fully regard them as the results of God's matchless excellence. Redemption gets *all* its glories here.

3. There is also the love of good-will. It manifests itself in pity to the miserable, in forgiveness to the injurious, in compassion to the weak, in pleasure at the good estate of those whom we love. God is infinitely above us, and never needs our compassion. Even Jesus Christ, the sufferings of whose human nature once held the inanimate creation in strange sympathy, suffers no more. He has overcome, and is set down on his throne. He was dead, but he is alive for evermore. God is holy, and has done us no wrong. We may in our pride complain of him, and dream of forgiving him; but the Judge of all the earth makes no mistakes, and is never unkind or unjust. Neither is Jehovah accountable to us. We cannot without presumption revise his decisions, or find fault with his judgments. Though we greatly need forgiveness from him, he has no need of ours. Nor can we be profitable unto God, as he that is wise may be profitable unto himself, or as he that is kind may be advantageous to his friend. It is no gain to

the Almighty that we cleanse our ways. But we can evince our good-will to those who are quite beyond the need of our aid. Towards God we can manifest it in many ways. We can show benevolence to his people, especially those of them who are greatly afflicted. Indeed, he has constituted them the receivers of our bounty in his place. Whatsoever is done to them is done to him. We can show our good-will towards God by honoring him, by rejoicing in the worship which others render to him, and by delighting in the advancement of his glory. This love is the great animating principle in heartily praying, "Hallowed be thy name: thy kingdom come; thy will be done in earth as it is done in heaven." This love is wonderful, passing the love of woman. It fills the heart with all gladness when God is glorified and his name exalted.

Though we thus distinguish the acts of love, yet they are all performed by the same person. They all proceed from the same pious affection. In many respects they all agree. They all strengthen a gracious character. All love to God has for its object the same Being, the Three in One, Him who is infinite, eternal, unchangeable in his wisdom, power, holiness, justice, goodness, and truth. All the exercises of love are refreshing. They awaken not painful emotions. All the kindly affections produce pleasant effects. Whoever enjoys the luxury of having his heart drawn out to God in gratitude, complacency, or good-will, would fain continue in that state always.

It is not of the nature of true love to God to count the cost, or to make much of its services. Even as Jacob served seven years for Rachel, and they seemed to him but a few days for the love he had to her; so the true friend of God is sustained through a life of trial and sorrow by his love to God.

"While duty portions out the debt it owes
With scrupulous precision and nice justice,
Love never measures, but profusely gives;
Gives, like a thoughtless prodigal, its all,
And trembles *then*, lest it has done too little."

True love is not selfish, cold, and calculating. "Charity seeketh not her own." "Greater love hath no man than this, that a man lay down his life for his friends." Here was the soul of martyrdom. The labors of love would be impossible, if they sprang from any other principle. Because they are the fruit of love, they are esteemed as nothing.

Where the love of complacency exists, there

will be a desire to be like the object beloved. No praise is so great as that which we render by imitating another. Therefore all who delight in God do hunger and thirst after righteousness, and are wholly pleased with God's law, and are deeply pained when they find their hearts inclined to corruption. They never will be satisfied till they awake in God's likeness. To be like him is their highest aim.

Those who love desire also to please God. This is very natural. Above all things, the righteous wish to please God. His will is their law. His favor is their life. His smile is their joy.

Love to God is a powerful principle. It becomes the master-passion. It is "strong as death." "Many waters cannot quench love, neither can the floods drown it: if a man would give all the substance of his house for love, it would utterly be contemned." Love roused and sustained Paul in all his toils and sufferings. It made the confessors take joyfully the spoiling of their goods. It has made heroes of babes, and martyrs of the most timid. No principle of human action is more efficient.

It is indeed not always of the same strength. Some love so little that they are constantly kept in doubt about their state, and are uncertain whether they love at all. In some, love is but a spark with some smoke. In others it is a strong, steady flame. If genuine, it will finally gain the victory over all opposing influences. It grows, so that in due time it sways every power of the mind, every inclination of the heart.

Love to God promotes the happiness of all whose hearts it rules. Believers know what Paul means by "the comfort of love." "He that dwelleth in love dwelleth in God, and God in him." Solomon says, "Better is a dinner of herbs where love is, than a stalled ox, and hatred therewith." This he speaks of love in a family. But how much more true is it of the love of God. It turns all bitter into sweet, converts all sorrow into joy. "All things work together for good to them that love God." Nor is our love to God a well-spring of life merely to the living: it wonderfully cheers and animates the dying, and keeps the best of them in a delightful strait. It makes them triumph over death. It goes still further: "Herein," says John, "is our love made perfect, that we may have boldness in the day of judgment." Of all things promised by God, nothing has surprised me more than this. Oh wonderful, wonderful love, to give "boldness in the day of judgment."

True love seeks union and communion. "How can we expect to live with God in heaven, if we love not to live with him on earth?" Aversion puts away its object, or withdraws from it; but love draws near its object, and rejoices to know and be known. Those who love God are looking for and hasting unto the coming of the day of God. They wait for him as the watchmen wait for the morning; as the thirsty land waits for the rain. He is their life. His coming will be their coronation-day. After that they shall be for ever with the Lord. Christ is the loadstone that lifts up their hearts to God. To be with him and to behold his glory will be the grand reward. But even in this life, the soul, by means of faith in God's word and through the agency of the blessed Spirit, has sweet communion with God. In this it greatly joys.

Paul offered a very benevolent prayer when he asked that his brethren at Philippi might "abound in love more and more." Love is a chief fruit of the Spirit. It is greater than faith or hope. It shall last and increase for ever. No wonder Jude, in the warmth of his affection for God's children, cried, "Keep yourselves in the love of God." This is the great business of the Christian. He who does this acts well his part. He who keeps himself in the love of God needs to know no other secret of happiness.

The qualities of the love which God requires are,

1. That it be sincere, not feigned, not in pretence. Here is the point where sad deficiency is found in the love of many. It is not hearty. Its professions are mere pretences.

2. Genuine love to God is supreme. It puts him before and above all others. It admits of no rivals in the heart. It does not hesitate to prefer him to every other object. Others may be *means* of good to us, but God is the *portion* of his people, the lot of their inheritance.

3. True love to God regards all his character, laws, and judgments. It does not find fault with his justice. It does not cavil at the strictness of his law. It approves of the purity of his ordinances, of the simplicity of his worship, and of the sovereignty of his authority.

4. There is in genuine love to God stability. It is not fitful. It loves always; not indeed with equal vigor, but yet with constancy. It is both an affection and a principle. Like other affections, it is liable to ebb and flow; but as a principle, nothing can change it while God upholds it.

We may know that we love God by our cheerful, earnest obedience to his will. "Now are ye my disciples, if ye do whatsoever I command you." "Love is the fulfilling of the law."

We may also prove our love to God by our love to his people. "We know that we have passed from death unto life, because we love the brethren."

We also evince our love to God by our possession of a childlike temper towards him. The Spirit of adoption always goes with love to God; so that all believers may say, "We have not received the spirit of bondage again to fear."

This love to God is essential to Christian character. None can be admitted to the heavenly mansions without it. We may be saved without science, without literature, without wealth, without genius, without renown, without family, without health, without the favor of man. But there is no admission to heaven without love. "We must be baptized in the fire of love, or burned in the fire of hell." "Though I speak with the tongues of men and of angels, and have not charity, I am become as sounding brass and a tinkling cymbal. And though I have the gift of prophecy, and understand all mysteries and all knowledge; and though I have all faith, so that I could remove mountains, and have not charity, I am nothing. And though I bestow all my goods to feed the poor, and though I give my body to be burned, and have not charity, it profiteth me nothing." John Angell James says, "Let the love we bear to God pervade and influence every thought and word and action. We shall *then* abhor that which he abhors, and depart from evil. We shall subdue our own will, and find our best happiness in doing *his*."

The importance of this love to God is seen at every step in the Christian life. Without it men are continually perplexed concerning their duty and their liberty. It is a remark of John Newton, that "love is the clearest and most persuasive casuist; and when our love to the Lord is in lively exercise, and the rule of his word is in our eye, we seldom make great mistakes." Cold reason can never safely settle questions which must chiefly be determined by the heart. Logic is a poor substitute for love. Right affections are often a better guide than all the rules of reasoning. This is so with the mother, in her sleepless care of her babe. It is so with the devoted husband, in his ceaseless watch over his helpless wife. It is so when filial piety sits down to watch the last flickerings of life in a venerable parent. It is eminently so in the love of a child of God to his Father which is in heaven.

He who finds his heart warmed with love to God need not trouble himself respecting his election. Leighton well says, "He that loves may be sure that he was loved first; and he that chooses God for his delight and portion may conclude confidently that God hath chosen him to be one of those that shall enjoy him, and be happy with him for ever; for that our love and electing of him is but the return and repercussion of the beams of his love shining among us." "Love begets love." This is most true of God's love to us. All our love to him is engendered by his love to us. And so if we choose him, we may know that he has chosen us, and ordained us, that we should bear much fruit to his glory.

He who thus loves God will surely be provided for. His temporal wants shall not be forgotten before God. Chrysostom says, "If thou have a concern for the things which are God's, he will also be careful of thee and thine." "Seek ye first the kingdom of God, and his righteousness; and all these things shall be added unto you." Matt. 6:33. Nor are the blessings of love confined to our bodily wants. "God is love; and he that dwelleth in love dwelleth in God, and God in him." It may not be given to mortals to know all that is thus promised; but surely such language implies very much. To all who love him, God is a rest and a refuge, a strong tower and a hiding-place, a portion and an eternal all.

# CHAPTER XVI.

## LOVE TO CHRIST.

In addressing the strangers scattered abroad throughout Pontus, Galatia, Cappadocia, Asia, and Bithynia, the apostle Peter admits that they had never personally seen Jesus Christ. He himself had often seen the Lord. He had seen him walking by the sea of Galilee. He had seen him walking on it. He had been with him on the holy mount, in the judgment-hall, and on the top of Olivet, when he ascended to glory. He had been his companion for years, had tasted of his mercy, had beheld his miracles, had been an eye-witness of his agony, of his betrayal, of his trial, of his resurrection, of his ascension, and of his glory and majesty. He had seen him in the depths of his humiliation. He had seen him in the first and second stages of his exaltation. Yet the apostle does not assert that those who had not been so highly favored as himself were destitute of right affections to the Redeemer, but says, "Whom having not seen, ye love."

1 Pet. 1 : 8. What a rich provision of mercy is that which so far puts all God's people on a level as to permit the saint of these latter days to love the Lord Jesus as fervently and as acceptably as if he had seen his blessed person and spoken with him face to face.

Though love to Christ is not different from love to God, yet it is worthy of distinct consideration. It is much spoken of in Scripture. It enters very fully into the experience of all saints. It is one of the strongest of all affections, and one of the most powerful principles. If the time shall ever come when such a theme shall be distasteful to professing Christians, then indeed the glory will have departed from the visible church. Yet the theme is always unpleasant to carnal men. Some satisfy themselves with not caring for these things; but others rail at the whole doctrine of love to the Son of God. The efforts of such are commonly directed to the denial of the reality of every thing vital in religion. Accordingly they make light of sin, they speak of human guilt as a trifle, they think a depraved nature a theological invention, they look upon heaven as a picture and hell as a dream. They deny all Christian graces, and in particular they regard all love to Christ as romance, confined to the weak and ignorant.

But the word of God rebukes all such wickedness. If God does not teach us the reality of love to Christ in all his people, he teaches us nothing. Else what shall we do with such scriptures as these? "Let him kiss me with the kisses of his mouth: for his love is better than wine. Thy name is as ointment poured forth, therefore the virgins love thee. We will remember thy love more than wine: the upright love thee. Behold, thou art fair, my beloved, yea, pleasant: also our bed is green. A bundle of myrrh is my beloved unto me; he shall lie all night betwixt my breasts. I sat down under his shadow with great delight, and his fruit was sweet to my taste. He brought me to the banqueting-house, and his banner over me was love. Stay me with flagons, comfort me with apples: for I am sick of love. His left hand is under my head, and his right hand doth embrace me. My beloved is mine, and I am his. I am my beloved's, and his desire is towards me. I found him whom my soul loveth; I held him, and would not let him go, until I had brought him into my mother's house. Set me as a seal upon thy heart, as a seal on thine arm. I charge you, O ye daughters of Jerusalem, if ye find my beloved, that ye tell him I am sick of love. Come, my beloved, let us go up early to the vineyards, let us see if the vines flourish. There will I give thee my loves. Make haste, my beloved, and be thou like to a roe, or to a young hart on the mountains of spices."

Such is some of the language of one of the short books of the Bible, which abounds indeed in imagery borrowed from the East, but which also abounds in the richest stores of Christian experience. Other portions of Scripture fully accord with the proofs already quoted. Christ himself said, "He that loveth me shall be loved of my Father, and I will love him, and manifest myself to him. If any man love me, he will keep my words, and my Father will love him, and we will come unto him, and make our abode with him. As the Father hath loved me, so have I loved you; continue ye in my love." Other portions of God's word are of like import. It is then undeniable that God's word calls for love to Christ as an essential proof of Christian character. Downright infidelity teaches nothing more dangerous than that we can have pious affections, pleasing to

God, without any love to the Lord Jesus Christ.

And God's people have the best ground of love to Christ. He is "the chiefest among ten thousand, and altogether lovely." He is perfect God and perfect man in two distinct natures and one person for ever. He is the author of eternal redemption, the Saviour of the world. To him we owe both our being and our well-being. His grace is rich, free, and unchangeable. His love to us has in it heights and depths, lengths and breadths, which can never be measured. It passeth knowledge. None ever loved us as Christ, who gave himself for us. Well do Solomon and Paul unite in calling him The Beloved. All the righteous do the same. We owe him all gratitude, all good-will, all complacency.

The first essential quality of love to Christ is that it be unfeigned. In it there can be admitted no double-mindedness. Paul closes one of his epistles with the solemn words, "Grace be with all them that love our Lord Jesus Christ in sincerity. Amen." Eph. 6 : 24. Insincerity spoils any profession; but a profession of love, not founded in the depths of the heart, is exceedingly hateful to God and man.

When even the worst of men see deception and guile in matters of friendship, their abhorrence is awakened. Let every man see to it that his love is real and genuine.

Love to Christ is a pure and holy affection. It is the reigning principle among the redeemed in glory. It is the bond of union among believers on earth. Love to Christ has for its object his glorious person. And yet it is not at all like the admiration and fondness we have for the comely appearance of men upon earth. There is nothing carnal or gross in the affections of a creature towards the Lord of life and glory. When upon earth, his pious followers loved him, although "his visage was so marred more than any man, and his form more than the sons of men." And it is so still. After his resurrection and before his ascension, he said to Mary, "Touch me not; for I am not yet ascended to my Father; but go to my brethren, and say unto them, I ascend unto my Father and your Father, and to my God and your God." John 20:17. Some think our Lord thus intended to remind Mary that it was not by touching his body, but by believing on him; not by handling him, but by spiritually laying hold on him, that he would have her approach him. Whether this passage bears such a construction or not, there is no doubt of the fact that thousands saw him, heard him, and touched him with their bodily faculties, and were never a whit the better for it all. Paul says, "Though we have known Christ after the flesh, yet now henceforth know we him no more." 2 Cor. 5 : 16. To his disciples no less than to his enemies Jesus said, "Ye shall seek me; and as I said unto the Jews, Whither I go ye cannot come, so now I say to you." John 13 : 33; compare John 8 : 21. "He is a Jew, which is one inwardly; and circumcision is that of the heart, in the spirit, and not in the letter; whose praise is not of men, but of God." Rom. 2 : 29.

True love to Christ is always grieved at having its sincerity seriously questioned. "Jealousy is cruel as the grave; the coals thereof are coals of fire, which hath a most vehement flame." Song 8 : 6. "Peter was grieved because Jesus said unto him the third time, Lovest thou me?" John 21 : 17. That question is never earnestly brought home to the bosom of any genuine follower of the Saviour without awakening the deepest concern; and until it can be satisfactorily answered, the soul is in deep waters. This must ever be the case. It is not possible for any to love the Lord Jesus without seeing something of his infinite excellency, without at the same time wishing to love him more, or without seeing that want of love to him would be the eternal undoing of the soul.

It should also be noted that there may be much imperfection even in genuine love to the Saviour. To deny this is to cut off the whole Christian world from a participation in the favor of Christ. If no man loves the Saviour, except he loves perfectly, then none but the redeemed above have any evidence that they are his. How sadly imperfect even genuine love may be, is seen in the case of David and Peter and many other Bible saints. At times their conduct was sadly opposed to the belief that they were good men. So now all the best men in this world are among the foremost to cry out, "In many things we all offend;" "Iniquities prevail against us;" "We abhor ourselves, and repent in dust and ashes;" "Unto us belong shame and confusion of faces."

Yet true love to Christ is not fitful. It is constant, not periodical. Like the fire of old kept burning on the altar, which at some times was much brighter than at others, yet at no time was entirely extinct, so the love of Christ never totally vanishes from the heart of a good man, although it is not always glowing. A gold dollar may be as genuine metal as a gold eagle. A live coal is as truly fire as the bowels of a glowing furnace. The new-born infant is as truly a human being as the full-grown man. Let us beware how we grieve whom God doth not grieve by denying them the rights and privileges of the sons of God. He who can give power to the faint, and increase might to him that hath no strength; he who can hold up the weak brother, and make the feeble among his people like David, will not forget his covenant nor quench the smoking flax.

It is a good sign when we can humbly and reverently appeal to Omniscience for the sincerity of our love. Appearances are sometimes against men, very good men. When this is so, they are deeply abased; but they will not therefore let go their hold on the divine mercy, nor deny their allegiance to Christ. This was the case with Peter. He had denied his Lord, and brought great reproach on the cause of God, and had deeply bewailed his wickedness; yet when thrice interrogated by Christ, his answers were, "Yea, Lord: thou knowest that I love thee;" "Yea, Lord: thou knowest that I love thee;" "Lord, thou knowest all things; thou knowest that I love thee." Every true child of God can sincerely pray, "Lord, if I am deceived, do thou undeceive me." To our Master in heaven we stand or fall; and when we can truly say, "Lord, to whom shall we go but unto thee? thou hast the words of eternal life," we have a right to rejoice and be glad.

Genuine love to Christ does not regard any service it can render, or any sacrifice it can make, as too great for the honor of Christ. True love to the Saviour, so far from being a dormant principle, is wonderfully active, and delights in paying the largest tribute it can possibly render. It is not of the nature of supreme love to begrudge any thing. Under the sway of such affection for Christ, Paul said of bonds and afflictions, "None of these things move me, neither count I my life dear unto myself, so that I might finish my course with joy, and the ministry which I have received of the Lord Jesus, to testify the gospel of the grace of God." Acts 20:24. Again he says,

"What things were gain to me, those I counted loss for Christ. Yea doubtless, and I count all things but loss for the excellency of the knowledge of Christ Jesus my Lord: for whom I have suffered the loss of all things, and do count them but dung, that I may win Christ, and be found in him, not having mine own righteousness, which is of the law, but that which is through the faith of Christ, the righteousness which is of God by faith." Phil. 3:7–9. It was the same mighty principle of love to Christ that sustained the martyrs of all ages, made them rejoice in the spoiling of their goods, and in all tribulation, and finally caused them to triumph over death in its most horrible forms.

True love to Christ is supreme. "If any man come to me, and hate not his father, and mother, and wife, and children, and brethren, and sisters, yea, and his own life also, he cannot be my disciple." Luke 14:26. That is, if a man does not put Christ above all these, and love them less than him, he is not a true Christian. Gregory Nazianzen said, "If I have any possessions, health, credit, learning, this is all the contentment I have of them, that I have somewhat I may despise for Christ, who is the all-desirable and the every thing desirable." Augustine said, "How sweet it is to deny these sinful sweets."

It is worthy of special notice that the exercise of love to Christ is not only pleasant, but is so in a high degree. The same may indeed be said of other pious affections, but this is so peculiarly true of love to the Saviour, that it deserves special consideration. The very first motions of this grace are so delightful, that even young converts regard a day of holy exercises of mind as worth more than years of sinful pleasure. They greatly wonder that they never had a just estimate of these things before. To love Christ is the very height of wisdom. Every Christian has the demonstration of this truth in his own blessed experience. The natural language of the renewed soul is, Who would not love Jesus? The wicked passions of our nature commonly bring with them great pain. Under their influence men grow pale, tremble in their whole frame, lose their appetite, become wakeful and restless, and often pine away. But the love of Christ produces none of these miseries. It opens fountains of joy before sealed up, and makes rivers to break forth in the wilderness.

In love to Christ, nothing is more pleasing than to witness its increasing strength and mellowness. At first, in all its feebleness it may yet manifest some rather fiery qualities; but when it becomes strong it acquires much of the gentleness of Christ. Our first love is often like new wine. Our matured love is like wine on the lees well refined. The former may burst even new bottles; the latter would not injure old ones. This matter may be well illustrated by the difference between a loving young groom and bride and the same persons after they have been partakers of each other's joys and sorrows for half a century. When young, there is a peculiar ardor and fondness not at all diminished by the novelty of the affection; but in old age, the heart and life of each are bound up in the other. If one of those young persons had died, the survivor would have been filled with grief, and perhaps have fallen into paroxysms; but in a few years at most, all would have seemed to pass away. But let one of those loving old people die, and the survivor, however strong and healthy at the time, will soon show signs of decay, and in a short time will sink into the grave. The young couple, with all their affection, were sometimes a little irritable, perhaps jealous or moody; but the old ones had a confidence in each other, and a natural tenderness which nothing could disturb. So the young disciple, though he loves sincerely, has but little stability compared with what he will have, if he shall serve God till he has a large experience.

There is also in true love to Christ a genuine modesty, which grows with all other right affections. This modesty leads even the babe in Christ to be dissatisfied with the amount of his devotion to the Saviour. More experience leads to yet more profound self-renunciation. Every fall into sin followed by recovery but deepens self-distrust. And although the child of God may not be ready to renounce his integrity nor deny his love, yet he is very willing to speak of himself and his love to Christ in the most unpretending manner.

It is also true, that he who loves Christ delights in commending and honoring him, and in seeing others do the same. It is impossible to love that which is not excellent or beautiful in our eyes. And so surely as any thing seems so to us, we wish others to unite with us in admiring it. Could therefore a converted man be found who was indifferent whether others were brought to love Christ or not, he would be such a monster in the spiritual world as has never yet made his appearance.

True love to Christ is to his whole person, to his human and his divine natures. He who hates or rejects either his divinity or his humanity hates and rejects him. Chrysostom says, "When thou hearest of Christ, do not think him God only or man only, but both together. For I know Christ was hungry, and I know that with five loaves he fed five thousand men, besides women and children. I know Christ was thirsty, and I know Christ turned water into wine. I know Christ was carried in a ship, and I know Christ walked on the waters. I know Christ died, and I know Christ raised the dead. I know Christ was set before Pilate, and I know Christ sits with the Father. I know Christ was worshipped by the angels, and I know Christ was stoned by the Jews. And truly some of these I ascribe to the human, others to the divine nature; for by reason of this he is said to be both together."

Of course he who loves Christ loves his Sabbaths, his worship, his truth, his laws, his people, and all that brings him to mind. To such the Sabbath is a delight, the holy of the Lord, and honorable. There is no uncharitableness in supposing that he who hates holy time hates a holy God and a holy Saviour. And if any man loves not the worship of Christ on earth, surely he cannot love the temper of the redeemed above; for nothing is more clearly revealed than that Christ receives the highest adorations of heaven. The same man, when he finds the words of Christ, will keep them and rejoice in them. They are to his soul meat and drink. They are to him a fountain of life, a well-spring of salvation. Even Christ's laws, with all their binding force, are the rejoicing of his heart. And to him God's people are the excellent of the earth, in whom is all his delight. Whoso loves God's image anywhere, will love it in his people. He who loves not his brother, whom he has seen, cannot love his Saviour, whom he has not seen.

One of the miseries of man is that he is apt to set his affection on unworthy objects. The more he loves such things, the more unhappy he is. But in loving Christ we know that the object is worthy of our supreme regard. Yes, he is worthy. Lady Huntington expressed common Christian experience when she said, "I am nothing; Christ is all: I disclaim as well as disdain any righteousness but his. I not only rejoice that there is no wisdom for his people but that from above, but reject every pretension to any but what comes from himself. I want no holiness he does not give me; I would not accept a heaven he did not prepare for me. I can wish for no liberty but what he likes for me, and I am satisfied with every misery that he does not redeem me from; that in all things I may feel that without him I can do nothing." Either Christ will be all our salvation, or he will leave us to perish. The righteous consent that it shall be so.

Would you have fervent love, labor for lively faith. Ardent love is sure to accompany strong believing. An old writer says, "Believe, and you shall love; believe much, and you shall love much; labor for strong and deep persuasions of the glorious things which are spoken of Christ, and this will command love. Certainly, did men believe his worth, they would accordingly love him; for the reasonable mind cannot but love that which it firmly believes to be worthiest of affection. Oh, this mischievous unbelief is that which makes the heart cold and dead towards God. Seek then to believe Christ's excellency in himself, and his love to us, and our interest in him, and this will kindle such a fire in the heart as will make it ascend in a sacrifice of love to him."

Love to Christ is sure to be requited by the love of the Father, of the Son, and of the Spirit. Christ himself said, "He that loveth me shall be loved of my Father, and I will love him and manifest myself to him." And the Spirit is as loving as the Father and the Son. And although that expression used by Paul, *the love of the Spirit*, is by many understood to mean "the love of which the Holy Spirit is the author," yet even that shows his loving nature perhaps no less than if thereby we understood his direct love to his people.

Love to Christ is a mighty principle. Let it control us, and we shall be able to meet all the storms of life with firmness, and do all the duties of life with alacrity. It will bear us up and on and through. John Newton says, "The love of Christ was the apostle's chief motive; it constrained him; bore him along like a torrent, in defiance of labor, hardship, and opposition." As for us, what are we without it but reeds shaken with the wind? But with it we become heroes, pillars, martyrs, victors, yea, more than conquerors. This is true at all times. On one occasion Dr. Doddridge interested himself in behalf of a condemned criminal, and at length obtained his pardon. On entering the cell of the condemned man, the pardoned man fell at his feet, and with streaming eyes exclaimed, "Oh sir, every drop of my blood thanks you, for you have had mercy on every drop of it. Wherever you go, I will be yours." How natural was all this. And how surely will one who feels that his soul is saved from wrath by the blood of the Lamb, be ready to give all, all to him. It is this love to Christ that makes God's people so dissatisfied with all their present attainments, and so long to depart and be with Christ. That eminent servant of God, Samuel Davies, on recovering from a dangerous illness, wrote to a friend, "Formerly I have wished to live longer, that I might be better prepared for heaven; but this consideration had but very little weight with me, and that for a very unusual reason, which was this: after a long trial, I found this world is a place so unfriendly to the growth of every thing divine and heavenly, that I was afraid if I should live longer, I should be no better fitted for heaven than I am. Indeed, I have hardly any hopes of ever making any great attainments in holiness while I live, though I should be doomed to stay in it as long as Methuselah. I see other Christians around me making progress; but when I consider I set out about twelve years old, and what sanguine hopes I then had of my future progress, and yet that I have been almost at a stand ever since, I am quite discouraged. Oh my good and gracious Master, if I may dare to call thee so, I am afraid I shall never serve thee much better on this side the region of perfection. The thought grieves me; it breaks my heart; but I can hardly hope better. But if I have the least spark of true piety in my breast, I shall not always labor under this complaint. No, my Lord, I shall yet serve thee, serve thee through an immortal duration, with the activity, the fervor, the perfection of the seraph that adores and burns. I very much doubt this desponding view of matters is wrong, and I do not mention it with approbation, but only relate it as an unusual reason for my willingness to die, which I never felt before, and which I could not suppress." The only thing very remarkable in this extract is that its learned and experienced author should have supposed that some strange thing had happened to him. All God's people long for perfect deliverance from sin; nor does their experience lead them to expect it here. They would be made perfect in love to Christ.

Child of sorrow, come and welcome to Jesus Christ. He will give you rest. His peace shall rule your heart. Blunt says, "Are you travailing with sorrow? Are you heavy-laden with the burden of oppression or woe? Christ will give you rest. Doubtless the heavy-laden with the burden of sin are first invited, but they exclude no other sufferers. There is no exception of age or rank or clime, the extent of the travail, or the weight of the burden; the childish sorrows of the weeping school-boy are as much the subject of the Saviour's sympathy as the matured wretchedness of the aged man; all come within the Saviour's invitation." Oh that all would receive him. How soon should the waters of bitterness be changed into fountains of joy, and the mournful dirge be given up for the song of triumph.

We can now see something of the force of that solemn declaration of Paul, "If any man love not the Lord Jesus Christ, let him be anathema, Maran-atha." The world hurls its anathemas after those who despise its follies and denounce its vices. The Council of Trent cry anathema on the man "whoever shall affirm that a true and proper sacrifice is not offered to God in the mass," or "whoever shall affirm that matrimony is not truly and properly a sacrament." But Paul says, "If any man love not the Lord Jesus Christ, let him be anathema, Maran-atha;" that is, let him be accursed when the Lord cometh.

# CHAPTER XVII.

## LOVE TO OUR NEIGHBOR.

WE need line upon line and precept upon precept. Although one clear and undeniable revelation of God's will binds the conscience and moulds the character of a child of God, yet it is with peculiar pleasure that the pious mind finds a duty inculcated in various forms, at different times, and by different men. This remark applies to the whole matter of love to our neighbor. In Leviticus 19:18, Jehovah says, "Thou shalt not avenge, nor bear any grudge against the children of thy people; but thou shalt love thy neighbor as thyself: I am the Lord." And in the thirty-fourth verse of the same chapter he says, "The stranger that dwelleth with you shall be unto you as one born among you, and thou shalt love him as thyself; for ye were strangers in the land of Egypt: I am the Lord your God." The evangelists Matthew, Mark, and Luke, inform us that Jesus Christ repeatedly called attention to the command, "Thou shalt love thy neighbor as thyself," and pronounced it the great

16*

pillar of morals. See Matt. 19 : 19; 22 : 39; Mark 12 : 31–34; Luke 10 : 27–37. In his epistles to the Romans and to the Galatians, Paul also quotes with high commendation the same law. Rom. 13 : 9, and Gal. 5 : 14. The apostle James does the same. Jas. 2 : 8. So that there is no room left for any doubt as to the importance and obligation of the duty enjoined. That great prophet Moses, Jesus the Son of God, Paul the great apostle to the Gentiles, and James the son of Alpheus, the brother of Jude and the near relative of our Lord, all in the name of Jehovah give us this command. It is distinctly repeated nine times in God's word.

Such a command is far from being unnecessary. A man who had lived much in society, said that his acquaintance would fill a cathedral, but a pulpit would hold all his friends. We are naturally slow to open our hearts in a comprehensive good-will. We are all by nature prone to narrow-mindedness. Carnal men are never in a mood to be pleased with a widely diffusive benevolence. They may admire its fruits as exercised by others, but its practice is irksome to the unrenewed mind. We love like snails to crawl into our little shells and there abide. The plan of God is to call us out and make us banish these contracted views. All the noble sentiments of the human heart are, like the widow's oil, increased by pouring out. God is as kind as he is holy in so ordaining that no man shall be strongly selfish and truly happy. If God gives you bread enough and to spare, and then brings to your knowledge the case of the poor and needy, he does you a great kindness; and you will be a better and happier man for having your soul drawn out to the hungry.

The Bible says, "Thou shalt love thy neighbor as thyself." And here we are met with the old question, "Who is my neighbor?" When a carping lawyer, who wished to justify himself, asked this question, Jesus Christ answered him thus: "A certain man went down from Jerusalem to Jericho, and fell among thieves, which stripped him of his raiment, and wounded him, and departed, leaving him half dead. And by chance there came down a certain priest that way; and when he saw him he passed by on the other side. And likewise a Levite, when he was at the place, came and looked on him, and passed by on the other side. But a certain Samaritan, as he journeyed, came where he was: and when he saw him, he had compassion on him, and went to him, and bound up his wounds, pouring in oil and wine, and set him on his own beast, and brought him to an inn, and took care of him. And on the morrow when he departed, he took out two pence, and gave them to the host, and said unto him, Take care of him; and whatsoever thou spendest more, when I come again I will repay thee. Which now of these three, thinkest thou, was neighbor unto him that fell among thieves? And he said, He that showed mercy on him. Then said Jesus unto him, Go and do thou likewise." Without dwelling on the striking incidents here brought out in detail, the great truth clearly taught is that any man is our neighbor to whom we can show a kindness. Although D. Kimchi, in remarking on Psalm 15:3, says, "A neighbor is every one with whom we have any dealing or conversation;" yet in the days of our Saviour the Jews regarded themselves as bound to love none except their own people. Their rule was, "Thou shalt love thy neighbor, and hate thine enemy." Between Jews and Samaritans there was no intercourse that could possibly be avoided. Yet Christ teaches that they are neighbors in the eye of God's law. No man who admits that God gave the command to love our neighbor, will deny that it obliges us to love our friends, our kindred, and our countrymen. Even the scribes and Pharisees always admitted thus much. Yet this is a very low standard of virtue. Christ said, "If ye love them which love you, what reward have ye? do not even the publicans the same? And if ye salute your brethren only, what do ye more than others? do not even the publicans so?" While he whose love goes not beyond his own little sphere, has but little deserving of the name of right affections; he who goes not thus far, is a monster of wickedness, and without natural affection.

It is also evident from Scripture that even our enemies are to receive the tokens of our good-will. Jesus Christ said, "Love your enemies; bless them that curse you; do good to them that hate you; and pray for them which despitefully use you and persecute you; that ye may be the children of your Father which is in heaven." Matt. 5:44, 45. Again, "Love ye your enemies, and do good, and lend, hoping for nothing again; and your reward shall be great, and ye shall be the children of the

Highest." Luke 6 : 35. Paul and Solomon teach the same doctrine: "If thine enemy hunger, feed him; if he thirst, give him drink: for in so doing thou shalt heap coals of fire on his head. Be not overcome of evil, but overcome evil with good." Rom. 12 : 20, 21; Prov. 25 : 21, 22. With these agree all the inspired writers. Now all consent that we should love our friends, and the Scriptures teach that we should love our enemies; and these two classes comprehend the whole human race with whom we have intercourse or dealings. Besides the foregoing explanations, it may be stated that the love of gratitude is confessedly binding on all the human race. There is no man so depraved as not to see gross iniquity in a flagrant act of injustice. It is a truth no less commonly confessed, that if men have great moral excellence, they ought to be loved on that account. But when we enforce the obligations of a pure and high benevolence to all the race, there is apt to be a withholding of the hearty consent of the mind. Yet from Scripture nothing is clearer than that such good-will is due to all as we have knowledge of them and opportunity to do them good.

This leads us to consider what are the

proper proofs and uniform fruits of such love to our neighbor as is enjoined in Scripture. In the nineteenth chapter of Leviticus there are many things specified as duties to our fellow-men, all of which are so fitly joined with love to our neighbor, that they may be properly mentioned here. One was this: "When ye reap the harvest of your land, thou shalt not wholly reap the corners of thy field, neither shalt thou gather the gleanings of thy harvest." Verse 9. Another was like unto it: "Thou shalt not glean thy vineyard, neither shalt thou gather every grape of thy vineyard; thou shalt leave them for the poor and stranger." Verse 10. Another was in these words: "Ye shall not steal, neither deal falsely, neither lie one to another." Verse 11. Again, "Thou shalt not defraud thy neighbor, neither rob him: the wages of him that is hired shall not abide with thee all night till the morning." Verse 13. One still more striking was, "Thou shalt not curse the deaf, nor put a stumbling-block before the blind." Verse 14. In other words, you shall take no advantage of the afflictions and powerlessness of men. Another precept was, "Ye shall do no unrighteousness in judgment; thou shalt not respect the person of the poor, nor honor the person of the mighty: but in righteousness shalt thou judge thy neighbor." Verse 15. Another rule of great importance was, "Thou shalt not go up and down as a talebearer among thy people." Verse 16. Nothing could be more inconsistent with love to our neighbor than such a practice. Another precept forbade any man to give false testimony, or to refuse to give true testimony. Verse 16. Another was in these words: "Thou shalt not hate thy brother in thy heart: thou shalt in any wise rebuke thy neighbor, and not suffer sin upon him." Verse 18. Then immediately comes the command, "Thou shalt love thy neighbor as thyself." From all this it is evident that love to our neighbor is the same in its fruits as the fulfilment of the second table of the law. And we have the authority of Christ for saying that on love to God and to our neighbor hang the law and the prophets. Matt. 22:40. Paul teaches the same when he says, "He that loveth another hath fulfilled the law. For this, Thou shalt not commit adultery, Thou shalt not kill, Thou shalt not steal, Thou shalt not bear false witness, Thou shalt not covet; and if there be any other commandment, it is briefly comprehended in this, Thou shalt love thy neighbor as thyself. Love worketh no ill to his neighbor: therefore love is the fulfilling of the law." Rom. 13:8–10.

The fruits of love to our neighbor are, first, benevolent wishes concerning him and his affairs. Hearty good wishes are far from being vain either in the sight of God or of good men. Oftentimes good wishes are the best, the only proof we can give of our good-will. Only let us see to it that they be sincere.

Again, we can express kind thoughts and charitable judgments of men and their conduct, and so prove that we love them. Towards ourselves we are at liberty to practise severity of judgment; but to others there must be lenity. "Judge not, that ye be not judged. For with what judgment ye judge, ye shall be judged; and with what measure ye mete, it shall be measured to you again." Matt. 7:1, 2. Some express contempt for kind words; but they really mean such as are hypocritical, or they know not what they say. Words of genuine kindness are of the highest value. Without them society is a source of constant misery.

When our love leads us to the throne of grace, and we are drawn out in fervent prayer for men, then the fruit of love is very pleasing. "Bless them that curse you, and pray for them that despitefully use you and persecute you." So says Paul, "I exhort therefore, that, first of all, supplications, prayers, intercessions, and giving of thanks, be made for all men: for kings, and for all that are in authority; that we may lead a quiet and peaceable life, in all godliness and honesty." 1 Tim. 2:1, 2. What mode of expressing good-will could be more appropriate than that commended in Psalm 20:1–5: "The Lord hear thee in the day of trouble; the name of the God of Jacob defend thee; send thee help from the sanctuary, and strengthen thee out of Zion; remember all thy offerings, and accept thy burnt sacrifice; grant thee according to thine own heart, and fulfil all thy counsel... The Lord fulfil all thy petitions." Let us often search and try our ways, and see if by our prayers we prove that we love our fellow-men.

True love to men will of course lead us to forgive those who have injured us. This is a point on which our blessed Saviour laid the greatest stress. There is no dispensing with it. "If ye forgive not men their trespasses, neither will your Father forgive your trespasses." Matt. 6:15. "Forgive, and ye shall be forgiven." Luke 6:37. Perhaps there is no better evidence of a renewed heart than a cordial forgiveness of injuries, nor a surer sign that we are yet in our sins, than carrying old grudges about with us. He that will not forgive, must soon have his heart filled with hatred; and he that hateth his brother is a murderer; and ye know that no murderer hath eternal life abiding in him. Of all the holy arts possessed by Christians, none is more admirable than that whereby they turn injuries to their own profit and to the divine glory. Mather says, "The injuries of life, if rightly improved, will be to us as the strokes of the statuary on his marble, forming us to a more beautiful shape, and making us fitter to adorn the heavenly temple." Genuine love to man will not only seem to forgive, but it will do that very thing. "It is the glory of a man to pass over a transgression." Prov. 19:11. Merely to pretend to such a thing, and not to do it, is but miserably to mimic goodness, while we are filled with all uncleanness. There are upon earth no worse and no more unhappy men than those who carry about old grudges, and retain a lively memory of wrongs long since committed against themselves. The Persians have a pleasing proverb: "The man who returns good for evil is as a tree which renders its shade and its fruit to those who cast stones at it." South says, "Love is never so blind as when it is to spy faults. It is like the painter who, being to draw the picture of a friend having a blemish in one eye, would picture only the other side of his face."

"Love ye your enemies." "This is the most sublime precept ever delivered to man. A false religion durst not give a precept of this nature, because, without supernatural influence, it must be for ever impracticable."

Another good fruit of love to man is mercifulness. "The righteous is ever merciful." Psa. 37:26. "Blessed are the merciful; for they shall obtain mercy." Matt. 5:7. "Be ye merciful, as your Father also is merciful." Luke 6:36. An habitual unrestrained inclination to harshness, cruelty, and oppression is one of the worst signs in the character of any man. On the other hand, an enlarged prevailing disposition to pity men's sorrows, alleviate their miseries, and promote their happiness is one of the best signs in the character of any man. There is in some men a fitful and variable tenderness to others, which seems to be a mere instinct. It sometimes burns with great heat, and soon subsides into indifference or aversion; but genuine love forms habits of kindness in the heart, and brings them forth in the life. The dispositions we display to the helpless, the guilty, the forsaken, are often the best tests of our real character. Nor is there any surer prelude of wrath than cruel dispositions. "He shall have judgment without mercy that hath showed no mercy." James 2:13. Tyrants, in any sphere of life, are hateful not only to all virtuous men, but also to God himself.

Love to man will always produce kindness to the poor and needy, the friendless and afflicted. "Blessed is he that considereth the poor: the Lord will deliver him in time of trouble. The Lord will preserve him, and keep him alive: and he shall be blessed upon the earth: and thou wilt not deliver him unto the will of his enemies. The Lord will strengthen him on the bed of languishing. Thou wilt make all his bed in his sickness." Psa. 41:1–3. "Pure religion and undefiled before God and the Father is this, To visit the fatherless and widows in their affliction, and to keep himself unspotted from the world." James 1:27. "Remember the words of the Lord Jesus, how he said, It is more blessed to give than to receive." Acts 20:35. These portions of Scripture form a basis broad enough for any sober scheme of genuine charity that has ever been devised. The word of God uniformly lays the greatest stress upon kindness to the poor and afflicted, as evidence of a heartfelt charity. "Whoso hath this world's good, and seeth his brother have need, and shutteth up his bowels of compassion from him, how dwelleth the love of God in him?" 1 John 3:17. So that the Scriptures deny the genuineness of all love which is without good fruits. Nor is any act of our lives more sure of reward than kindness to the needy. "He that hath pity on the poor lendeth unto the Lord; and that which he hath given will he pay him again." Prov. 19:17.

But love is never at a loss for some way to evince itself. If it can do no more, it will cheer with a smile, it will rejoice or weep with those it loves, it will soften a pillow or smooth a bed, it will watch with those to whom nights of vanity are appointed, it will whisper encouragement to the faint, it will in some way make itself felt for good. A preacher once said, "If you know any thing that will make a brother's heart glad, run quick and tell it; but if it is something that will only cause a sigh, bottle it up, bottle it up."

God's word requires that thou shouldest "love thy neighbor *as thyself*." The measure of love due to our neighbor is a matter of chief importance. Very few persons in a Christian country will deny that it is our duty to bear some good-will to those around us. But many deny the extent of the obligation. Some respectable writers have expressed great difficulties on the subject. But surely it is no presumption to prefer the plain teachings of God's word above those of any mortal. Here is a command repeated in Hebrew and Greek by Moses, Christ, Paul, and James, in all nine times, without any variation, and in very plain terms. Nor is it pretended that there is any philological difficulty in the case. The translation is correct. There is no room for doubt in this respect. What right therefore has any man to say that the command so often repeated means no more than that we should love our neighbor generally and indefinitely as ourselves? To clear the matter, the following remarks are offered, with confidence in their entire justice:

1. It is evidently the design of the inspired writers to fix the degree in which we are bound to love our neighbor. They distinctly require us to love God supremely, above all others, admitting no rivals, no comparisons. They as distinctly say that we should love our neighbor as ourselves. There is no reason why inspired men should so often have added the words "as thyself," unless they thus designed to determine how far we should love others.

2. In alluding to our love of self, the inspired writers did not refer to such love of ourselves as is inordinate, and therefore properly selfish and sinful. All inordinate affection, whether towards ourselves or others, is contrary to God's word and will; and its excesses in one case cannot justify its excesses in another. Besides, it is simply impossible, in the nature of things, that the human mind should love God supremely, and at the same time go out inordinately both towards one's self and one's neighbor.

3. There is a difference between selfishness and self-love. The former is the excess and outlawry of the latter. The former is

wicked, and consists in a persistent looking on our own things and a constant caring for ourselves, let others do as they may. The latter is an enlightened and lawful regard to our own welfare, and is the standard and measure approved of God for regulating our affections towards others. "Thou shalt love thy neighbor *as thyself.*"

4. It is not denied that in a sense we may care and act more for the immediate good of ourselves and families than of others more remotely connected with us. We are urged by the instinct of self-preservation to protect from harm our own bodies more than those of others. But the commandment relates not to instincts, but to moral affections. So also by natural affection the mother is led to forget the rest of the world for a season, that she may watch her own languishing babe. But the law we are now considering does not relate to natural affection, which is more or less discoverable even in brute animals. It is a moral law, given to moral agents. And so there is no violation of its spirit in a man's providing for his own, and especially for those of his own household. Not to do so would prove him "worse than an infidel."

5. There is nothing in this law which requires us to do a natural impossibility. Thus it is commonly in our power to do much more for ourselves and families than for others. Most persons are commonly not within our reach. They are out of our sight and beyond the compass of our voice. But we can reprove, exhort, warn, and encourage ourselves when we will. We can often do the same to those near us. But this does not prove that we may love ourselves and families more than all others. The mother may not lawfully love the child at her side more than she may love his little brother captured by savages and carried into the wilderness. Yet a man would not be esteemed sane who should assert that this same mother was bound to do as many acts of daily kindness for one child as for the other. It would be literally impossible.

6. The law of love to our neighbor has an excellent practical exposition in what has long been called the *golden rule*, which is in these words: "All things whatsoever ye would that men should do to you, do ye even so to them: for this is the law and the prophets." None can deny that this law binds us to all the acts of love to our neighbor which we may lawfully

desire him to perform towards ourselves. If therefore we are bound to yield the fruits of love to others as we seek them from others, why should we not love our neighbor as we do ourselves? Where is any flaw in this reasoning? This golden rule affords an excellent test by which to judge both of our selfish and of our benevolent feelings. When we wish others to do something for us, let us ask first whether, in an exchange of circumstances, we should be ready to do the same for them.

7. The Scriptures do commend a very high degree of love to men. They say that "peradventure for a good man some would even dare to die." Rom. 5:8. This is evidently spoken not in censure, but in praise of the self-sacrificing man. John is yet more explicit, and says that in certain cases "we ought to lay down our lives for the brethren." 1 John 3:16. Paul furnishes us with an example of what John here teaches when he says to the Philippians, "If I be offered upon the sacrifice and service of your faith, I joy and rejoice with you all." Phil. 2:17. Now Paul did not love others more than the law requires; yet he was willing to suffer martyrdom, if thereby he could be most useful to his fellow-men. Surely this

is loving our neighbor as ourselves. The thing is therefore not impracticable. Greater love than this is not required.

8. We do most effectually promote our own happiness when we cultivate the most benevolent affections towards our neighbor. Nor is there any limit to this remark. Who that ever hoarded up wealth was as happy as John Howard? What lazy, selfish minister ever enjoyed life like Paul, who rejoiced even in tribulation? Home says,

> "The truly generous is truly wise;
> And he who loves not others lives unblest."

I have never known an unhappy philanthropist. I have never had a doleful letter from a foreign missionary. It is on the selfish that ennui and satiety and discontent and anguish prey. Wilcox says,

> "Wouldst thou from sorrow find a sweet relief?
> Or is thy heart oppressed with woes untold?
> Balm wouldst thou gather for corroding grief?
> Pour blessings round thee like a shower of gold."

Thus it is clear that we ought to love our neighbor as much as we love ourselves; we ought to be as ready to give as to receive justice, kindness, truth, pity, and bounty; in our dealings with others, we should be as careful to fulfil to all men the duties required, and to avoid the sins forbidden in the second table of the law, as we are free to regard them bound to do and to avoid the same. In some things, we may even give others the advantage. "In honor preferring one another;" and, "Let each esteem other better than themselves," are forms of speech which show that where there seems to be a conflict between our love to ourselves and our love to our neighbor, there are cases where he is to have the benefit of the doubt, and to take the precedence. This love will make us put a proper estimate upon the worth of our neighbor, construe all his conduct in as charitable a manner as truth will permit, proffer assistance whenever it is required and we can afford it, be careful to say nothing contrary to "the royal law," take pleasure in the welfare of others, and especially with diligence seek their spiritual and eternal good. The highest charity is that which aims at men's salvation. "He that winneth souls is wise."

It remains that a few words be said in presenting motives for the performance of this duty. The motive twice presented in the nineteenth chapter of Leviticus, is the awful authority of God: "I am the Lord;" "I am the Lord your God." A due consideration of God's authority, and a due regard to it, are sufficient to command the assent and the consent of all who have the love of God in them. But this saying, *I am the Lord*, may mean more than this. It may call us to a large benevolence, corresponding in our measure to the love manifested by God himself. Thus Paul says, "Be ye followers," imitators, "of God, as dear children; walk in love, as Christ also hath loved us, and hath given himself for us." Eph. 5:1, 2. God "maketh his sun to shine on the evil and on the good, and sendeth rain on the just and on the unjust." Matt. 5:45. Even where whole nations have forsaken God, practised idolatry, and walked in their own ways, "he left not himself without witness, in that he did good, and gave them rain from heaven, filling their hearts with food and gladness." The Lord's mercies are "new every morning." Lam. 3:23. "Herein is love, not that we loved God, but that he loved us, and sent his Son to be the propitiation for our sins. Beloved, if God so loved us, we ought also to love one another." 1 John 4:10, 11.

The example of our blessed Saviour is often presented as a powerful motive to this very duty. He went about doing good. We should walk as he walked. He has set us an example, that we should follow his steps. Ye know the grace of our Lord Jesus Christ, that though he was rich, yet for our sakes he became poor, that we through his poverty might be made rich.

In this way we can also best commend our religion to others, and put to silence the ignorance of foolish men, and win those who are of a contrary part.

Nothing more fatally hinders our prayers than the want of love to men. All correct moral feelings are shocked at prayer mingled with malice. Who ever heard of a happy or thriving church where the spirit of love was not? Leighton says, "To pray together, hearts must be consorted and tuned together; otherwise, how can they sound the same suits harmoniously? How unpleasant in the exquisite ear of God, who made the ear, are the jarring, disunited hearts that often seem to join in the same prayer, and yet are not set together in love! And when thou prayest alone, while thy heart is imbittered and disaffected to thy brother, although upon an offence done to thee, it is as a mistuned instrument; the strings are not accorded, are not in tune among themselves, and so the sound is harsh and offensive. Try it well thyself, and thou wilt perceive it; how much more He to whom thou prayest! When thou art stirred and in passion against thy brother, or not lovingly affected towards him, what broken, disordered, unfastened stuff are thy requests! Therefore the Lord will have this done first—thy heart tuned. "Go thy way," says he; "leave thy gift, and be reconciled to thy brother; then come and offer thy gift." Every enlightened conscience must approve this method. No other consists with sincerity or holiness.

One of the great excellences of love to our neighbor is, that it is an immortal principle. "Charity never faileth." "It will survive the wreck of worlds," says Dr. John James, "out-time time itself, and be for ever the work of the servants of God."

# CHAPTER XVIII.

## LOVE TO THE BRETHREN.

JUST before he laid down his life, our Lord Jesus Christ said to his disciples, "A new commandment I give unto you, That ye love one another; even as I have loved you, that ye also love one another." John 13:34. In explaining this passage, critics have found difficulty from the use of the word *new*. They say that love to God's people as such is no new thing under the gospel. This is certainly true. Saints have always esteemed each other the excellent of the earth, in whom was all their delight. Psa. 16:3. David says, "I am a companion of all them that fear thee, and of them that keep thy precepts;" and "mine eyes shall be upon the faithful of the land, that they may dwell with me." Psa. 119:63; 101:6. Solomon says, "He that walketh with wise men shall be wise: but the companion of fools shall be destroyed." Psa. 13:20. So in the days of Malachi, "they that feared the Lord spake often one to another." Mal. 3:16. It is impossible for two children of God to know and not to love each other. This was as true three thousand years ago as it is now. Many regard the friendship between David and Jonathan as based in this love. If this be correct, we have a very strong case of brotherly love furnished under the old dispensation. The word *new* is not then to be taken in the sense of novel or unheard of. Christ does not intend to say, "I give you an additional commandment." Some have thought that the difficulty might be removed by supposing that the word *new* here signifies superior, better, or excellent. Now although the word might have this sense, and in some cases has it, yet this command is not better than that which binds us to love God with all the heart, and our neighbor as ourselves; and so this sense cannot be here admitted.

Sometimes the word *new* seems to mean *strange*, and so some would read it, "I give you a strange commandment," meaning thereby a precept that will seem strange to the masses of men, being so unusual in human history. But this is hardly the sense of the word here. We are not driven by any necessity to such a construction. The meaning is not that the duty of love to man or to good men is now first taught, but that we are called to love good men *as Christ's disciples*, and *because they are such*, and that in a previously unknown degree and for an unusual motive, namely, Christ's love to all his people. We are to love Christians as Christians. We are to love them after the pattern of Christ's love to us. And we are to love them because he thus loved us. In these senses and in no others is this commandment *new* or novel. In these senses it was new until Christ came.

*Fifty-seven* years after Christ uttered these words, John wrote respecting this commandment of love to Christian brethren, "Not as though I wrote a new commandment unto you, but that which we had from the beginning, that we love one another." Dr. John Brown of Edinburgh thus paraphrases these words: "Though the commandment to love one another cannot now be called a new one, as if just issued forth—for from the beginning of the gospel it was announced as the distinctive command of our one Lawgiver—yet it may well be called new so far as he is concerned, for no one gave it till he did it; and so far as you are concerned, for it was a law to which you were strangers till you assumed his easy yoke and light burden." Jesus Christ differed from all the philosophers and teachers among the ancients, because he inculcated love among his disciples, and so in the sense explained he gave them a new commandment concerning love to their brethren.

It is worthy of notice that other portions of Scripture urge the same duty. Thus Christ says, "This is my commandment, That ye love one another, as I have loved you." John 15:12. Paul says, "Be kindly affectioned one to another with brotherly love." Romans 12:10. Again, "The Lord make you to increase and abound in love one toward another." 1 Thess. 3:12. Again, "We are bound to thank God always for you, brethren, as it is meet, because that your faith groweth exceedingly, and the charity of every one of you all toward each other aboundeth." 2 Thess. 1:3. Peter says, "Be ye all of one mind, having compassion one of another; love as brethren, be pitiful, be courteous." Again, "Above all things have fervent charity among yourselves." 1 Peter 3:8, and 4:8. John says, "This is the message that ye heard from the beginning, that we should love one another." 1 John 3:11. The same is taught in many other places.

The first essential quality of this love is that it should be real, not feigned. Thus John says, "My little children, let us not love in word, neither in tongue, but in deed and in truth." 1 John 3 : 18. So also Peter speaks of "unfeigned love of the brethren." 1 Pet. 1 : 22. Every Christian grace may be counterfeited. Even all love to the people of God is not what the Scripture requires. John Newton well says, "There is a *natural* love to the brethren. People may sincerely love their relations, friends, and benefactors who are of the brethren, and yet be utter strangers to the scriptural love the apostle speaks of. So Orpah had a great affection for Naomi, though it was not strong enough to make her willing with Ruth to leave her native country and her idol-gods. Natural affection can go no further than to a personal attachment; and they who thus love the brethren, and upon no better grounds, are often disgusted with those things in them for which the real brethren chiefly love one another.

"There is likewise a *love of convenience*. The Lord's people are gentle, peaceful, benevolent, swift to hear, slow to speak, slow to wrath. They are desirous of adorning the doctrine of

God their Saviour, and approving themselves followers of him who pleased not himself, but spent his life in doing good to others. Upon this account they who are full of themselves, and love to have their own way, may like their company because they find more compliances and less opposition from them than from such as themselves. For a while Laban loved Jacob: he found him diligent and trustworthy, and perceived that the Lord prospered him on Jacob's account; but when he saw that Jacob flourished, and apprehended he was likely to do without him, his love was soon at an end; for it was only founded in self-interest.

"A *party-love* is also common. The objects of this are those who are of the same sentiment, worship in the same way, or are attached to the same minister. They who are united in such narrow and separate associations, may express warm affections without giving any proof of true Christian love; for upon such grounds as these not only professed Christians, but Jews and Turks may be said to love one another: though it must be allowed that believers being renewed but in part, the love which they bear to the brethren is too often debased and alloyed by a mixture of selfish affections." It is a great matter when love unfeigned to God's people fairly gets possession of the man.

Again, our love to the brethren should be lasting, and not occasional or temporary. "Let brotherly love *continue.*" Heb. 13:1. The reasons which should lead us to brotherly love at one time are of perpetual force, nor can we innocently deny their power or refuse their control. All affections which seem to be of good quality, but are temporary in duration, are spurious. This is as true of temporary faith or sorrow for sin, as of love. True grace is not like Jonah's gourd, which "came up in a night and perished in a night."

Our love to the brethren should also be fervent. Well did Peter say, "See that ye love one another with a pure heart fervently." 1 Pet. 1:22. Love wholly without fervor cannot exist. There is no such thing. But love without considerable fervor will make many of our duties to our brethren irksome. Besides, we are naturally timid. Pride might embolden us, but pride is officious and offensive. On the other hand, love is as humble as it is diligent, and begets a sweet and obliging disposition, and prepares us to do good on a large scale.

Nor can differences of nationality hinder this. I have heard of a Hindoo and a New Zealander who met upon the deck of a missionary ship They had been converted from their heathenism, and were brothers in Christ, but they could not speak to each other. They pointed to their Bibles, shook hands, smiled in one another's faces, but that was all. At last a happy thought occurred to the Hindoo. With a sudden joy he exclaimed, "Hallelujah!" the New Zealander, in delight, cried out, "Amen!" Those two words, not found in their own heathen tongues, but given them by the gospel, were to them the beginning again of "one language and one speech."

The true basis of love to God's people is not merely the gratitude we may owe them for their kindness, or the good-will we bear to them in common with others, but it is especially the image of God that is in them. We love them in the Lord. It is loving them because they are disciples. One Christian loves another chiefly because he has a likeness to Christ, and lives for the glory of Christ.

Nothing can damp the ardor of true love. For a while Joseph of Arimathea was a disciple secretly, for fear of the Jews; yet at the crucifixion he goes and begs the body of Jesus. The terrible persecution which broke out three or four years after Christ's resurrection, could not so intimidate the church but that "devout men carried Stephen to his burial, and made great lamentation over him." Acts 8:2. Trying occasions do commonly draw out this pious affection in a surprising manner. My brother in sorrow is still my brother, and the heavier his grief, the more fitness is there in my loving him and refusing to let him go unnoticed. Charnock says, "At the last day, the trial of men is by *their acts towards God's people* in time of their persecutions." And in proof, he refers to Christ's account of the final judgment as given in Matthew 25. He is right. If we are ashamed of the bonds of God's people, it is idle for us to pretend to love them after a godly sort when they are in prosperity.

In the early history of the Christian religion, nothing was more remarkable than the love which one disciple bore to another. This was noticed by friends and foes. Lucian scoffingly says of the Christians of his time, "Their Lawgiver has persuaded them that they are all brethren." Another heathen says, "Christians do love one another before they are acquainted, if they but know that they are Christians." Indeed it was often said among the heathen, "See how these Christians love one another, and how ready they are to die for each other." Tertullian says, "This surprised them beyond measure, since they are accustomed to hate one another—that one man should be ready to die for another."

The proper proofs of our love to the brethren are found in our making common cause with them in all their sufferings for righteousness' sake, in being very slow to take offence at their conduct, in abhorring all bigotry and haughty exclusiveness, in embracing all the friends of God of every rank and condition, of every name and nation, and especially in loving most fervently those who give the highest proof of having been born again; for this brotherly love supposes that our brethren have their hearts drawn out to us just in proportion as they see us wear the image and manifest the spirit of Jesus Christ.

True love to our brother will make no man a bigot. John Foster thus describes a bigot: "He sees religion not as a sphere, but a line, and it is a line in which he is moving. He is like an African buffalo—sees right forward, but nothing on the right or left. He would not perceive a legion of angels or devils at the distance of ten yards on the one side or on the other."

This love to Christ's people is among the best evidences of a renewed state. "We know that we have passed from death unto life, because we love the brethren. He that loveth not his brother, abideth in death." 1 John 3:14. "The more believers love God, the more they will love one another; as lines, the nearer they are to the centre, the nearer they are to one another."*

Perhaps there is no method of teaching the true nature of any grace so well as by example. Take then for your consideration and imitation the case of John, the disciple whom Jesus loved. Respectable historians say that, after the ascension of our Lord, he remained in Judea fifteen or twenty years, and was present at the Council at Jerusalem. After that he spent most of his time in Asia Minor, and particularly at Ephesus. He survived all the other apostles, and lived to be a hundred years old. He has been celebrated for two thousand years as a very loving brother. Yet his love

* Charnock.

was not blind and fond. It did not make him pretend brotherly love to those enemies of righteousness who had crept into the church under false pretences. "Charity rejoiceth in the truth." "It rejoiceth not in iniquity." When John lived at Ephesus, he went to bathe, and seeing in the bath a celebrated heretic, who had denied the divinity of our Lord, he hastily retired, saying, "Let us flee, lest the bath should fall while this enemy of the truth is within." This story is given by Irenæus, who had it from those to whom Polycarp, the disciple of John, had told it. John was now the only living apostle. Cerinthus and Ebion were industriously spreading the contagion of their false doctrines, denying the Lord that bought them. John loved his Lord, he loved the souls of men, he loved his Christian brethren too well to favor or seem to favor heresy, by voluntarily companying with the enemies of his Lord and Master in any way that seemed to sanction their errors. John practised as he taught. In his second epistle he says to the elect lady, "If there come any unto you, and bring not this doctrine, receive him not into your house, neither bid him God-speed; for he that biddeth him God-speed is partaker of his evil deeds." 2 John 10, 11. John would have us cease from the instruction that causeth to err. His threatening language concerning Diotrephes, in his third epistle, verses 9, 10, shows that he never regarded it as proof of brotherly love to permit bad men to destroy or even disturb the flock of Christ.

It is stated that in a tour through the churches he became much interested in a young man, who was soon brought into the Christian church. Very soon the young man fell into temptation, was much in evil company, became idle, intemperate, and dishonest, finally heading a band of robbers. John, hearing of the sad change, went near his haunts, and allowed himself to be taken by the robbers. "Bring me," says he, "to your captain." As soon as the leader saw John coming, and knew who he was, he was filled with shame, and fled. The apostle pursued him, crying, "My son, why fleest thou from thy old and unarmed father? Fear not; even yet there is hope of salvation. Believe me, Christ has sent me." The young man stopped, trembled, and wept bitterly. The apostle prevailed on him to forsake his sins, brought him back to the society of the Christians, and had the pleasure of seeing him leading a pious and blameless life. "Brethren, if any of you do err from the truth, and one convert him; let him know, that he which converteth the sinner from the error of his way shall save a soul from death, and shall hide a multitude of sins." James 5 : 20. Brotherly love never willingly leaves one to perish in his ignorance, errors, or vices. It goes after the lost sheep. It pities the wanderer.

When John was very old, and unable even to walk to the places of public worship, he was still carried to the Christian assemblies, where, when he could not say much, he at least cried out, "Children, love one another." "Being asked why he told them but one thing, he answered that nothing else was needed." The truth of this narrative is, I think, generally admitted. And surely it presents to the mind one of the most lovely examples and lessons of brotherly kindness that we have on record. Who can refrain from expressing his admiration of so exalted worth? The Lord grant that we all may love as John loved.

In this subject there is furnished us very great help in the work of self-examination. Love to the brethren is as essential a mark of true piety as is faith. So teaches God's word. "This is his commandment, that we should believe on the name of his Son Jesus Christ, and love one another, as he gave us commandment." 1 John 3 : 23. It is not easy for us to press this matter too much on our own attention. Do we love the disciples of Christ because they learn of him and are taught of God? Do we study to promote their usefulness, comfort, and honor out of a special delight in their character? When we see a brother or a sister naked and destitute of daily food, do we say, Depart in peace; be ye warmed and filled; and yet decline to give them those things which are needful to the body? Do we put away from us all bitterness and wrath and anger and clamor and evil-speaking, with all malice? Are we kind one to another, tender-hearted, forgiving one another, even as God for Christ's sake hath forgiven us? Do we walk in love? Do we sympathize with John Wesley in his prayer, "Lord, if I must dispute, let it be with the children of the devil; let me be at peace with thy children?" Do we limit our warm charities to those of our own communion; or do we fervently love all who love our Lord Jesus Christ?

The motives presented in Scripture for Christians loving one another are such as these:

1. In the world they have tribulation. They weep and lament and are sorrowful. John 16:20. To him that is afflicted, pity should be shown. To him who is persecuted by the enemies of God, great friendship should be manifested by the friends of God, lest his sorrows should overwhelm him.

2. The world hates God's people, and nothing but the love of the brethren can compensate for so much malignancy from others. Christ said, "If the world hate you, ye know that it hated me before it hated you. If ye were of the world, the world would love his own; but because ye are not of the world, but I have chosen you out of the world, therefore the world hateth you." John 15:18, 19. All this is spoken by Christ to enforce brotherly love.

3. Love to the brethren is to the world a powerful proof of the divinity of the Christian religion. Jesus says, "By this shall all men know that ye are my disciples, if ye have love one to another." John 13:35. No other founder of a sect or religion ever made love a test and mark of belonging to him. And it is

a fact fully sustained by church history, that whenever the gospel has unusual power over men's minds, it is always preceded or accompanied by much love to the brethren.

4. We are urged to brotherly love by the sweet and awful authority of Jesus Christ: "A new COMMANDMENT give *I* unto you, that ye love one another." Even advice from Christ we should be bound to follow; but his *command* none may innocently forget. "These things I *command* you, that ye love one another." John 15:17. To rebel against such authority must be truly perilous.

5. The love of Christ towards us should constrain us to love our brethren. Christ himself urged this consideration: "As I have loved you, even so do ye love one another." Let us love our brethren, not for our own sakes, nor chiefly for their own sakes, but for Christ's sake. This consideration binds, and is felt to be powerful by all who love our Lord Jesus Christ. "LET BROTHERLY LOVE CONTINUE." Heb. 13:1.

In this and the three preceding chapters, the subject of love has been brought before the attention of the reader. A more heavenly theme could not be found. God is love; heaven is love. Christ is love incarnate; religion is love in exercise. Nothing is of more importance to any one's happiness, usefulness, or salvation than that he be filled with love. True, men are not saved for their love, but they cannot be saved without it. Nor can any mortal utter a kinder wish for all to whom he wishes well, than to say with Paul, "This I pray, that your love may abound yet more and more in knowledge and in all judgment; that ye may approve things that are excellent; that ye may be sincere and without offence till the day of Christ; being filled with the fruits of righteousness, which are by Jesus Christ, unto the glory and praise of God." Phil. 1:9–11.

# CHAPTER XIX.

## PEACE.

PEACE is the opposite of war, persecution, temptation, condemnation, alarm, tumult, strife, contention, controversy, quarrelling.

In the Scriptures, the word *peace* relates to several different things. By nature we are all enemies to God, and by wicked works we evince and strengthen our aversion to God and holiness. But "being justified by faith, we have peace with God, through our Lord Jesus Christ." Rom. 5 : 1. By this peace with God we are freed from condemnation. We are no longer hostile to God, nor he to us. We no more contend with the Almighty, nor he with us. Christ is our Surety, our Sacrifice, our Peace. "Thorns grow everywhere, and from all things below; and from a soul transplanted out of itself into the root of Jesse, peace grows everywhere too from Him who is called Our Peace, and whom we still find the more to be so the more entirely we live in him, being dead to the world and self and all things besides him." The repose of the soul in its God and Saviour is wonderful. "Thou wilt keep him in perfect peace whose mind is stayed on thee; because he trusteth in thee." Isa. 26 : 3. This "peace of God passeth all understanding." Phil. 4 : 7. In its basis and in its effects no mortal has adequate conceptions of its richness as a blessing from God. "When he giveth quietness, who then can make trouble?" said Job, chap. 34 : 29. And Jesus Christ himself said, "Peace I leave with you, my peace I give unto you: not as the world giveth give I unto you." John 14 : 27. Nothing can finally destroy this peace. "Who is he that condemneth? It is Christ that died, yea rather, that is risen again, who is even at the right hand of God, who also maketh intercession for us." Rom. 8 : 34.

This is one of God's richest blessings. It is the sum and beginning of all mercies. It is a pledge that we shall never perish. This counsel of peace is between God and every soul that flees to Jesus. "The chastisement of our peace was upon him." Isa. 53 : 5. By Him we have access to God. We are entitled to call him our Father and our God. God is in Christ reconciling the world unto himself, not imputing their trespasses unto them. When God thus pardons and accepts us, every creature in the universe, whose friendship can do us permanent good, is made to be on our side. The angels become ministering spirits to aid and befriend us as God shall commission them. The stars in their courses no longer fight against us. He has even made a covenant for his chosen "with the beasts of the field, and with the fowls of heaven, and with the creeping things of the ground." Hos. 2:18. We may therefore speak boldly to all who have made peace with God by Jesus Christ, and say, "All things are yours; whether Paul, or Apollos, or Cephas, or the world, or life, or death, or things present, or things to come: all are yours; and ye are Christ's, and Christ is God's." 1 Cor. 3 : 21–23. Paul seven times uses a phrase nowhere else found in Scripture. It is this, "The God of peace." And surely a more striking delineation of the blessed character of God could not be given in so few words, unless we except those words of John, "God is love." Let every man "acquaint himself with God, and be at peace." Job 22 : 21. So also our Saviour is "The Prince of peace." In him we have reconciliation with

God and all other good things. He was sent "to guide our feet into the way of peace." Luke 1 : 79. His "kingdom is not meat and drink; but righteousness, and peace, and joy in the Holy Ghost." Rom. 14 : 17. So "to be spiritually-minded is life and peace." Rom. 8 : 6. And so also no greater blessing could be asked on others than this: "Grace be unto you, and peace, from him which is, and which was, and which is to come; and from the seven spirits which are before his throne; and from Jesus Christ, who is the faithful Witness, and the First-begotten of the dead, and the Prince of the kings of the earth." Rev. 1 : 4, 5.

From peace with God through Christ naturally flows peace of conscience. This is a vast treasure. Nothing can compensate the want of it. Nothing can make us happy without it. In the angels above, peace of conscience is the fruit of innocence. In man it is the purchase of a Saviour's blood. We must have our hearts sprinkled from an evil conscience, else the sting will remain and rankle for ever. Heb. 10 : 22. Yea, we must have our consciences purged from dead works, or we never can acceptably serve the living God. Heb. 9 : 14. If we are ever to be made perfect as pertaining to the conscience, it cannot be "without blood." Heb. 9 : 7, 9. The blood of Christ "turns our fears into hopes, and our sorrows into songs; it settles the agitations of our spirits; it silences troubles in us; it is a ground of peace to us. That which hath been a sweet savor to pacify God, wants not a savor to appease our consciences." The great misery of the wicked is that to them "there is no peace." Isa. 48 : 22, and 57 : 21. "The way of peace they know not." Isa. 59 : 8; Rom. 3 : 17. Conscience of sin remaining, no man can be otherwise than a poor trembling, self-condemned creature. Nor can he by hardening his heart erect any strong bulwarks against the sudden invasion of extreme terrors.

This peace of conscience is often interrupted by our sins and follies. When worldliness takes the place of a tender walk; when principle is impinged on; when practice is made to conform to temptation; when time seems more important than eternity; then we may know that sooner or later there will be an uproar in our consciences. But "great peace have they which love thy law." Psa. 119 : 165. It is in vain for any one to hope for a blessing when he is saying, "I shall have peace, though

I walk in the imagination of my heart." Deut. 29 : 19.

A third kind of peace is when God disposes our fellow-men to regard us with so much favor as to let us alone, not to tease, torment, persecute, or make war upon us, but to think, speak and act in a friendly way towards us. This is a great blessing, and when it is made sure to us we ought to give hearty thanks to God for it, for he is its author. "When a man's ways please the Lord, he maketh even his enemies to be at peace with him." Prov. 16 : 7. Thus for a long time Solomon "had peace on all sides round about him." 1 Kings 4 : 24.

It is true that this peace is not, like the others, essential to our piety or our happiness. Jesus Christ said, "Think not that I am come to send peace on earth : I came not to send peace, but a sword." Matt. 10 : 34. And the effect of true piety under all dispensations has been to provoke the malice of wicked men, though oftentimes it is restrained by the good providence of God. He turns men's hearts whithersoever he will.

But the word peace is also applied to our habits, pursuits, and dispositions towards others. "Follow peace with all men." Each of the other kinds of peace is a rich blessing. This is a weighty duty. On this point the Scriptures are very clear and full. Thus even to Nabal David sent this message: "Peace be both to thee, and peace be to thy house, and peace be unto all that thou hast." 1 Sam. 25:6. So Jeremiah sent a letter to all his brethren, captives in Babylon, saying, "Build ye houses, and dwell in them; and plant gardens, and eat the fruit of them;... and seek the peace of the city whither I have caused you to be carried away captive, and pray unto the Lord for it: for in the peace thereof shall ye have peace." Jer. 29:5, 7. The circumstances of the people to whom this message was sent were such that, if any thing in the shape of wrong could have justified revenge, they surely would have been at liberty to seek the ruin of the city that had dealt so proudly and cruelly with them. But God, by the mouth of his prophet, condemns all such proceedings, and requires a line of conduct quite the opposite. The prophet delivers his message in an extreme case, and yet with the utmost clearness and consistency with other parts of God's word. Paul also says, "Let us follow after the things which make for peace." Rom. 14:19.

"God hath called us to peace." 1 Cor. 7:15. "The fruit of the Spirit is peace." Gal. 5:22. "Live in peace." 2 Cor. 13 : 11. "Endeavor to keep the unity of the spirit in the bond of peace." Eph. 4 : 3. He also commands us to pray for our rulers, "that we may lead a quiet and peaceable life, in all godliness and honesty." 1 Tim. 2:2. The apostle James also says, "The wisdom that is from above is first pure, then peaceable ;" and, "the fruit of righteousness is sown in peace of them that make peace." James 3 : 17, 18. Our blessed Saviour also said to his disciples, "Have peace one with another." Mark 9 : 50. So that there is not left the shadow of a doubt respecting the binding obligation upon all men to have and to manifest peaceable dispositions at all times. Nor should we ever forget that the duty is enjoined with great frequency and solemnity. We should therefore address ourselves to this with much seriousness and earnestness. Nor are we at liberty to limit our endeavors after peace to friendly relations. We must "follow peace with *all* men." We are not at liberty to confine our efforts in this behalf to a few, and those of our own circle or party. We must let our endeavors extend to all with whom we have dealings. "If a stranger sojourn with you in your land, ye shall not vex him." Lev. 19 : 33.

What then is enjoined on us in maintaining peace with our fellow-men? The answer is, that first of all we are bound to entertain peaceable and friendly thoughts respecting all men. In the heart is the seat of every virtue. "As a man thinketh in his heart, so is he." If men be not in their temper and disposition peaceable, it is certain that they do in their hearts violate the whole spirit of the gospel. Nor will it be possible for such to make their outward conduct conform to the scriptural standard. "It is hard to act a part long; for where truth is not at the bottom, nature will always be endeavoring to return, and will peep out and betray herself one time or other."

Another thing to be done in fulfilment of our duty is, to speak peaceably. The peace of neighborhoods is often destroyed by words. "Grievous words stir up anger." Prov. 15:1. "Where no wood is, the fire goeth out; so where there is no talebearer, the strife ceaseth." Prov. 26 : 20. "The words of a talebearer are as wounds." Prov. 18 : 8. "Render not railing for railing." 1 Pet. 3:9. Paul warns us against "strifes of words." 1 Tim. 6:5; 2 Tim. 2:14. Rash words may have as ill an effect as those which are the fruit of a truly malignant design in destroying the peace of families and of neighborhoods. "A whisperer separateth chief friends," Prov. 16:28; and "an angry man stirreth up strife." Prov. 29:22. We cannot therefore be too guarded in our speech. "Death and life are in the power of the tongue." Prov. 18:21. And every prudent man will pray, "Set a watch, O Lord, before my mouth; keep the door of my lips." Psa. 141:3. A good man has said, "Before we allow ourselves to find fault with any person behind his back, we should ask ourselves three questions: 1. Is it true? 2. Is it kind? 3. Is it necessary?" A little heart-searching, even a little reflection before a hard speech, would effectually prevent much misery.

John Newton says, "In mixed conversation, it is a good rule to say nothing, without a just cause, to the disadvantage of others." Again, "I was once in a large company, where very severe things were spoken of Mr. W——, when one person seasonably observed, that though the Lord was pleased to effect conversion and edification by a variety of means, he had never known anybody convinced of error by what was said of him behind his back. This was about thirteen years ago, and it has been on my mind a useful hint ever since."

Another matter required of us is, to act peaceably. "A man that hath friends must show himself friendly." Prov. 18 : 24. And here the Scriptures furnish us both with rules and with examples. Take the case of Abram and Lot, the uncle and the nephew. These two great men had each many flocks and herds and tents. "And the land was not able to bear them, that they might dwell together: for their substance was great, so that they could not dwell together. And there was a strife between the herdmen of Abram's cattle and the herdmen of Lot's cattle... And Abram said unto Lot, Let there be no strife, I pray thee, between me and thee, and between my herdmen and thy herdmen; for we be brethren. Is not the whole land before thee? Separate thyself, I pray thee, from me: if thou wilt take the left hand, then I will go to the right; or if thou depart to the right hand, then I will go to the left." Gen. 13 : 6–9. Strife can hardly subsist where such a temper is manifested. There is no fuel to keep the fire burning. The wisdom of the course adopted by Abram was conspicuous in these things: 1. In keeping separate interests from clashing. It is a great trial when good men are so situated that they cannot avoid collision of interests. Here is an example. Let them follow it. 2. Abram refused to listen to the stories of his servants. They seem to have been men ready for strife. It is hard, but it is wise, to avoid mingling ourselves with the quarrels into which our servants get with others. 3. Abram showed his wisdom by leaving all his interests in the hands of God. If we will mind his glory, he will mind our welfare.

The last generation was adorned by one who, in some respects, and especially in faith and peaceableness, particularly in his latter days, was a child of Abraham. I refer to the pious Simeon of Cambridge, England, who said, "The longer I live, the more I feel the importance of adhering to the rules which I have laid down for myself in relation to the following subjects:

1. "To hear as little as possible what is to the prejudice of others.

2. "To believe nothing of the kind till I am absolutely forced to it.

3. "Never to drink into the spirit of one who circulates an ill report.

4. "Always to moderate as far as I can the unkindness which is expressed towards others.

5. "Always to believe that, if the other side were heard, a very different account would be given of the matter.

"I consider love as wealth; and as I would resist a man who should come to rob my house, so would I a man who would weaken my regard for any human being. I consider too, that persons are cast in different moulds; and that to ask myself, What should *I* do in that person's situation? is not a just mode of judging. I must not expect a man that is naturally cold and reserved to act as one that is naturally warm and affectionate; and I think it a great evil that people do not make more allowances for each other in this particular. I think religious people are too little attentive to these considerations."

It is hardly possible that a man honestly holding and practising such views should fail to be esteemed a good man, and in a time of freedom from legal persecution, should fail to enjoy general quietness of life and the respect of all good men who know him.

One of the most serious hinderances to the peace of many men and many communities is found in occasional outbursts of bad temper. Some men are constitutionally moody. They are not, and without a miracle they could not be, uniform. Their feelings vary with the wind, with the state of their stomachs, and with other mutable things. Others are nervous, and are easily provoked to tears or to passion. Some are naturally choleric and excitable. Many from early infancy have had bad precepts and worse examples held up before them. Some are fretted and crossed in childhood and youth, until they are like the trained whelps of the tiger. All this is to be greatly deplored; for "a wrathful man stirreth up strife." Proverbs 15:18. Indeed, the first bursts of passion are often like coals thrown among shavings. There is no telling what will be the end of the mischief done.

It would vastly conduce to peace if men could be induced to guard against all causes, occasions, and beginnings of discord. "The beginning of strife is as when one letteth out water: therefore leave off contention, before it be meddled with." Prov. 17:14. "Nip the evil in the bud," is one of the best rules.

Nor do we follow peace when we allow ourselves to be made parties to contests which do not concern us. "He that passeth by, and meddleth with a strife not belonging to him, is like one that taketh a dog by the ears." Prov. 26 : 17.

One of the greatest disturbers of peace is pride. It is sure to be insolent. It struts, and boasts, and vapors, and provokes others. "He that is of a proud heart stirreth up strife." Prov. 28 : 25. "Only by pride cometh contention." Prov. 13 : 10. There is a "wrath of pride." Prov. 21 : 24.

Ambition also begets many contests. There never was a more unhappy state of feeling in the family of our Saviour than when "there was a strife among them which of them should be greatest." Luke 22 : 24.

It would greatly conduce to the advancement of peace, if men could be induced to put a just estimate on its value. In the eyes of a wise and good man, it is always of great price. In Scripture it is mentioned side by side with the most excellent things. By one prophet God says, "Love the truth and peace." Zech. 8 : 19. By one apostle he says, "Follow peace with all men, and holiness, without which no man shall see the Lord." Heb. 12:14. So that if truth and holiness are of great price in the eyes of God and good men, so is peace. In his old age John Newton wrote, "Peace and holiness are the peculiar characteristics of a disciple of Jesus; they are the richest part of the enjoyments of heaven; . . . and they are more inseparably connected between themselves than some of us are aware of. The longer I live, the more I see of the vanity and sinfulness of our unchristian disputes; they eat up the very vitals of religion."

Our great guaranty against a disturbed, distracted existence is to be found in God alone. He is our refuge as well as our strength. Thus says David, "Thou shalt hide them in the secret of thy presence from the pride of men; thou shalt keep them secretly in a pavilion from the strife of tongues." Psa. 31:20.

Nor can we easily overestimate the evils that flow from a state of carnal strife between man and man, or between the sections of a community. "Where envying and strife is, there is contention and every evil work." Jas. 3:16. See also Gal. 5:15.

Yet so inveterate is this spirit of contention, and so dreadfully does it blind the mind, that it is with great difficulty men of strife can be brought to believe that they are injuring and degrading themselves by all their malice. "It is an honor for a man to cease from strife; but every fool will be meddling." Prov. 20:3. Such a sentence is either not heeded by them, or it strikes terror into their consciences. Other portions of God's word are no less explicit. Paul puts wrath and strife in a list of vices of the most hateful character. Gal. 5:19–21. James says, "If ye have bitter envying and strife in your hearts, glory not, and lie not against the truth." Jas. 3:14.

Nothing should more arouse us to this duty than the example of our blessed Lord, of whom it was foretold that "he shall not strive nor cry; neither shall any man hear his voice in the streets." Matt. 12:19. "When he was reviled, he reviled not again; when he suffered, he threatened not."

We can now see why our blessed Saviour spoke as he did concerning those who, with a good will, seek to promote peace around them. "Blessed are the peacemakers; for they shall be called the children of God."

And can any imagine a more interesting

sight than a community regulated by such principles as the gospel enjoins on this subject, where would be nothing to hurt or destroy in all God's holy mountain?

But the question arises, How far are we to bear and forbear; how much must we yield for peace? Is it possible for us to control other people's minds and acts in this matter? And here it is pleasant to be able to say that the Bible prescribes no impossible tasks. Its language is, "If it be possible, as much as lieth in you, live peaceably with all men." Rom. 12:18. How plain and how safe is this rule. Up to the measure of our ability we must go, but the law extends no further. Nay, the Scriptures tell us of one great and good man whose lament was, "My soul hath long dwelt with him that hateth peace. I am for peace; but when I speak, they are for war." Psa. 120:6, 7. They go further, and tell us of some who "preach Christ even of envy and strife." Phil. 1:15, 16. There is no limit to the contentious propensities of some. They introduce virulence even into their most solemn public acts in religion. Some do all this, and yet add all the time great professions of love. Thus in the days of Micah, God speaks of "prophets that make my people err, that bite with their teeth, and cry, Peace; and he that putteth not into their mouths, they even prepare war against him." Micah 3 : 5.

We are then not at liberty to forsake God or deny his truth, in order to promote peace. On the contrary, we must obey God rather than man. We must contend earnestly for the faith once delivered to the saints. We must never make shipwreck of faith. We must never part with a good conscience. "Buy the truth, and sell it not"—sell it not even for peace. The world asks too dear a price for its smiles or its favor, when it asks us to renounce the faith of God's people, or purity of mind.

Nor is it necessarily proof of a wrong spirit in us to refuse to surrender our just and legal rights merely because others choose to attempt to take them from us. Paul exclaimed, "I am a Roman citizen." "I appeal to Cæsar." Nor can any sober man deny that his retention of his rights in these cases was every way justifiable. This will suggest our right course respecting lawsuits. We should not engage in these from ambition or a love of contention. We should not be litigious. Oftentimes "a bad settlement is better than a good lawsuit." Those who love to resort to courts seldom thrive. As the wolf spends all his strength in escaping from the dogs and the hunters, although he eats many sheep, so the enormous expenses of the practised litigant, even when successful, very much exhaust his means, and keep him poor.

## CHAPTER XX.

### COURAGE.

I ONCE asked a great general what proportion of men might be regarded as naturally brave without discipline? He said it was impossible to answer the question with precision, but that the number was very small. If the inquiry had related to the tempers of men in the performance of their moral and religious duties, the number of the naturally courageous might have been stated as still less. Sin has made cowards of us all. Without the grace of God no man has heroism enough left to enable him to do his duty to God or man. We are not only averse to holiness, but we have a very peculiar dread of those things which by the wicked are inflicted on the conscientious. We have need of constant support and encouragement in the path of rectitude. Accordingly no small part of all good writings, inspired and uninspired, are designed to give boldness in the profession and practice of that which is right. Thus in Psa. 27 : 14 we read, "Be of good courage, and he shall strengthen thy heart;" and in Psa. 31 : 24, "Be of good courage, and he shall strengthen your heart, all ye that hope in the Lord." When Joshua sent away the spies, his chief exhortation to them was to "be of good courage." Num. 13 : 20. Among the dying counsels of Moses to Israel, in view of the conquest of Canaan, was this: "Be strong and of a good courage, fear not, nor be afraid of them: for the Lord thy God, he it is that doth go with thee; he will not fail thee, nor forsake thee." Deut. 31 : 6. The same exhortation is given by God himself through Joshua. Josh. 1 : 6, 9; 10: 25. A part of David's dying advice to Solomon was, "Be strong and of good courage; dread not, nor be dismayed." 1 Chron. 22 : 13. Again, "Be strong and of good courage, and do it; fear not, nor be dismayed, for the Lord God, even my God, will be with thee; he will not fail thee, nor forsake thee." 1 Chron. 28 : 20. Words of similar import have often been addressed to armies about to engage in battle. 2 Sam. 10 : 12; 1 Chron. 19 : 13. Indeed, so surely as the spirit of piety revives among any people, there will be a great revival of courage. See Ezra 10 : 4, and many other places, especially Acts 4 : 13, 29, 31. In like manner

Paul exhorts the Corinthians: "Watch ye, stand fast in the faith, *quit you like men, be strong*." Of like import are those numerous exhortations in both Testaments to "be strong," to "be strong in the Lord," etc. In fact the Scriptures often speak in tones of high commendation of doing things courageously, and greatly censure such as are not valiant for the truth. Indeed, when sin is impudent and brazen-faced, it is not right that piety should be timid and sneaking. Accordingly the genuine people of God have in all ages manifested more or less intrepidity in the cause of truth. And as inspired men, so also uninspired men, who have gained a just influence in the church of God, have always commended this virtue. Indeed what can be done without it? A timid, discouraged, despondent, cowardly person is ill prepared to meet the rough assaults of the enemies of virtue. He will yield the citadel of truth, and flee as one ashamed. He will betray the best interests of his cause. He will defend nothing, and uphold nothing good. He will be a poor help and a poor reliance in the day of trouble.

But what is the courage which the Scriptures commend? This is a question of great importance. There are in our language four words which are often used confusedly. These are, *bravery*, *courage*, *valor*, and *fortitude*. Bravery belongs to the animal part of our nature; courage to the mental. The former depends on physical temperament; the latter on the reason. Bravery is an instinct; courage is a virtue. One may be brave without thought. He cannot be courageous unless he calmly reflects. Bravery is often headlong and headstrong; courage is cool and reasonable. The former acts upon an impulse; the latter upon conviction. By delay bravery dies away; by delay courage gains strength. Bravery is blind and furious; courage is far-seeing and prudent. Men are brave in common with the war-horse; they have courage in common with the great patriots and bleeding martyrs of all ages. A man may be brave without courage, and courageous without bravery. He may be unmoved because he has no sense of danger. Or his nerves may be upset by apprehensions of peril, and his constancy of mind be wholly unshaken.

*Valor* is supposed to have all the best qualities of both bravery and courage. It glories in risking all upon a just occasion. It looks far ahead and is wise. But its counsels would be madness in the timid. Men are never valiant except as they are moved by the higher aims and passions of our nature. No man can be valiant for a trifle or a sordid end. The love of country, the love of truth, the love of God, or something high and noble must always actuate the valiant man.

There is also, in strict propriety of language, a difference between courage and *fortitude.* Courage faces and resists danger; fortitude endures pain. Courage is sometimes used in a bad sense; fortitude never. Courage is for action; fortitude for suffering. In this sense fortitude differs little from constancy and patience. Yet by many good writers these words are used interchangeably. Indeed all these words are at times used in a good sense and synonymously. In this chapter the word *courage* will be used, and in a good sense only. There is a Christian grace of that name. It is of great value. It is the quality Peter points out when he says, "Add to faith *virtue.*" So highly did the ancient Greeks and Latins esteem courage, that often in their classics the word by which they express it is the word by which they express the idea of virtue generally; as if they would assert that it was either the sum or the index of all virtue. In the sense of courage, it is by many held that Peter uses it in the words just quoted. Merely to believe is not the whole of our work. To our faith we must add courage. We have great need of this grace. But like all other Christian virtues, courage has its counterfeits. It is therefore very important for us soundly to discriminate. True courage is wise and calculates. It thinks soberly, and

> "Is not the appetite
> Of formidable things, nor inconsult
> Rashness; but virtue fighting for a truth."

It has that prudence which foreseeth the evil, and hideth itself. It looks well to its ways. It chooses the best ends and the best methods of attaining them. It never cries, "There is no danger," but is suspicious of mere appearances. It admits the real difficulties in its way, and provides for their removal. It is full of wisdom and forethought. In this it wholly differs from fanaticism, which is blind and furious, and commonly blind in proportion to its fury. The Bible everywhere commends "a sound mind." It is as truly at war with folly as with sin. Would you have a courage quite dauntless? Choose such a course of life as God unquestionably approves, such a course as you know you will yourself approve when standing before God in judgment. Thus you will always be supported by your own understanding and conscience. Having no mental misgivings, you will not grow pale at the shaking of a leaf or of a spear. This true courage seeks worthy objects and noble aims, and

> "Is seen in great exploits
> That justice warrants, and that wisdom guides;
> All else is towering frenzy and distraction."

It is not low and mean in its aims and plans. It is expansive in its desires. It lives for God's glory and man's happiness.

True Christian courage is also humble. It vaunteth not itself, and is not puffed up. It greatly boasteth in God, but not at all in the flesh. It emptieth itself, but finds its fulness in God. Just so surely as one trusteth in himself that he is strong and can do exploits, just so surely is he a poor, weak, cowardly thing. Look at Peter. He cries out, "Though all men forsake thee, yet will not I." It is but a few hours till he denies his Lord with oaths. Boasters are like clouds and wind without rain. When we lay hold on God, we are girded with omnipotence; but when we are left to ourselves we are as weak as water.

Evans says, "Courage in general is a temper which disposes a man to do brave and commendable actions without being daunted at the appearance of dangers and difficulties in the way."

Buck says, "Courage is active fortitude, that meets dangers and attempts to repel them."

Seneca, whose mind was unenlightened by Christianity, yet says, "Courage is properly the contempt of hazards *according to reason;* but that to run into danger from *mere passion*, is rather a daring and brutal fierceness than an honorable courage."

Cicero, in some respects the greatest of the heathen philosophers, says, "That sort of courage which disregards the rules of justice, and is displayed not for the public good, but for private selfish ends, is altogether blamable; and so far from being a part of true virtue, it is a piece of the most barbarous inhumanity."

Plato says, "As that sort of knowledge which is not directed by the rules of justice, ought rather to have the name of design and subtlety than wisdom and prudence; just so that bold and adventurous mind which is hurried on by the stream of its own passions, and not for the good of the public, should rather have the name *fool-hardy* and *daring*, than valiant and courageous."

The Duke of Sully says, "That which arms us against our friends and countrymen, in contempt of all laws, as well divine as human, is but a brutal fierceness, madness, and real pusillanimity."

Another says, "That hardy rashness which many account valor is the companion of ignorance; and of all rashness, boldness to sin is the most witless and foolish."

Addison says, "Courage that grows from constitution very often forsakes a man when he has occasion for it; and when it is only a kind of instinct in the soul, it breaks out on all occasions without judgment or discretion; but that courage which arises from a sense of duty and from a fear of offending Him that made us, always acts in a uniform manner and according to the dictates of right reason." He also says courage "is that heroic spirit inspired by the conviction of our cause being just, and that God will not forsake us."

Mr. Burke says, "The only *real* courage is

generated by the fear of God. He who fears God fears nothing else." Indeed the Scriptures justify the remark that no man has true courage except so far as he is a good man. "The righteous are as bold as a lion; but the wicked flee when no man pursueth."

> "Stand but your ground, your ghostly foes will fly:
> Hell trembles at a heaven-directed eye.
> Choose rather to defend than to assail;
> Self-confidence will in the conflict fail.
> When you are challenged, you may dangers meet—
> True courage is a fixed, not sudden heat;
> Is always humble, lives in self-distrust,
> And will itself into no danger thrust.
> Devote yourself to God, and you will find
> God fights the battles of a will resigned.
> Love Jesus. Love will no base fear endure.
> Love Jesus, and of conquest rest secure." Bp. Ken.

Collier says, "True courage is the result of reasoning. A brave mind is always impregnable. Resolution lies more in the head than in the veins, and a just sense of honor and of infamy, of duty and of religion, will carry us further than all the force of mechanism."

From all this it appears that true courage is calm, rational, firm, controlled by a sense of justice, free from raving and madness, from hatred and malignity. It is truth, justice, and honor sitting on a throne of virtue. Because it fears God, it has not that fear of man which bringeth a snare. Trials do but evince and evoke it. "True courage never exerts itself so much as when it is most pressed; and it is then we most enjoy the feast of a good conscience when we stand in the greatest need of its support."

Dymond well says, "The courage which Christianity requires, is to bravery what fortitude is to daring—an effort of the mental principles rather than of the spirits.. It is a calm, steady determinateness of purpose, that will not be diverted by solicitation, or awed by fear." And he very properly cites as an illustration of his meaning those immortal words of Paul: "Behold, I go bound in the spirit unto Jerusalem, not knowing the things that shall befall me there; save that the Holy Ghost witnesseth in every city, saying that bonds and afflictions abide me. But none of these things move me, neither count I my life dear unto myself."

So much for the general nature of courage. It may be either active or passive. Active courage leads to bold deeds; passive courage is not moved by fears in times of peril and suffering. By active courage Jonathan and his armor-bearer captured the strong-hold of the Philistines; by passive courage Joseph sustained himself in the dungeons of Egypt. By the former David performed the great exploits of killing the lion, the bear, and the giant of Gath; by the latter he endured the contumely of Shimei as he was retreating from the holy city. Daniel was passively courageous when in the lions' den; he was actively courageous when, in unfaltering tone and with awful solemnity, he pronounced sentence of death on Belshazzar. Active courage bestirs itself, and uses all its resources to avert, remove, or diminish evils; passive courage defies the worst evils that can come, and preserves equanimity in the midst of convulsions, disasters, revolutions, and death in all its frightful forms. The principle of all courage is the same. He who is possessed of the genuine virtue in one set of circumstances, will not want it when circumstances change.

Perhaps no historical book of equal length gives more instruction as to the nature and obligation of active courage than that of Nehemiah. It contains an account of one of the greatest and most difficult enterprises ever accomplished. There was peril at every step; yet Nehemiah was never daunted. "Shall such a man as I flee?" was the short but stern reply he gave to those who would tempt him to cowardice. But one must read the whole book with care in order to understand the heroism of that great governor. Verily he obtained a good report, and on the best grounds. Leighton well says, "It is the battle tries the soldier, and the storm the pilot. How would it appear that Christians can be not only patient but cheerful in poverty, in disgrace and temptations and persecutions, if it were not often their lot to meet with them?" It is a great thing for us when we know our calling, and understand why we are made to suffer severely.

One of our capital errors is, that we often fall into a dreamy state, and forget that life is full of severe realities.

"I slept, and dreamed that life was beauty;
I woke, and found that life was duty.
Was then thy dream a shadowy lie?
Toil on, sad heart, courageously,
And thou shalt find thy dream to be
A noonday light and truth to thee."

Let every man say with Romaine, "My time is short; I must be up and doing; I must go briskly on with my work, leaving it to my Lord to find me strength for it and success in it. His blessing I expect here and for ever; not for any thing I have done; and yet I would labor as hard as if heaven was to be the reward of my labors." True Christian courage is loudly demanded in our day. Every duty may bring it to the test.

It is not possible for us to be too entirely and intrepidly devoted to the service of God. Yet we cannot be too guarded as to our motives in undertaking any service for Christ. Let us not seek our own ease, our own honor or advantage; let us not be moved by any unholy bitterness, nor by party-spirit; let us not follow blind impulses, nor indulge in temporary excitements; let us not neglect the duties of the closet for those of the platform; but still let us boldly and earnestly serve the Lord day and night.

Important as is a stirring, active courage, a passive courage is no less so. This we commonly need in all our Christian course. The world is never pleased with the people of God. The son of the bond-woman still strives with the son of the free-woman. Opposition to all that is good is stern, instant, and determined. Nothing but divine grace can ever enable a child of God to endure the fearful hostility of the enemy. Our Saviour's word is still fulfilled: "I am come to set a man at variance against his father, and the daughter against her mother, and the daughter-in-law against her mother-in-law; and a man's foes shall be they of his own household." The offence of the cross has not ceased. It never can cease but by the conversion of the soul to God. "If ye were of the world, the world would love his own; but because I have chosen you out of the world, therefore the world hateth you." Men of the world have no better temper towards Christianity than when they crucified its Author, and cast his followers to the wild beasts. He who would be a Christian must be so at the risk of all he counts dear in this life. The world will heap odium upon him, will vex his righteous soul from day to day, and if possible, turn him away from his tender walk with God. Of three devices the enemies of the saints are very fond: one is seduction; another is scorning; the third is bloody persecution. The first is used at all times. To seduce God's people from the path of rectitude is the business of thousands. Whether they really design it or not, their principles and their practices are alike evil and corrupting. They are always spreading snares for the feet of the unwary. They use every blandishing art. They allure by means of winning manners. They use cunning craftiness. They profess great friendship for the very objects of their arts; but they regard Christian principle as unnecessarily strict and severe. They glory in not being bound by the unbending laws of God's people; yet their example makes them uneasy. Besides, having no love to God and holiness, they cannot endure the exemplary life of consistent Christians. Yet they are not prepared to show all the venom of the adversary, and so they satisfy themselves with attempts to seduce God's servants.

Others go further, break friendship with consistent professors, affect to esteem them fanatics, and vent upon them the utmost virulence of their scorn. They practise those "cruel mockings" of which Paul speaks; cruel mockings, than which nothing is harder to be borne with an unruffled spirit. Many take delight in subjecting to all manner of mortification those whose minds seem made up to walk in the paths of scriptural piety. In every age, the world has exhausted its vocabulary of abuse against the people of God. Nazarene,

Galilean, obstinate, precisian, Puritan, Lollard, enthusiast, fanatic, are but a few of the terms of reproach used by the world towards consistent Christians. I have known a man told to his face that he was a fanatic, because he would not go with a man of the world to view his earthly possessions on the Lord's-day, and he professing a warm friendship all the time. There is cruelty in the scorning of the scorners. They delight in their trade. They love to afflict the heritage of God. They shoot out the lip.

When seductions and scornings fail, the world will, as it can, try more formal persecutions. For three centuries together, at the first preaching of Christianity, the blood of the martyrs hardly ceased to flow. Although the laws of some countries, and the public sentiment of the world, do much oppose bloody persecutions in our day, yet even to this present time dungeons and death are the portion of some of God's people. It is but a short time since in one year *eight thousand* persons were by edict doomed to death on the island of Madagascar, because they professed to love the Lord Jesus Christ. The Inquisition still has its dungeons and its tortures and secret deaths and burials. A large body of men in the nominally Christian world are by profession trained to regard themselves as doing God service when they violate all the laws of charity towards those who differ from them in religious doctrine and practice. Whether much of the blood of the saints is likely again to be shed on the earth, is a point on which good men differ. But prophecy does seem to foretell days of great trial yet to come on the church, and that before her final triumph and universal dominion. Should that day of trial come, who is prepared? who is full of courage? who is ready to be offered upon the sacrifice and service of the church's faith? Such a day will demand the faith and fortitude of martyrs.

That many cherish the principles of persecutors is evident, by the malice they show in many forms, and by their open, bold avowals. The Shepherd of the Valley, a Roman-catholic paper in our country, says, "If the Catholics ever gain, as they will do, though at a distant day, an immense majority, religious freedom is at an end." It also says, "Heresy and unbelief are crimes; that is the whole of the matter; and in Christian countries, as Italy and Spain for instance, where all the people are

Catholic, and where the Catholic religion is an essential part of the public law of the land, they will be punished as other crimes."

This is but the echo of the dogmas of Romish doctrines for centuries past. Let not the supine wrap themselves up in the cloak of indifference, and say that there is no danger. Every bishop and archbishop in that apostate communion is a sworn persecutor to the utmost of his power. Ungodly men everywhere may suddenly have all restraints removed, and then they will be wild beasts in the heritage of God.

If any would have examples of high Christian courage both in doing and suffering the will of God, let them study the history of the church in all ages. Moses, Joshua, Gideon, Barak, Samson, Jephthah, Ehud, Stephen, Paul, Peter, and John, in inspired history, with scores and hundreds in later ages, stand forth as bright patterns of the grace here commended. They "subdued kingdoms, wrought righteousness, obtained promises, stopped the mouths of lions, quenched the violence of fire, escaped the edge of the sword, out of weakness were made strong, waxed valiant in fight, turned to flight the armies of the aliens. Women received their dead to life again: and others were tortured, not accepting deliverance; that they might obtain a better resurrection: and others had trial of cruel mockings and scourgings, yea, moreover, of bonds and imprisonment: they were stoned, they were sawn asunder, were tempted, were slain with the sword: they wandered about in sheep-skins and goat-skins; being destitute, afflicted, tormented; (of whom the world was not worthy:) they wandered in deserts and in mountains, and in dens and caves of the earth."

Nor were examples of great courage confined to the days of inspiration. The pious Flavel has collected several pleasing instances of this grace. When Valens the emperor in a great rage threatened Basil the Great with banishment and torture, he replied, "As to the first, I little regard it, for the earth is the Lord's and the fulness thereof; as for tortures, what can they do upon such a poor thin body as mine, nothing but skin and bone?" Luther had such a courage in the cause of truth, that in his last sickness he expressed sorrow that "he must carry his blood to the grave," and so not be permitted to die a martyr's death.

Tertullian testifies of the Christians of his day, "Our women and children—not to speak of men—overcome their tormentors, and the fire cannot fetch so much as a sigh from them."

In conclusion, take the following principles and observations for guidance in this duty.

The Scriptures enforce courage both by precepts and examples.

Our circumstances urgently demand that we should possess and practise this grace.

It is not probable that we shall have courage in any high degree unless we set a high value upon it.

Mere natural courage is of no use in enabling us to resist spiritual foes and fears. We must therefore seek true courage by faith in Christ Jesus. He who is readily discouraged cannot rise to great eminence in any thing, surely not in the divine life.

Scriptural modes of arguing are the best to inspire courage. They are such as these: "Because I live, ye shall live also;" "As thy days, so shall thy strength be;" "I will never leave thee, nor forsake thee;" "If God be for us, who can be against us?"

All true spiritual heroism is based in the precious blood and righteousness of Jesus

Christ. "Time will neither wear out the guilt of sin, nor blot out the records of conscience." But the blood of Christ cleanseth from all sin. It speaks better things than the blood of Abel. His righteousness is enough for us all.

Nor should we hesitate to look at anything in the most serious and solemn manner. "Those who cannot bear to hear their duty, may prepare soon to hear their doom." Those who will not permit their thoughts to travel beyond the bounds of time, will be, must be greatly surprised by eternal things. The thoughtless and frivolous must expect eternity to flash damnation in their consciences. It is mournful that in a world like ours it should be said of but one here and there, "He is a thoughtful man." It is as shocking as it is dangerous for those who possess the powers and responsibilities of men to aim at no higher end than is attained by the brutes that perish. Those who would grow wiser and better, must not turn away their minds from any subject simply because it excites painful emotions. The thoughtless die as soon as others—not as safely.

Would you have dauntless courage in all coming duration, die unto sin, hold fast the covenant and oath of God, and let Christ be all in all to you. He that would not be filled with shame, must first count the cost of all he undertakes.

God's word and Spirit are always on the side of truth and duty, and may be infallibly relied on.

The enemy has no arts nor devices that have not been thwarted a thousand times. He can be beaten. He has been vanquished.

Never do evil that good may come. Choose your weapons. Maintain a good conscience.

Pray to know the depths of Satan and the cunning sleight of men, whereby they lie in wait to deceive. If it were possible, they would deceive the very elect.

Divine desertion will make cowards of the bravest, fools of the wisest. As soon as the Spirit of the Lord deserted Saul, an evil spirit rested on him.

Leave character as well as soul and body in the hands of God. Clamor and falsehood cannot harm you if truth is your buckler and God your refuge.

Set your face as a flint. Trust in the Lord, and do good. "Nothing but cowardice ever finally lost the victory in the cause of God."

## CHAPTER XXI.

### CONTENTMENT.

OUR libraries abound with treatises on contentment. Some of them are written with great ability. Nor has there ever been much formal disputation among writers on morals respecting the obligation and excellence of this attainment. It produces results so happy, and is enforced by so many urgent reasons, that a man must be particularly blinded before he can regard discontent as either lawful or slightly criminal. The difficulty therefore is not so much in the want of good rules and strong reasons for guiding us into a state of contentment, as in the deep-rooted aversion of our hearts to a duty which requires our submission to the will of God. We *know* better than we *do*. Seeing the *right*, we pursue the *wrong*. We smile at the folly, or frown at the wickedness of discontent in others, and then follow their example.

But what is contentment; and how may it be known from evil states of mind somewhat resembling it? Contentment is not carelessness or prodigality. It is not obtuseness of sensibility. It is a disposition of mind in which we rest satisfied with the will of God respecting our temporal affairs, without hard thoughts or hard speeches concerning his allotments, and without any sinful desire for a change. It submissively receives what is given. It thankfully enjoys present mercies. It leaves the future in the hand of unerring wisdom. Nor is there any thing in true contentment to make men satisfied with the world as a portion or as a permanent abode. The most contented person may long for the day when Christ shall call him home. He may, like Paul, be in a strait betwixt two, not knowing whether to desire to abide in the flesh for the sake of others, or to depart and be with Christ, which is far better. God never required any man to be willing to live here for ever. Nor is there any thing stoical in contentment. It is not bluntness of feeling. True religion does not make men dream that a prison is a palace, nor make them reckless of their own happiness. Refined sensibility is promoted by true religion.

We may form some correct idea of contentment by considering its opposites. Of these, one of the most prominent is envy, than which there is not a more vile, nor a more violent passion. It is full of deadly malice. When a man's heart grows sick at the superior worldly success of others, and hates them on that account, he is not far from ruin. Evans says, "Envy is an infallible mark of discontent. Duty to God, and charity to our neighbor, would induce us to take pleasure in the welfare of others, whether we immediately share in it or not." If thine eye is evil towards thy neighbor because God is good to him, it is proof that thou quarrelest with Providence. This is the more inexcusable, because God has expressly informed us that men of the world have their portion in this life. He has provided for his friends a portion better than was ever enjoyed on earth by any man, even by Adam before his fall. And if God should give to one of his children more than he gives to you, has he not a right to do what he will with his own?

Contentment is also opposed to corroding care about our worldly condition. The command of the New Testament is, "Be careful for nothing; but in every thing by prayer and supplication with thanksgiving let your requests be made known unto God." Phil. 4 : 6. Similar to this is the exhortation, "Cast all your care upon him, for he careth for you." 1 Pet. 5 : 7. To the same purport spoke our Lord: "Take no thought for your life, what ye shall eat, or what ye shall drink; nor yet for your body, what ye shall put on. Is not the life more than meat, and the body than raiment?" Matt. 6 : 25. It is of the greatest importance to our peace and usefulness, that we settle it in our minds that all fretting care about the things of this life is both a sin and a folly. It is to these immoderate cares that our Lord refers when he says, "Take heed to yourselves, lest at any time your hearts be overcharged with surfeiting, and drunkenness, and cares of this life, and so that day come upon you unawares." Luke 21 : 34. Seest thou a man eager after the things of time, behold one in great peril—peril heightened by his success. Our hearts are very deceitful. Jonah may be too much taken up with his gourd, as well as Solomon with his vast public works.

Contentment is opposed to covetousness. "There are two words in the Greek Testament which may be rendered *covetousness.* The one literally signifies *the love of money;* the other *a desire of more*, in Eph. 4:19 rendered *greediness*. These two senses are coincident, for no man desires more of that which he does not love; and as he that loveth silver cannot be satisfied with the silver which he already possesses, he will of course desire more. To both of these contentment is the opposite. It loves not inordinately what it has, nor is greedy for more. So says the Scripture: "Let your conversation," your life, your behavior, "be without covetousness, and be content with such things as ye have." Heb. 15:5. "Having food and raiment, let us be therewith content." 1 Tim. 6:8. What a man parched with the thirst of dropsy needs is not more water, but more health. It is as impossible to remove the restlessness of a covetous mind by heaping wealth upon it, as to extinguish fire by pouring oil upon it. It is a great thing to learn that "a man's life's consisteth not in the abundance of the things which he possesseth." Luke 12:15. So that "if a man is not content in that state he is in, he will not be content in any state he would be in." Evans says, "We see people arriving at one enjoyment after another, which once seemed the top of their ambition; and yet so far from contentment, that their desires grow faster than their substance, and they are as eager to improve a good estate when they are become masters of it, as if they were still drudging for food and raiment." "Beware of covetousness."

Contentment is also the opposite of pride. "Humility is the mother of contentment." "They that deserve nothing should be content with any thing." When we become lifted up with pride, and think we deserve something good at God's hands, it is impossible to satisfy us. But with the lowly is wisdom, quietness, gentleness, contentment. He who expects nothing, because he deserves nothing, is sure to be satisfied with the treatment he receives at God's hands. So that "a little that a righteous man hath is better than the riches of many wicked;" for "the wicked, through the pride of his countenance, will not seek after God." The proud is like a bullock unaccustomed to the yoke. He is turbulent and fiery. He alienates friends; he makes enemies. He has much trouble and sorrow where the humble pass quietly along. Pride and contentment do not go together.

Neither do contentment and ambition at

all agree. "Seekest thou great things for thyself? I say unto thee, Seek them not." Our actual wants are not many; but the ambitious create a thousand demands, which it is hard, if not impossible to meet. If men are bent on gratifying the strong desires of a wicked ambition, it will require more resources than any mortal possesses to meet the half of them. If a wise man cannot bring his condition to his mind, he will honestly endeavor to bring his mind to his condition. But this the ambitious will not do. He will be content with nothing gained, because each elevation widens his horizon, and gives him a view of something else which he greatly longs for, and so he is tossed from vanity to vanity, a stranger to solid peace. Art thou ambitious? then thou art thine own tormentor.

Contentment is opposed to murmurings and repinings against God's providence, and dwells with her sisters gratitude, submission, resignation. Like Hezekiah, she exclaims concerning all God's orderings, "Good is the word of the Lord." Isa. 39 : 8. This is a great point. If you can say nothing clearly to the glory of God, it is wise to be dumb and not open your mouth. Psa. 38 : 13; 39 : 2.

Contentment is also opposed to distrust of God, and to despondency respecting the orderings of his providence. Instead of waiting on the Lord, and relying on him for strength of heart, how many forebode ill from all that occurs to them, or is anticipated by them. They have little if any cheerfulness. Their souls are never as mount Zion, which cannot be removed, but abideth for ever. Apprehension takes the place of confidence. True contentment will break up this state of things. It will settle, confirm, and establish the soul.

The proper fruits of contentment are many, pleasant, and easily discerned.

1. It begets cheerfulness and thankfulness of speech. He who is always singing dirges, and has no songs of praise; he who is perpetually filling the ear of friendship with his complaints, and has nothing to say of loving-kindness, is not blessed with true contentment. It tells a different tale. It does not charge God foolishly. If it sings of judgment, it sings also of mercy.

2. True contentment makes men conscientious and exact in religiously performing their duties to all around them. They trust in the Lord, and do good. They do good to all men,

especially to the household of faith. If God takes away one friend, they will endeavor more meekly and assiduously to render all that is due to those who remain. If he takes half one's worldly goods, the residue is more than ever conscientiously employed for his glory. If such cannot do as they wish, they will do as Providence permits.

3. The truly contented will not resort to wicked or to doubtful expedients for relieving their own wants and distresses. They had rather suffer wrong than do wrong. To them want is not so bad as ill-gotten wealth. They prefer to endure a hard lot rather than to drive a hard bargain. Stealing, cheating, wild speculation, or any fraud, is to them worse than poverty. They go not down to Egypt nor over to Assyria for help, when they have been told to trust in Jehovah alone. They are willing to be rid of want or straits, but not at the expense of a good conscience.

4. If the truly contented have been disobliged by men, they are not malignant, but benevolent towards them. They look upon their enemies as God's hand and God's sword, the rod of his anger, the scourge of his people. Their enemies may be violent and unreason-

able, and so wholly culpable, but they do not forget who has said, "Vengeance is mine; I will repay." All is committed to unerring wisdom and eternal love.

The matters of discontent are chiefly such as relate to wealth, honor, or pleasure. These are the objects of both lawful and unlawful care and desire. It is quite reasonable that we should be contented in regard to each of them.

1. As to wealth. The judgment of the sober, and especially of the wise and good of all ages, might reasonably be expected to have some influence over us to check our discontent on this point. Sages and saints, teachers from earth and teachers sent from God have united in bearing a solemn testimony against the love of money, and in favor of contentment with our lot. Hear their words:

Socrates: "Content is natural wealth."

Democritus: "If thou dost not desire much, a little will seem to thee an abundance."

Horace: "Care and thirst for more attend a growing fortune."

Woolstoncraft: "The middle rank contains most virtue and abilities."

Clarkson: "There is no greater calamity

than that of leaving children an affluent independence."

Dymond: "The most rational, the wisest, the best portion of mankind, belong to the class who possess neither poverty nor riches."

Wilberforce: "A much looser code of morals commonly prevails among the rich than in the lower and middling orders of society."

Lord Bacon: "Certainly great riches have sold more men than they have bought out. As baggage is to an army, so are riches to virtue. It hindereth the march, yea, and the care of it sometimes loseth or disturbeth the victory."

Mrs. Hannah More: "It is to be feared that the general tendency of rank, and especially of riches, is to withdraw the heart from spiritual exercises."

Mason: "To have a portion in the world is a mercy; but to have the world for a portion is a misery." "We must answer for our riches; but our riches cannot answer for us." "If the world be our portion here, hell will be our portion hereafter."

Johnson:

"Wealth heaped on wealth nor truth nor safety buys,
The dangers gather as the treasures rise."

When his vast estates were confiscated for

his adherence to God's truth, the Marquis of Vico said, "Their gold and silver perish with them who count all the wealth of the world worth one hour's communion with Christ."

Pollok:

> "Gold many hunted, sweat and bled for gold;
> Wasted all night, and labored all the day.
> And what was this allurement, dost thou ask?
> A dust dug from the bowels of the earth,
> Which, being cast into the fire, came out
> A shining thing, that fools admired, and called
> A god; and in devout and humble plight
> Before it kneeled, the greater to the less;
> And on its altar sacrificed ease, peace,
> Truth, faith, integrity, good conscience, friends,
> Love, charity, benevolence."

Bunyan: "Nothing more hinders a soul from coming to Christ than a vain love of the world; and till a soul is freed from it, it can never have a true love for God."

Beveridge: "There is one piece of folly which all mankind are naturally guilty of, and that is desire of riches, whereby men love and long for fine houses and lands, and silver and gold, and such like things. Just as we may have sometimes seen an idiot pleasing himself with having his pocket full of stones or dirt; or rather, as distracted persons desire swords or such like weapons, whereby to destroy themselves; so others that have lost their senses and the right use of their reason, nothing will serve them but a great deal of wealth, howsoever they come by it, and therefore they go through a thousand temptations and dangers to get it; and when they have got it, what then? Then they are in a thousand times worse condition than they were before."

Richard Baxter shows the malignity of the sin of worldliness in several particulars. "1. It is a sin of deliberation. 2. It is a sin of choice set up against our chief interest. 3. It is idolatry. 4. It is contempt of heaven, when it must be neglected and a miserable world preferred. 5. It shows that unbelief prevails in the heart. 6. It is a debasing of the soul of man. 7. It is a perverting of the very drift of a man's life. 8. It is a perverting of God's creatures to an end and use clean contrary to that which they were made and given for."

Owen: "Learn to be contented with your lot. He is wise also who took a view of it and measured it and found it just commensurate to your good: had he known that a foot's breadth more had been needful, you would have had it."

Thomas Scott: "*Reliance* on increasing

riches, however obtained, is idolatry, and totally inconsistent with the life of faith."

Arndt: "Riches are like a stream, which soon flows to a person, and may also soon flow away."

Horne: "Of all things here below, wealth is that on which poor deluded man is chiefly tempted, even to the loss of life, to place his confidence; and when 'riches increase,' it proves a hard task for the human heart to keep its affections sufficiently detached from them."

Such are the views of some of the wits, poets, philosophers, statesmen, nobles, and divines who have warned us of the folly of loving gain. These men spoke from their natural sense, or were guided by religious principle; but they were all uninspired. When we open the oracles of God, they speak in a manner still more clear and solemn.

King David, who had personally tried both humble life and great wealth, said, "A little that a righteous man hath, is better than the treasures of many wicked." "If riches increase, set not your heart upon them." Like unto his is the testimony of his son.

Solomon says, "He that is greedy of gain,

troubleth his own house." "Riches profit not in the day of wrath." "He that trusteth in his riches shall fall." "There is that maketh himself rich, yet hath nothing: there is that maketh himself poor, yet hath great riches." "A good name is rather to be chosen than great riches." "Labor not to be rich: for riches certainly make themselves wings; they fly away as an eagle towards heaven." "He that maketh haste to be rich shall not be innocent."

Ezekiel says, "Behold, this was the iniquity of thy sister Sodom, pride, fulness of bread, and abundance of idleness was in her and in her daughters, neither did she strengthen the hand of the poor and needy."

Agur: "Two things have I required of thee; deny me them not before I die: Remove far from me vanity and lies; give me neither poverty nor riches; feed me with food convenient for me; lest I be full, and deny thee, and say, Who is the Lord? or lest I be poor and steal, and take the name of my God in vain."

John: "Love not the world, neither the things that are in the world. If any man love the world, the love of the Father is not in him."

James: "Go to now, ye rich men, weep and howl for your miseries that shall come upon you. Your riches are corrupted, and your garments are moth-eaten. Your gold and silver is cankered; and the rust of them shall be a witness against you, and shall eat your flesh as it were fire. Ye have heaped treasure together for the last days."

Paul: "They that will be rich fall into temptation and a snare, and into many foolish and hurtful lusts, which drown men in destruction and perdition. For the love of money is the root of all evil; which while some coveted after, they have pierced themselves through with many sorrows." "Charge them that are rich in this world, that they be not high-minded, nor trust in uncertain riches, but in the living God, who giveth us richly all things to enjoy; that they do good, that they be rich in good works, ready to distribute, willing to communicate; laying up for themselves a good foundation against the time to come, that they may lay hold on eternal life."

But of all the teachers ever sent by God to men, his dear Son spoke the most fully and clearly respecting riches. Jesus Christ said, "It is more blessed to give than to receive."

"Lay not up for yourselves treasures upon earth, where moth and rust doth corrupt, and where thieves break through and steal; but lay up for yourselves treasures in heaven, where neither moth nor rust doth corrupt, and where thieves do not break through nor steal: for where your treasure is, there will your heart be also." "Ye cannot serve God and mammon." "Seek ye first the kingdom of God and his righteousness, and all these things shall be added unto you." "Take heed, and beware of covetousness." "Seek ye not what ye shall eat, or what ye shall drink, neither be ye of doubtful mind. For all these things do the Gentiles seek after; and your Father knowest that ye have need of these things." "It is easier for a camel to go through a needle's eye than for a rich man to enter into the kingdom of God." "Make to yourselves friends of the mammon of unrighteousness; that when ye fail they may receive you into everlasting habitations. If ye have not been faithful in the unrighteous mammon, who will commit to you the true riches?" "The cares of this world and the deceitfulness of riches choke the word." "Blessed be ye poor; for yours is the kingdom of God. Blessed are ye that hunger now; for ye shall be filled. Blessed are ye that weep now; for ye shall laugh. But woe unto you that are rich; for ye have received your consolation. Woe unto you that are full; for ye shall hunger. Woe unto you that laugh now; for ye shall mourn and weep."

Thus spoke the Messiah, the one Mediator between God and man. Shall not we be wiser for all these instructions? The Author of our religion was the only sinless being ever born of woman. He lived and died in poverty. He knows, and he has felt, the humiliation of dependence.

God has greatly honored virtuous poverty in every age, as the history of science, of literature, of philosophy, of poetry, and of piety in every country shows. He takes the poor from the dunghill, and sets him among princes. Though poverty is no virtue, yet most of the striking examples of virtue have been from humble life. Poverty brought on by indolence or waste is a disgrace, because it is a punishment; but wealth is the great corrupter of all who have it, and have not with it unusual grace.

A few of our race live and labor, that they may have the means of doing good to others.

This is scriptural: "Let him that stole steal no more; but rather let him labor, working with his own hands the thing that is good, that he may have to give to him that needeth." Eph. 4:28. One of the calmest and profoundest writers on political economy some years ago said, "I suppose the British and Foreign Bible Society, during the twenty or thirty years that it has existed, has done more direct good in the world—has had a greater effect in meliorating the condition of the human species—than all the measures which have been directed to the same ends by all the prime ministers of Europe during a century." Oh that men everywhere were moved by that "insatiable benevolence which, not contented with reigning in the dispensation of happiness during the contracted term of human life," or on the narrow theatre of its own vicinage, "strains with all the graspings and reachings of a vivacious mind to extend the dominion of its bounty beyond the limits" of one country or of one generation. Were such the temper of all men, we should have no need of preaching sermons to check the rapacity or moderate the desires of each succeeding generation, and bring human wishes within the limits of a holy contentment.

People devoted to doing good are commonly a cheerful and happy class of persons.

2. As to honor, rank, standing in the world, much needs not be said to make a wise man more contented with his lot. For what is more fickle than popular favor? The man whose name is to-day mingled with shouts of welcome, is to-morrow met with hisses and hootings. The very crowd that spread branches in the way, and cried, "Hosanna, blessed is he that cometh in the name of the Lord," as Jesus entered Jerusalem in the triumph which prophecy had decreed to him, did in three days vociferate, "Not this man, but Barabbas," "Away with this fellow," "Crucify him, crucify him." The very city that murdered the prophets also built their sepulchres. It is the habit of popular opinion to shift incessantly. Men are constant only in fickleness. But if popular favor was perfectly settled, what is it but a puff of wind? What good can it do any man? If the praise of others is undeserved, it is but flattery, and may lure us to self-conceit and ruin. If it is merited and just, we are apt to know our own virtues soon enough, without having them trumpeted by others.

Besides, the best men that ever lived have

had their names cast out as evil—have been far more frequently under the ban than under the smile of their generation, and in many cases have died amid the execrations of their contemporaries. He has the best name who gets the "white stone, and in the stone a new name written, which no man knoweth saving he that receiveth it." How often men are warned not to seek the favor of the world. In one of the great contests in England for a seat in parliament, one of the candidates was suddenly called out of time. Burke, the survivor, on that occasion uttered a sentence which has become like one of our proverbs: "What shadows we are, and what shadows we pursue."

3. But some are not content because they have so few worldly pleasures. Do they not know that all pleasure but that which springs from lawful sources leaves a sting behind? Communion with God has its pleasures that do not cloy the appetite. "She that liveth in pleasure is dead while she liveth." Commonly the more worldly pleasure the less happiness there is. The more pleasure, the more sin also. The more pleasure, the more dreadful the last account. Bunyan says, "The epicure, that delighteth in the dainties of this world,

little thinketh that these very creatures will one day witness against him." The pleasures of sin are but for a season, and that season so short. The pleasures of the table are in the end followed by dreadful forms of disease and anguish. The pleasures of sense are wholly insufficient to give permanent enjoyment. "The eye is not satisfied with seeing, nor the ear with hearing."

Contentment is a most reasonable duty. It is best that your will should not control your affairs. Your health, ease, success, wealth, reputation, and enjoyment deeply concern you; but are you fit to direct respecting them? If God should give you your way, how much would satisfy you? Would not your desires soon be drowned in cares and crimes and sorrows? Is it best for you to have uninterrupted health? Without *some* bodily pain, you might forget that you were mortal. It would be more painful to a truly pious man to say when, how long, and how severely he should be sick, than it would be to be sick all his life. A greater name than you now have might be your downfall. More ease might subject you to dreadful diseases. Make not your lot worse by sinful repinings.

You have not shown wisdom sufficient to direct any of your own affairs. It is a mercy to us all that "it is not in man that walketh to direct his steps." Human knowledge is ignorance, human prudence folly, human strength weakness, human virtue a slender reed. God may cross you without doing you any injustice. Your will is the will of a sinner. Sometimes God has tried you by gratifying your desires for something new, something different. The result has not generally been favorable. "He gave them a king in his anger, and took him away in his wrath." You have often done worse when full than when empty. "Jeshurun waxed fat and kicked." Good Hezekiah greatly desired life, and God gave him fifteen years more; but in that time he greatly erred, and left a sad blot on his name. A man may live too long for his own peace, or honor, or usefulness. Your wishes are not always wise. A child was sick. His mother was almost frantic. She fasted, she fainted, she wept, she screamed. God restored her boy to health, and at manhood he committed felony, was arrested, imprisoned, convicted, executed, and broke her heart. How much less would she have suffered had he died in childhood. Your views are liable to be full of error.

But God is fit to govern you and all things. He knows what is best for you, how much you can bear, and when a smile or a stroke will do you most good. His grace is great, and so are his truth, and power, and wisdom. If he shall direct, all things will go right. He is never deceived nor outwitted. He is gentle and kind. "He knoweth our frame; he remembereth that we are dust." His will is holy, just, and good. He keepeth mercy for thousands. His faithfulness is unto all generations. You should be glad that Jehovah governs the universe, that he governs you. If wise, thou wilt "trust in the Lord and do good, and verily thou shalt be fed;" for he hath said, "I will never leave thee, nor forsake thee." What a promise! what a promise!

Learn, in whatever state you are, therewith to be content. "You are the borrower, not the owner of created comfort." Suppress the first risings of ambition, covetousness, self-will, restlessness, and the spirit of murmuring. Rest quietly in God. The future will bring a full explanation of the present. Treasure up in your heart the blessed promises of God.

Incessantly ask the Lord to increase your faith. Diligently perform all known duties, especially relative duties. Be of good courage, and he shall strengthen your heart. Say not, God hath forgotten, or is as a stranger that tarrieth for a night. Resist all unworthy thoughts of your Saviour and heavenly Father. Stand in your lot, and leave results with him who governs all things after the counsel of his own will. So shall you walk safely, and light shall be your burden, and soon the Almighty shall call you to himself, and "the days of thy mourning shall be ended." But till that day of joy shall come, rest in the Lord, and wait patiently for him, remembering that "we brought nothing into this world, and it is certain we can carry nothing out." It was one of the greatest attainments ever made, when Paul was able to say, "I know both how to be abased, and I know how to abound; everywhere, and in all things, I am instructed both to be full and to be hungry, both to abound and to suffer need."

Bishop Hall says, "If a man would be rich, honorable, or aged, he should not strive so much to add to his wealth, reputation, or years, as to detract from his desires. For certainly in these things he hath the most that desireth least. A poor man that hath little and desires no more, is in truth richer than the greatest monarch who thinks he hath not what he should or what he might, or who grieves that there is no more to have. It is not necessity but ambition that sets men's hearts on the rack."

There are three considerations which should quite reconcile us to be without much of what mankind are generally so greedy after.

The first is, that God generally gives the great amount of the wealth, honors, and pleasures of this world to his foes. How seldom do the potentates of earth fear God. How few very rich men love prayer. The sons of pleasure are never the sons of God. No wise man should care much for that which God habitually bestows on those who have no share in his saving mercy, and shall never see his face in peace.

The second consideration is, that the arts by which these things may be, and often are gained, are of the lowest kind. It requires neither much sense nor much virtue to build up a great fortune, to have many praising you, or to be called a man of pleasure. One great secret in the lives of many who rise to eminence in these things is, that first of all they deny God, and give themselves over to irreligion. They part with a good conscience. They may speak much of honor, but often there is no honor there. If a man will but agree to flatter and cozen, lie and defraud, oppress and banter; if he will allow his selfishness to reign supreme; if he will harden his heart against the demands of justice, the dictates of equity, and the urgencies of charity; if he will hold fast all he gets, and get all he can, he may be rich; and if he can once acquire wealth, there are always some that will sound his praise; and so he may by money and flattery buy his way to power and notoriety. It is the deliberate judgment of many close observers, that the mass of the successful in worldly schemes do not possess the average of intellect, and are below the average in want of good feeling and good conduct. This may seem strange to some, but let every man look over the list of his acquaintance, and see if it is not so. The butt of many a family dies worth more than all the rest of his father's children. "Godliness with contentment is great gain."

The third consideration is, that nothing can make us happy if our minds are restless and grasping; but that contentment is itself riches, honors, and pleasures. "The sleep of the laboring man is sweet, whether he eat much or little; but the abundance of the rich will not suffer him to sleep." The Persians have this proverb: "Ten poor men can sleep tranquilly upon a mat; but two kings are not able to live at peace in a quarter of the world." And one of our own poets has said,

> "Contentment gives a crown
> Where fortune hath denied it."

## CHAPTER XXII.

### PATIENCE.

IN the Greek Testament are two words which we translate patience. One of these is rendered by Robinson *longanimity*, *long-suffering*, *forbearance*, *patient endurance*, *patience*. In Scripture it is used to express the forbearance or patience of God towards sinners in delaying their just punishment. Rom. 2 : 4; 9 : 22; 2 Pet. 3 : 15. It also expresses human forbearance, or the patience of one man towards another. Matt. 18 : 26, 29; Eph. 4 : 2. The verb from which it is derived is used to express the delay of God to deliver his persecuted people. Luke 18 : 7. And another signification is, that of man's quietly and confidently awaiting blessings from God, as Gal. 5 : 22. In general this patience is opposed to all hastiness of spirit towards God or man.

The other word in the Greek Testament rendered patience is perhaps of still more frequent use, and signifies endurance, constancy, patience. It often occurs in the epistles of the New Testament. In many cases it clearly conveys the idea of perseverance in duty at all risks and hazards with hope towards God.

Buck defines patience to be "that calm and unruffled temper with which a good man bears the evils of life."

Barrow says, "Patience is that virtue which qualifieth us to bear all conditions and all events, by God's disposal incident to us, with such apprehensions and persuasions of mind, such dispositions and affections of heart, such external deportments and practices of life, as God requireth and good reason directeth."

Evans says, "Christian patience is a disposition that keeps us calm and composed in our frame, and steady in the practice of our duty under the sense of our afflictions or in the delay of our hopes."

Charnock says, "In regard of God, patience is a submission to his sovereignty." . . . "To be patient because we cannot avoid or resist it, is a violent, not a loyal patience; but to submit because it is the will of God to inflict it, to be silent because the sovereignty of God doth order it, is a patience of a true complexion."

Mason says, "Christian patience is not a careless indolence, a stupid insensibility, mechanical bravery, constitutional fortitude, a daring stoutness of spirit, resulting from fatalism, philosophy, or pride: it is derived from a divine agency, nourished by heavenly truth, and guided by scriptural rules."

Bates says, "The insensibility of God's hand inflicting evils is as different from Christian patience and constancy, as a mortal lethargy is from the quiet, soft sleep of health: nothing kindles his anger more than neglecting it; it is equally provoking with the despising of his love; it is a symptom of a wretched state of soul: if there proceed no sighs and groans, no signs of grief from the sense of God's displeasure, it is a sad evidence there is no spiritual life. Indolence under the effects of God's anger is like the stillness of the Dead sea, whose calm is a curse."

Dilwyn says, "A phlegmatic insensibility is as different from patience as a pool is from a harbor. Into the one indolence naturally sinks us; but if we arrive at the other, it is by encountering many an adverse wind and rough wave, with a more skilful pilot at the helm than self, and a company under better command than the passions."

From what has been said it appears that

patience has various objects. Towards God it is resigned, and says, "I will bear the indignation of the Lord." Towards Christian men, who justly reprove us, it is meek, and says, "Let the righteous smite me." Towards wicked and unreasonable men, who love to see others afflicted, it says, "Rejoice not against me, O mine enemy." Towards the ills under which we are called to suffer, it is not violent and imperious, but rather gives them a kind entertainment. Under provocation it is gentle and not resentful. It blesses and curses not. It bears insults and injuries without malice. It is "patient toward all men." Under affliction it is quiet and submissive. It will use no wicked measures to relieve even great distresses. It is "patient in tribulation," in the extremest sufferings. Under delays it is still constant. It loves to leave every thing in the hands of the Father. To this Paul refers when he says, "Ye have need of patience, that, after ye have done the will of God, ye might receive the promise. For yet a little while, and he that shall come will come, and will not tarry." Heb. 10 : 36, 37.

The duty of patience is illustrated in the Scriptures by several different similes. The first is that of the farmer. "Be patient therefore, brethren, unto the coming of the Lord. Behold, the husbandman waiteth for the precious fruit of the earth, and hath long patience for it, until he receive the early and latter rain." Jas. 5 : 7. The precious seed is often sown in autumn. For moisture it is dependent on dews and rains, over which the farmer has no control. Nor can he either send or withhold the snow for its protection against the rigors of winter. Nor can he defend it against blight and mildew and the caterpillar and the army-worm. Nor can he reap his harvest for months after the seed-time. So that "long patience" is required. At last the precious fruits come, and all his toils are rewarded and all his hopes realized.

Another mode of representing patience is by the life and habits of a city watchman. Thus the psalmist says, "I wait for the Lord, my soul doth wait, and in his word do I hope. My soul waiteth for the Lord more than they that watch for the morning: I say, more than they that watch for the morning." Psalm 130 : 5, 6. The night may be dark and long and stormy, but the longest night has its morning, the darkest night has the day-spring coming after it, and the most stormy weather is followed by calm and sunshine. The weather-beaten watchman knows that he will be allowed to cease his rounds and at last rest in his bed. He rejoices in hope of sure release. He longs for the time to come. Yet he frets not because it seems to tarry. He knows he cannot hasten it. If he could do away with night altogether, it would but spoil his business. If he could materially abbreviate it, he would but diminish his gains. So he enters upon his beat and its duties with firmness and constancy.

A third mode of representing this patience is by the duties and habits of a servant. "Behold, as the eyes of servants look unto the hand of their masters, and as the eyes of a maiden unto the hand of her mistress; so our eyes wait upon the Lord our God, until that he have mercy upon us." Psa. 123 : 2. The context shows that the state of mind here described had special reference to the state of the righteous as called to endure the contempt and scorning of the proud.

A quiet patient spirit is also set forth in God's word by the behavior of a weaned child. David says, "Surely I have behaved and quieted myself as a child that is weaned of his mother: my soul is even as a weaned child." Psa. 131 : 2. This process, when first commenced, produces wakefulness, restlessness, fretfulness; but when completed, it produces quietness and submission. An illustration so familiar to all parents needs no further explanation.

Job uses another simile to set forth the same thing, that of a hireling, who watched the lengthening shadows of the evening, and longed for his reward. He had too much principle to desert his work or to attempt to defraud his employer. But at the going down of the sun he looked for release. This seems to be a favorite mode of expressing the views of life entertained by Job in the time of his great and sore afflictions. Job 7 : 1, 2; 14 : 6.

When examples of patience are demanded, we can be at no loss. James says, "Take, my brethren, the prophets, who have spoken in the name of the Lord, for an example of suffering affliction, and of patience. Behold, we count them happy which endure. Ye have heard of the patience of Job, and have seen the end of the Lord; that the Lord is very pitiful, and of tender mercy."

Time would fail us to tell of Isaiah royally descended, who for his fidelity is said to have been nailed up in a box and sawn asunder; of Jeremiah and all his suffering in the slimy pit and elsewhere; of Daniel in the lions' den; of the faithful Hebrews in the fiery furnace; and of all those great sufferers for the truth and honor of God in ancient times. Look also at our forefathers in Scotland, England, Ireland, France, Holland, and Germany.

But the apostle James selects Job as a special example. And indeed he was the most patient of all merely human sufferers. What did he not lose without one sinful word? Seven thousand sheep, three thousand camels, five hundred yoke of oxen, five hundred she-asses, a great retinue of servants, seven sons and three daughters, and bodily health were all taken, yet in all this his patience seems not once to have failed. His grief was heavier than the sand of the sea. The arrows of the Almighty were within him, and their poison was drinking up his spirits. Yea, the terrors of God set themselves against him. Yet more than fifteen hundred years afterwards James points to him as the brightest example of patience among the ancient servants of God.

The most illustrious sufferer and the best pattern of patience was Jesus Christ. None suffered so greatly, none suffered so patiently. He endured mockery, contradiction, scourging, and death at the hand of man. He also bore the wrath of God. The violence of men and the wrath of God, treachery and desertion by his disciples, and the hiding of his Father's face, all came on him at once. Yet he bore it all in a blameless manner. "When reviled, he reviled not again; when he suffered, he threatened not, but committed himself to him that judgeth righteously." "For this cause," says he, "came I to this hour." "Not my will, but thine be done." None can be at a loss for a safe guide, if he will but turn his eyes to Christ. There all is constancy, forbearance, quiet, unmurmuring endurance, unflinching obedience; nature indeed lifting up both hands in terror and amazement, but principle and piety triumphing over all temptations. Blessed be God, our Guide and Pattern has left us a perfect example.

This patience is the fruit of God's Spirit. Paul prayed that his Colossian converts "might walk worthy of the Lord unto all pleasing, being fruitful in every good work, and increasing in the knowledge of God; strengthened with all might, according to his glorious power, unto all patience and long-suffering, with joyfulness." Col. 1:10, 11. Every good gift comes from heaven. Nature is impatient, self-willed, restless, turbulent. Men must be taught of God, or they never will know any thing to purpose. Used as men are to some kinds or degrees of inconvenience, conscious as they ought to be that they deserve far worse than ever befalls them, yet all this is to no purpose until God by his Spirit gives them affections and principles which are quite above the measure and strength of nature.

That this grace enters into the essentials of Christian character, is certain from the fact that it is twice so catalogued. In 1 Tim. 6:11, Paul exhorts Timothy to "follow after righteousness, godliness, faith, love, patience, meekness." And in Galatians 5:22, 23, he says the fruit of the Spirit is love, joy, peace, long-suffering," or patience, "gentleness, goodness, faith, meekness, temperance." He who dares erase from either catalogue a single word, takes great liberties with sacred things, and brings his soul into jeopardy. It is also obvious from the very nature of holiness, and from the nature of heavenly things. Would not a fiery, impatient spirit be every way as unlovely and as unfit for the society above as the spirit of revenge, of pride, or of covetousness?

If we have an impatient temper, occasions and temptations will not be wanting to elicit it. The world is full of evil-doers and evil-doings, of evil-speakers and evil-speeches, of evil-surmisers and evil-surmisings. "Fret not thyself because of evil-doers, neither be thou envious against the workers of iniquity. For they shall soon be cut down like the grass, and wither as the green herb. . . . Fret not thyself in any wise to do evil." Psa. 37:1, 2, 8. Sometimes the power of wicked men is fearful, and wielded in the most wanton and oppressive manner. The beast which rose out of the sea, having seven heads and ten horns, and upon his horns ten crowns, and upon his heads the name of blasphemy, has always had a mouth speaking great things and blasphemies; and has often had power to make war with the saints, and to overcome them; and all whose names are not written in the book of life of the Lamb slain from the foundation of the world, do at times worship him. And he carries God's people into captivity, and he slays them with the sword. In such a state of things as this, we see "the patience and the faith of the saints." Rev. 13:10. As a roaring lion, Satan goeth about seeking whom he may devour.

Doubtless there is a just anger, a righteous indignation against wrongs and wrong-doers. It is based on a sense of justice. But anger which results from our evil tempers, which is violent or perpetuated, does no good. It torments him who exercises it. It grieves his best friends; it terrifies his dependents. It makes intercourse with him a source of misery. It is commonly followed by dreadful reproaches of conscience. It drives away many who would otherwise delight to do one a service. It mends no mistakes, relieves no pains, repairs no losses. And it is infectious, and in turn communicated to those around us.

A time of sickness generally tries one's patience. There is always much sickness in the world. No man can entirely escape it but by a sudden death, which in a moment calls him into eternity. Some sicknesses waste the frame without beclouding the mind. Others beget stupor, which destroys sensibility to pain. But generally sickness renders men less capable of reasoning soundly and feeling kindly than before. To him who is of a patient spirit, sickness may, without a miracle, be a means of great enjoyment. It enables a good man to test his principles. The severer the sickness in such cases, the richer the blessings following. Probably the happiest person in many a large city in Christian lands is some child of God, whose bodily health makes him a stranger to sound sleep, and a stranger also to the house of God. There is still living a man who says he has seen four very happy days. One was the day of his conversion; another was the day of his marriage; the other two were days spent in a sick-bed far from home.

The church has had few brighter ornaments than the celebrated Andrew Rivet. As a student, a writer, a preacher, a professor, he was full of life and energy; yet he said he "had learned more divinity in ten days' sickness than in fifty years' study."

The pious Halyburton, in a state of great weakness and pain, said, "Verily there is a reality in religion. The little acquaintance I have had with God within these two days, has been better than ten thousand times the pains I have all my life been at about religion.

These fourteen or fifteen years I have been studying the promises; but I have seen more of the book of God this night than in all that time. If I had my students about me now, I would give them a lesson of divinity."

In 1826, one of my class-mates was taken sick. His illness became extreme. His life was in great peril. At times his pains were excruciating. He was not at ease one moment. Yet all who visited him were witnesses of his patience and joy. Their report led others to his sick-bed. Many a fellow-student dropped his books every day, and said, "I will now turn aside and see this great sight." This good man died not then, but lived to proclaim for several years the unsearchable riches of Christ. He bore with patience many trials, and carried with him through life a sweet savour of Christ, and has now fallen asleep. This happy sufferer was the Rev. Jacob Beecher, afterwards of Winchester, Va. Every pastor sees cases of this kind. Every evangelical church furnishes them. If God so blesses us in sickness, we need not dread its sharpest pangs. They prepare us for sweet mercies. Even if we have no transports, we may yet have quietness. Though we may not exult, we may endure. God may appoint to us wearisome nights and days of vanity, scaring us in visions, or holding our eyes waking. Our bed may not comfort us, nor our couch ease our complaints. For a time God may hide his face from us, or our consolations may be small. Yet it is a great attainment to lie passive in God's hands, and know no will but his.

Some are impatient respecting the future. Their faith is perhaps weak, their nerves are not strong, their circumstances not easy, and they have great disquiet. Indeed most men have alternate hopes and fears concerning coming days. It would greatly tend to check such thoughts if we would remember that the future, which we so much dread, may never come to us. There is nothing more certain than death, and nothing more uncertain than the time when death may overtake us. The human mind easily grows weary when prying into the future. A wise man can do nothing better than look up to God, and say, *My times are with thee.* I cannot see far; I am very blind. But God sees the end from the beginning. He is wise and mighty. Issues are with him; duty is mine. If I can do what God requires, I need not fear results. Times may change; revolution may swiftly follow revolution; friends and scenes and seasons may change; I myself may undergo many changes; but God, his word and plans and counsels never change. They are all holy and perfect.

To do one's duty and leave results with God is scriptural. "Trust in the Lord, and do good." "Offer the sacrifices of righteousness, and put your trust in the Lord." What better can a man do? What else can he do, unless he fret and sin? A great means of curing impatience is a close attention to present duties, some of which are always instant and urgent. One of these is the maintenance of a devout spirit. He who has no heart to pray and praise, to read God's word, to meditate on divine things, and to try his own ways, has not begun to do his duty, and lays himself open to the assaults of impatience. Whatever is unfriendly to a spirit of devotion is dangerous. We all need fire, fire from heaven, to consume our sacrifices. The love of Christ must be shed abroad within us. If prayer were always "the key of the day and the lock of the evening," we should have far fewer impatient speeches. The man who finds God's words and eats them, who meditates on divine things in the night-watches, who searches his heart as with candles, who is in the fear of the Lord all the day long, who praises the Lord seven times a day, cannot be under the sway of impatience.

Let a man also set himself to the imitation of Christ, whose example is perfect and lovely; let him follow the Lamb whithersoever he leadeth; let him walk in the footsteps of his great Forerunner; let him be careful to do this with exactness and alertness, and impatience shall not be his master.

Let him delight in the law of God after the inward man, let him esteem God's precepts concerning all things to be right, let him love the law which reproves his sins, let him take it as a rule for all his thoughts, words, and deeds, and he will have so much to do that he will find impatience yielding before a hearty performance of duty.

Let him watch his own heart, let him see to it that he be not merely "converted from the sins of men to the sins of devils," as from drunkenness, gluttony, and lewdness to envy, malice, and spiritual pride; but let him see to it that he is turned from sin to holiness, from Satan unto God, and he will by degrees gain a sure victory over impatience.

Let him die unto the world, let him die daily; let it be his rule, "I will lend, but not give myself to worldly matters;" let him quit the world before it quits him; let him learn that it is a cheat and a liar, not by always seeking to it, but by obeying the lessons of past experience and the teachings of God's word, and his impatience concerning the future will give way. Let him learn to avoid the habit of complaining, let him labor to take cheerful views of things, so far as this can in truth be done.

> "The wise in secret always hide their pain;
> And only when redress is sure, complain."

Or if the sorrow of the mind be great, let him go chiefly to God with it. A man may complain *to* God, but let him never complain *of* God. Let him never tire in his Master's service, always making Christ's righteousness his righteousness, God's will his will, God's Son his bright and morning star; let him consent to be nothing, that God may be all and in all; let him live by faith, and walk by faith; let him diligently run the race that is set before him, and he will find sinful impatience leaving him more and more, till at last it shall be a vanquished foe, and he shall rise to dwell with God. Above all things, look to God himself.

Perhaps old age has begun to come upon you, and you find there comes with it a certain spirit of impatience. It is sometimes said that the old are liable to peevishness. Great changes have taken place in the world since their habits were formed. Such conduct is often exhibited before them as makes them feel that others wish their place or their property. They see but little reverence for grey hairs. They have many infirmities. They are often kept from the house of God. Disappointment sometimes sorely tries their temper. They often see mean advantages taken of their age or weakness. Sometimes they have no means of occupying their time. They cannot see to read, or they did not form the habit of reading when young, and so cannot now enjoy it. Early in life Bishop Hall wrote, "There is nothing more odious than fruitless old age. And as no tree bears fruit in autumn, unless it blossoms in the spring, so that my age may be profitable, and laden with fruit, I will endeavor that my youth may be studious, and flowered with the blossoms of learning and observation." It is a great thing for old people to love reading. If the Bible alone is their companion and joy, they will surely find "solitude sweetened." It is a great matter for any, and especially for the aged, to learn to control their tongue and temper; to be economical without stinginess, liberal without prodigality, cheerful without levity, humble without meanness, strict without bigotry, devout without fanaticism, and obliging without laxity of principle. The angry passions by all men, especially by the aged, should be kept under strict control.

Earnestly cry to God for guidance, support, and comfort in old age. No wit, no learning, no renown in early life can of themselves preserve one from contempt in old age. Dean Swift was a great student, scholar, and wit; in old age he became stupid, helpless, senseless. He was fed like a child, and was actually exhibited by his servants for reward as a show to visitors. No man ever made a deeper impression on England than the duke of Marlborough. At court his sway was above that of all but the queen. In France his name was a solemn caution to men to live peaceably. All Europe resounded with the fame of his deeds. Yet his last days were full of misery.

He was an idiot. God alone and God only can protect the aged from all harm. Look to him. "Trust in the Lord, and do good; so shalt thou dwell in the land, and verily thou shalt be fed. Delight thyself also in the Lord, and he shall give thee the desires of thy heart. Commit thy way unto the Lord; trust also in him, and he shall bring it to pass; and he shall bring forth thy righteousness as the light, and thy judgment as the noonday. Rest in the Lord, and wait patiently for him." He can cause that the hoary head being found in the way of righteousness shall be a crown of glory.

If you are old, remember that as long as you live, one of your most solemn duties is to set an example of cheerfulness and patience; that as memory fails, it needs to be often refreshed by the perusal of God's word; that as your time on earth is short, you should be careful that none of it run to waste; that your sufferings on earth will not last long; and that God's promises to pious old age are very full and gracious. Listen to his words: "Thine age shall be clearer than the noon-day: thou shalt shine forth; thou shalt be as the morning." Job 11:17. "They shall still bring forth fruit in old age; they shall be fat and flourishing; to show that the Lord is upright: he is my rock, and there is no unrighteousness in him." Psa. 92:14. Again he says, "Even to your old age I am he, and even to hoar hairs will I carry you: I have made, and I will hear; even I will carry, and will deliver you." Isa. 46:4. Surely with such promises we may safely trust an unseen God even in the midst of the trials and weaknesses of age. How memorable that saying of an eminent servant of God, "I have had six children, and I bless God that they are either with Christ or in Christ, and my mind is at rest concerning them. My desire was that they should have served Christ on earth; but if God will rather choose to have them serve him in heaven, *I have nothing to object to it.*"

Are you a teacher of the young? Are you endeavoring to form the minds of others to virtue and knowledge? Be patient. Rule your own spirit; teach the same lesson over and over again; upbraid not others for their dulness. Persevere. *Be pleasant.*

Are you laboring for the conversion of others, and do they seem very dull and obstinate? Be patient with them. As long as God spares them there is hope. Who can tell but the

Lord will be gracious in the last extremity? Hope and plead with them. Hope and pray to God. Never cease your endeavors till life is extinct.

Are you slandered? Be not revengeful. Jesus Christ was more reviled and misrepresented than you have ever been. Make him your pattern. It is better to be slandered than to be a slanderer. It will do you more harm to lose your self-control and fall into sin, than to have all manner of evil spoken against you falsely.

Are you poor? Jesus Christ was more so. Be patient under trials. Christ passed through those that are worse. If men despise you for your poverty, it may drive you to the mercy-seat; and will not that be good for you?

Have you bodily pain? Learn to distinguish between those effects which show sinful impatience and those which are purely physical. A man may indulge very sinful impatience towards God, and yet not utter a sigh or a groan. Another may be in a state of mind highly pleasing to God, and yet every breath may be a groan or a sigh. It is not sinful for men to give natural expression to their sense of pain.

The motives which may properly be urged upon us to exercise patience are many and strong.

1. The impatient man is unhappy, and nothing can hinder his being so but a change of temper. He doubles all his sorrows. Those around him are apt to imitate him, and their impatience reacts on him. In prosperity and adversity, he is alike destitute of solid peace of mind.

2. The impatient brings on himself every sort of evil, and especially great guilt in the sight of God. "He that hath no rule over his own spirit is like a city that is broken down and without walls." Prov. 25:28. That is, he lies open to the invasion of all evils; he is protected against none of them. In a thousand respects, "the patient in spirit is better than the proud in spirit." Eccl. 7:8.

3. However sharp our pains and great our sufferings may be, they will not last always. The apostle says, "Be ye also patient; establish your hearts: for the coming of the Lord draweth nigh."

4. Patience is one link in the golden chain which holds us safe on earth in the midst of enemies and perils. Nor is there a brighter

link in that chain. Paul says, "We glory in tribulations also, knowing that tribulation worketh patience; and patience, experience; and experience, hope; and hope maketh not ashamed; because the love of God is shed abroad in our hearts by the Holy Ghost which is given unto us." Rom. 5:3–5. James also says, "The trying of your faith worketh patience. But let patience have her perfect work, that ye may be perfect and entire, wanting nothing." Chap. 1:3, 4. It was a noble exclamation in Fenelon when his library was on fire, "God be praised that it is not the dwelling of some poor man."

5. God has mercifully condescended to instruct us on this whole subject by divine example. To his enemies how amazingly patient is God. How he bears with sinners, and forbears to punish them. Indeed, ungodly men in all ages have hardened themselves in sin because God was so good. They have long and blasphemously cried, "Where is the promise of his coming? for since the fathers fell asleep, all things continue as they were." How long did the patience of God wait in the days of Noah. How many thousands of offences, even open and daring sins, do multitudes commit, and yet

God spares them, giving them time for repentance. Even the worst criminals are commonly permitted to live long enough to repent, if they have a heart to do so. Shall God show patience under such fearful provocations, and shall we be impatient under any wrongs committed against us? Oh let us "be followers," imitators, "of God, as dear children."

6. Especially has our Lord Jesus Christ left us an illustrious example of forbearance, meekness, and patience: "He was brought as a lamb to the slaughter; and as a sheep before her shearers is dumb, so he opened not his mouth." His forbearance towards his enemies when on earth was amazing. Legions of angels would have fought his battles with men, if he had bid them do so. But his hands and his heart were both full of blessings, not curses. He bore all, he endured all, he murmured not, he fretted not, he said no hard things, he felt no unkindness, he was all gentleness and love. In all this he left us an example, that we should follow his steps. "If we suffer with him, we shall also reign with him."

7. "Finally, be ye all of one mind, having compassion one of another; love as brethren, be pitiful, be courteous: not rendering evil for

evil, or railing for railing; but contrariwise blessing; knowing that ye are thereunto called, that ye should inherit a blessing. For he that will love life, and see good days, let him refrain his tongue from evil, and his lips that they speak no guile: let him eschew evil, and do good; let him seek peace, and ensue it. For the eyes of the Lord are over the righteous, and his ears are open unto their prayers: but the face of the Lord is against them that do evil. And who is he that will harm you, if ye be followers of that which is good? But and if ye suffer for righteousness' sake, happy are ye: and be not afraid of their terror, neither be troubled." 1 Pet. 3:8–14. "If when ye do well, and suffer for it, ye take it patiently, this is acceptable with God." 1 Pet. 2:20. "For it is better, if the will of God be so, that ye suffer for well-doing than for evil-doing." 1 Pet. 3:17. Every wise man has found trial good for him.

Lord Campbell, Chief-justice of England, says, "Little do we know what is for our permanent good. Had Bunyan been discharged, and allowed to enjoy his liberty, he no doubt would have returned, filling up his intervals of leisure with field preaching; his name would not have survived his own generation, and he would have done little for the religious improvement of mankind. The prison doors were shut upon him for twelve years. Being cut off from the external world, he communed with his own soul, and inspired by Him who touched Isaiah's hallowed lips with fire, he composed the noblest allegory, the merit of which was first discovered by the lowly, but which is now lauded by the most refined critics; and which has done more to awaken piety and to enforce the precepts of Christian morality, than all the sermons that have been published by all the prelates of the Anglican church."

In God's plan, to descend is first; to ascend comes afterwards. We must sink that we may rise. Good old Berridge says, "Afflictions, desertions, and temptations are as needful as consolations. Jonah's whale will teach a good lesson as well as Pisgah's top; and a man may sometimes learn as much from being a night or a day in the deep, as from being forty days in the mount. I see Jonah come out of a whale cured of rebellion. I see Moses go up into the mount with meekness, and come down in a huff and break the tables. Further, I see three picked disciples attending their Master into the mount, and falling asleep there. It is well for you to be clothed in sackcloth while you tarry in the wilderness. Look upward, and press forward. Heaven's eternal hills are before you, and Jesus stands with arms wide open to receive you. One hour's sight and enjoyment of the Bridegroom in his palace above will make you forget all your troubles on the way."

Three remarks are offered in conclusion:

1. We see the unspeakable value of religious truth. It is a stay and a joy when all comforts and resources of earth fail. Even wicked men have often confessed its power. Before his own mind was influenced by religious hopes or principles, Richard Cecil made the following observations:

"I see two unquestionable facts. 1. My mother is greatly afflicted in circumstances, body, and mind, and yet she cheerfully bears up under all by the support she derives from constantly retiring to her closet and to her Bible. 2. My mother has a secret spring of comfort of which I know nothing; while I, who give an unbounded loose to my appetites, and seek pleasure by every means, seldom or never find it. If, however, there is any such secret in religion, why may I not attain to it as well as my mother? I will immediately seek it from God."

Indeed, so cold, so barren is infidelity, so destitute of consolatory power, that many have borne a testimony like that of Cecil, and these not merely the weak, but also the strong. The prince among German historians was Niebuhr. He was not merely a great sceptic, he was an infidel. He was a rationalist, and received nothing as true in revelation except what he chose. This man had a son, whose happiness lay near his heart. Did he wish him to be educated an infidel? Had he found his own system full of consolation? No. He says that he intends his boy "shall believe in the letter of the Old and New Testaments, and *I shall* nurture in him from his infancy a firm faith in all that I have lost or feel uncertain about."

2. Of course it is very important to study God's word. Would that we had once more a race of great Bible readers. There have been such, and they have been fat and flourishing. Jerome seems to have had the whole Scripture stored in his memory. Erasmus says of him, "Who ever learned by heart the whole Scriptures, or imbibed or meditated on them as he did?"

After his conversion, Tertullian was occupied day and night in reading God's word. He committed much of it to memory.

That great divine Witsius was able without a concordance to recite almost any passage of Scripture in the original words, and tell the book, chapter, and verse.

A few years since I had an acquaintance on the bench of the Supreme court of his own state, who quoted Scripture with readiness and accuracy, which showed that the word of God dwelt in him richly. In fact, eminent Christians the world over are characterized by constant and profound meditation on God's word. Oh that men would be persuaded to make God's testimonies their constant delight! Locke says, "If any man will obtain a true knowledge of the Christian religion, let him study the holy Scriptures, especially in the New Testament. Therein are contained the words of eternal life. It has God for its author, salvation for its end, and truth, without any mixture of error, for its matter."

3. Let us follow Christ. Let us be content to live and suffer with him. Robertson of Dublin says, "We hear in these days a great deal respecting rights—the rights of private judg-

ment, the rights of labor, the rights of property, and the rights of man. Rights are grand things, divine things in this world of God's; but the way in which we expound those rights, alas, seems to me to be the very incarnation of selfishness. I can see nothing noble in a man who is for ever going about calling for his own rights. Alas, alas for the man who feels nothing more grand in this wondrous, divine world than his own rights. Two thousand years ago, there was One here on this earth who lived the grandest life that ever has been lived yet—a life that every thinking man, with deeper or shallower meaning, has agreed to call divine. I read little respecting his rights, or of his claims of rights; but I have read a great deal respecting his duties. Every act he did he called a duty. I read a very little in that life respecting his rights; but I hear a vast deal respecting his wrongs—wrongs infinite—wrongs borne with a majestic, godlike silence. His reward? His reward was the reward that God gives to all his true and noble ones—to be cast out in his day and generation, and a life conferring death at last—those were his rights!"

## CHAPTER XXIII.

### JOY.

Joy is delight at something esteemed good in possession or in prospect. It is one of the most powerful affections of the mind, and under the various names of satisfaction, cheerfulness, gladness, mirth, triumph, exultation, and glorying, enters in various degrees into the experience of mankind. Accordingly there are different words in the original Scriptures, as in our English text, signifying different degrees of joy.

The Scriptures draw a wide distinction between lawful and unlawful joy. This should always be maintained. The hypocrite, no less than the true servant of God—the stony-ground hearers, no less than those who received the word into good and honest hearts, had joy. This was very different in the two classes, but real in both. Unlawful joys are such as are not warranted by God's word or providence; such as spring from a thing of naught; such as have their basis in our wicked feelings; or such as have some iniquity as their exciting cause. They always prove men depraved, and always make men worse.

Lawful joys are of various kinds, some of which are common to mankind in all ages, such as the joy of mothers in beholding their smiling infants, the joy of the husbandman in harvest time, the joy of full health and vigor, inclining us to leap and run. There are also lawful joys in the exercise of our intellects, in solving difficulties, in achieving mental triumphs, in finding out hidden causes and dark sayings. True friendship has its joys. The soul, enlightened, comforted, transported by the power of God's Spirit, has great joy. It cannot be otherwise. The joy which we have in things temporal is inferior to that in things eternal. Things of sense cannot give such delight as the things of religion. It would be a calamity if any thing on earth was equal to the joys above.

One of the oldest and most mischievous slanders against religion is that it is unfriendly to enjoyment. Some admit that it makes ample provision for future blessedness, but contend that in this life it makes no proper return for the pleasures from which it cuts us off. This objection assumes many shapes, and is urged with various degrees of zeal and subtlety. More men feel its power than are ready to confess it. Particular answers may properly be given to particular forms of it. But some general remarks meet the objection in its leading principles.

1. Suppose it were a fact that God's people lose all joy on earth, and in this life have only sorrow and mortification, but a sure hope of being eternally saved; who is wise, the man that weeps for a day and rejoices for ever, or the man who is merry for a day and mourns for ever? No wise man doubts what answer should be given to that interrogatory. It is better to endure even a great evil for a moment than to have a comparatively small evil inflicted for a long time. It is agreeable to reason that great enjoyments are not to be sought if they will be followed by long-continued evils. To burn down a house to avoid the chilliness of a night, to take a powerful narcotic to relieve a slight pain, cannot be justified at the bar of reason. Can any temporal evil compare with everlasting sorrow? Can any earthly good compare with an eternity of bliss? What is an hour of joy to ages of woe? What is a day of weeping to ages of bliss? Even if in this

life piety gave nothing in lieu of what it takes away, and yet secured eternal life, it would be the height of wisdom to fear God and keep his commandments.

2. It is a suspicious circumstance that this objection is never made by the people of God, but only by those who know not whereof they affirm. No enemy of God has any experience by which he could possibly be qualified to judge whether the exercises of piety are conducive to enjoyment. What does an unconverted man know of faith, penitence, hope, peace, or the comfort of love? No more than a blind man knows of the colors of a rainbow; no more than the dead man knows of the joyousness of life. The unrelenting sinner knows nothing of the beauties of holiness, nothing of joy in the Holy Ghost, nothing of the attractions of Christ. To all such our Saviour is as a root out of a dry ground. To them his name has no music, nor is it as ointment poured forth. They are in darkness. They are blind. To those who cannot see, one painting has as few attractions as another. What do the deaf know of harmony? To them thunder and the flute, the roar of the lion and the song of the nightingale are the same.

Here is a miser. His joy is in heaping up gold, counting it over, increasing it, and beholding it with his eyes. A very sordid joy this is, but still it is a joy. Next neighbor to him lives the man who loves to feed the hungry, clothe the naked, bless his race, and make the widow's heart to sing for joy. See his eagerness and alacrity in doing good. His face beams with pleasure as he makes others glad. His dreams are of deeds of mercy. He rests not well unless he has done his best to make men happy, wise, and good. Then he sleeps as if he had nothing else to do. Is that miser a fit man to sit in judgment on this philanthropist? Can he weigh his deeds in the scale of sober truth, and tell the sum of all the joys that spring from a life of love? No more can a sinner tell what joys a saint may have.

3. This is the more certain as the joys of salvation consist of things invisible to the eye and unappreciable by any natural man. "The secret of the Lord is with them that fear him, and he will show them his covenant." Communion with God is wholly secret. Even one Christian knows not except on testimony when the richest blessings descend upon his brother. The child of God says,

In secret silence of the mind,
My heaven, and there my God I find.

Not so the wicked. When they have much joy, they kindle bonfires, they fire cannon, they get up processions, and march about with music. They mingle in the dance with the sound of the viol. How can he whose mirth finds scope in noise and revelry, be a judge of him whose joys make him love his closet and lead him to "be still?" Will mankind never learn the truth that true religion exposes not all to the gaze of uncircumcised men? Cecil says, "The joy of religion is an exorcist to the mind; it expels the demons of carnal mirth and madness." All Christians may adopt the language of one of the ancients: "We change, but do not lose real delights." Carnal men can never understand that saying of Augustine, "How sweet it is to want your sinful sweets."

4. Moreover the joys of God's people are sober things. Even Seneca said, "True joy is a serene and sober motion; and they are miserably out that take laughing for rejoicing." All our best joys are somewhat sober. The purer and greater they are, the more will they partake of seriousness. The husbandman who sees his abundant harvests secured; the mer-

chant whose risks in honorable trade have returned him many fold; the father whose child surpasses all his fond expectations; the teacher whose pupil is winning golden opinions from his generation—all have joys, but they are not to be expressed by laughter. Never does a noble father feel less like noisy merriment than when for the first time he hears the strains of a commanding eloquence poured forth from the lips of his darling son. So the joys of the saints are sober things. They are more: they are solemn; they are the joys of the Lord. They spring from forgiveness of sins, from peace with God, from glorious views of the great and dreadful God, from fellowship with the Father and the Son, through the Holy Ghost.

5. In true and great joy there is a calmness and stillness which men of the world do not understand. A little drop of joy in a human mind will agitate it. But when the fulness of divine comforts is poured upon the heart, it is quiet. It sits, admires, adores, walks softly, and is afraid of losing its hold on God. Reverence abounds in proportion to its joys. If a little joy makes one giddy, much will make him quiet; it may even overwhelm

him. For joy the disciples at first believed not the resurrection of Christ.

6. Besides, the joy of a wicked man is either in sin or in God's changing creatures. But the joy of the pious is chiefly in things the most pure, permanent, and powerful. So that they "rejoice evermore;" they even "rejoice in tribulation." If they have beyond most a keen sense and a sad experience of the ills of life, they have also a sovereign antidote. To them, as to others, affliction is not joyous, but grievous; nevertheless God reigns, Jesus lives, the covenant is ordered in all things and sure, and floods break forth to them in a dry and thirsty land where no water is, and thus they are made glad. It was not the unwashed stripes, nor the stocks, nor the innermost prison, nor midnight darkness, nor the gratuitous cruelty of the Philippian jailer, that made Paul and Silas sing praises unto God. These were all evils, and some of them very great grievances, but they could not drown the joys these holy men had in God through the hope of glory, and by the power of the eternal Spirit. When the Sun of righteousness arises in the soul with healing in his wings, midnight becomes noon, prisons are transformed into pal-

aces, and rills of sorrow are transmuted into rivers of delight. Did the martyrs die like abjects? Do real Christians weep and howl like the wicked when in trouble?

7. Add to this that all of us, even wicked men, have seen cases where joy expressed itself by tears. It is often so when one returns home after long absence or great perils. It is often so when enmities are buried, and a reconciliation is effected between old friends who had been sundered by strife and feuds. Why should it not be so when reconciliation with God through Jesus Christ is effected? Those tears of penitence which are shed by the child of God at the foot of the cross, are so sweet that he would fain weep them always. His gratitude often melts him down. Is thankfulness in its highest exercises painful to the virtuous mind? God's people may weep much without proving them unhappy.

8. It is also true that the pious often weep over the wicked who are deriding them as miserable. They mourn to see men rushing headlong to ruin. For twenty years that pious, delicate, refined lady has wept for the sins and follies of her son, father, or husband. Tears have been her meat day and night, while

he for whom they are shed seems more than ever bent on wickedness. She knows that unless he is speedily and thoroughly changed, she must soon bid him an eternal farewell. In God she is happy; by grace she is upheld. But rivers of water run down her eyes as she sees him sell himself to do evil. Long has she hoped for a change in his character; but hope deferred makes her heart sick. Her spirit almost dies within her. She weeps in secret places. He surprises her in tears, and charges all her sadness to religion. His vileness and impenitence are the cause of the sorrows he sees. Were all men seeking the Lord and walking in his ways, the righteous would not have half the griefs that now afflict them. Is it fair, is it just, by our wickedness to cover with sadness our best friends, and then to accuse their piety as the cause of their sadness?

9. God's people have also cause of grief in their own hearts. They are but partially sanctified. They have a world of trouble, not with their personal holiness, but with their want of more entire conformity to God. It is not the new man, but the old man; not the image of Christ, but the body of death that casts them down.

10. Finally, "out of the mouth of two or three witnesses shall every word be established." The witnesses in any matter must be both competent and credible. In the matter before us, God's people are capable of giving testimony. They have tried a life of sin, and found it vanity. They have tasted and seen that the Lord is gracious. They know both sides by experience. They can tell the truth if they will. And they are credible witnesses. The testimony of any two or three of millions of them would bring any man to prison or the gallows. What do these persons say? Without a dissenting voice in any age or country, they declare that "the ways of wisdom are ways of pleasantness, and all her paths are peace;" that they choose "to suffer affliction with the people of God, rather than enjoy the pleasures of sin for a season;" that Christ is a good Master, and his service freedom and joy. They all sing, "Blessed are they that dwell in thy house; they will be still praising thee." The Bible is full of such testimonies. God would never command his people to "rejoice evermore," if they had no cause for joy. Uninspired writers of all classes of God's people speak the same language with those who spoke

as they were moved by the Holy Ghost. Scripture and Christian experience alike declare, "True religion is joyful."

Haldane, on Rom. 5 : 2, says, "The Christian should speak nothing boastingly so far as concerns himself, but he has no reason to conceal his sense of his high destination as a son of God and an heir of glory. In this he ought to exult, in this he ought to glory, and in obedience to his Lord's command, to rejoice because his name is written in heaven. The hope of eternal salvation through the grace of our Lord Jesus Christ cannot but produce joy; for as there can be no true joy without such a hope, so it carries with it the very essence of joy."

Matthew Henry said, "You have been used to take notice of the sayings of dying men; this is mine, That a life spent in the service of God and communion with him, is the most comfortable and pleasant life that any one can live in this world."

His distinguished sister Mrs. Savage, dying, said, "I here leave the testimony of my experience, that Christ's yoke is easy, and his burden light."

In his commentary on the Galatians, Luther says, "Where Christ is truly seen, there must needs be full and perfect joy in the Lord, with peace of conscience."

Joseph Alleine said to his wife, "I live a voluptuous life; but it is upon spiritual dainties, such as the world knows not and tastes not of."

John Newton says, "I am sure the real Christian, who has peace with God and in his own conscience, has both the best title to joy and the best disposition for it."

Evans says, "It is the habitual and fixed judgment of every sincere Christian's mind, that Christ and his benefits are more to be rejoiced in than all worldly good."

Dr. Barrow says, "It is a scandalous misprision, vulgarly admitted, concerning religion, that it is altogether sullen and sour, requiring a dull, lumpish, morose kind of life, barring all delight, all mirth, all good-humor; whereas, on the contrary, it alone is the never-failing source of true, pure, steady joy, such as is deep-rooted in the heart, immovably founded in the reason of things, permanent like the immortal spirit wherein it dwelleth and like the eternal objects whereon it is fixed, which is not apt to fade or cloy, and is not subject to any impressions apt to corrupt or impair it."

It is a very noticeable fact, that true piety promotes joyfulness just in proportion as it is fervent, constant, and full of devout meditation. Bishop Horne having finished his commentary on the Psalms, and calling to mind the sweet thoughts he had had of God, says, "And now, could the author flatter himself that any one would take half the pleasure in reading the following exposition which he hath taken in writing it, he would not fear the loss of his labor. The employment detached him from the bustle and hurry of life, the din of politics, and the noise of folly; vanity and vexation flew away for a season, care and disquietude came not near his dwelling. He arose fresh as the morning to his task; the silence of the night invited him to pursue it; and he can truly say that food and rest were not preferred before it. Every psalm improved infinitely upon his acquaintance with it, and no one gave him uneasiness but the last; for then he grieved that his work was done. Happier hours than those which have been spent in these meditations on the songs of Zion he never expects to see in this world. Very pleasantly did they pass, and moved smoothly and swiftly along; for when thus engaged, he counted no time. They are gone, but have left a relish and a fragrance upon the mind, and the remembrance of them is sweet." In his commentary on the Romans, Dr. Chalmers quotes the above as "an actual specimen of heaven upon earth as enjoyed for a season of devotional contemplation on the word of God."

When such sentiments are rehearsed in the audience of God's people, they win their hearty and unanimous approbation. Are not all these witnesses to be believed? Who knows the truth, if they do not? Why do they thus agree, if they speak not the truth? What motive have they for giving false testimony?

All these views are heightened by a just comparison of the joys of the wicked and of the righteous, so far as they are different. For the righteous are not cut off from lawful delights even here; and the joys of all the wicked are strongly mixed with pains. "Many sorrows shall be to the wicked," says God. And although for a long time the enemies of God may seem joyful, may have great outward prosperity, may be very skilful in concealing their wounds, yet it is still true that "the wicked" have "many sorrows."

Their *consciences* are ill at ease. This is

true of all God's enemies. In the checks and clamors and forebodings of the monitor within are found present sorrows and infallible tokens of coming wrath. A man had better quarrel with his generation than with his conscience and his God. The righteous have peace with God, and their consciences are purged from dead works.

The wicked are sources of sorrow to *each other*. There are many aspirants for every post of honor, many rivals for preëminence in every profession, and many haughty despisers of the unfortunate and unsuccessful. Both in this life and the next, the wicked often torment each other. The righteous have pleasure in each other.

No amount of worldly success can ever *satisfy* the demands of wicked men. Their ambition, pride, covetousness, revenge, and envy burn the more vehemently the more they are gratified. To indulge them is to give them new power. They kindle a terrific, tormenting flame in every bosom, which is never extinguished but by the grace of God. "In all worldly joys there is a secret wound." But sin has lost its dominion over God's people. The truth has made them free. The Son of

God has wrought their deliverance. The very truths of religion, which gladden the hearts of believers, are sources of sorrow to the wicked. It is pleasing to the righteous, but dismal to the wicked, that this life will soon be over. It rejoices the humble, but afflicts the haughty, to know that God resisteth the proud and will surely abase them. The resurrection of the dead and the general judgment, two events quite essential to the completeness of Christian joy, are among the most gloomy of all topics of reflection to the wicked. The Lord reigns, says God's word, and the righteous shouts for joy; while the wicked says, "If that be so, my doom is sealed, and my damnation certain."

The wicked are not secured, but plagued by the covenant, promises, and perfections of God. Is God almighty? then he *can* destroy them. Is he righteous? then he *will* mark iniquity. Is he kind? they have provoked his displeasure by despising his mercy. Is he faithful and true? his threatenings will as certainly be executed as his promises.

Then the wicked are against themselves. They are self-destroyers. They hate life, and refuse good. They give their souls the wounds they feel. They stand in their own light. They fasten their own chains upon themselves. They will *for ever* do what many of them often do here; that is, curse their own folly.

And all nature is against them. The stars in their courses fight against them. Yea, "the stone shall cry out of the wall, and the beam out of the timber shall answer it." The fowls of the mountain, the beasts of the field, the serpents in the wall, and all the elements are ready at any moment to break out against the wicked, whenever God shall give them permission.

And their best joys are so short-lived. "As the crackling of thorns under a pot, so is the laughter of the fool." Eccl. 7:6. "The time is short. It remaineth that both they that have wives be as though they had none, and they that rejoice as though they rejoiced not." 1 Cor. 7:29, 30. And the end of their joys is sorrow, and the end of their sorrow is wailing and howling. So that always, in all worlds, "their vine is of the vine of Sodom and of the fields of Gomorrah; their grapes are grapes of gall, their clusters are bitter; their wine is the poison of dragons and the cruel venom of asps. Is not this laid up in store" for them? The joys of the righteous, on the other hand, are pure. They never cloy the appetite. They are salutary, and do good as a medicine. They last. They outlast the sun. Where the joy of the saints begins to be absolutely perfect, there the joy of sinners ends for ever.

> "See their short course of vain delight
> Closing in everlasting night."

O the impenetrable gloom of despair! O that night which will have no morning!

The objects of Christian joy are clearly set forth in Scripture. The chief of these is God himself. So says David, "I will go unto the altar of God, unto God my exceeding joy." Psa. 43:3. Paul says, "And not only so, but we joy in God." Rom. 5:11. Again, "Rejoice in the Lord always; and again I say, rejoice." Phil. 4:4. Isaiah says, "I will greatly rejoice in the Lord; my soul shall be joyful in my God; for he hath clothed me with the garments of salvation; he hath covered me with the robe of righteousness, as a bridegroom decketh himself with ornaments, and as a bride adorneth herself with her jewels." Isa. 61:10. In Psalm 5:11, we read, "Let all those that put their trust in thee rejoice; let them ever shout for joy, because thou defendest them; let them also that love thy name be joyful in thee." So also in many other places we are exhorted and commanded to rejoice in the Lord. Above all, God is fitted to be an object of unfailing joy, because he is God, infinite, eternal, and unchangeable in all conceivable perfections. The fulness that is in him meets all our wants. The pious delight in God; so that prayer, which would otherwise be a task, and praise, which would otherwise be a mockery, are refreshing to the soul as it cries, "Abba, Father," and "Hallelujah." In like manner all the duties of the Christian life become pleasant by our joy in God. Our Rock is perfect. In him is no darkness at all. He is an ocean of love, an infinitude of matchless loveliness. When he speaks peace, none can give trouble. When he makes glad, none can give sorrow. The mind of the child of God has no more fears that the resources which are in God will ever fail, than the mariner has that the sea will go dry. There is none like Jehovah, none before him, none with him, none to be compared to him, none besides him.

Our Lord Jesus Christ is a special object of joy. "Whom, having not seen, ye love; in whom, though now ye see him not, yet believing, ye rejoice with joy unspeakable and full of glory." 1 Pet. 1: 8. None like him gives "the oil of joy for mourning, and the garment of praise for the spirit of heaviness." Isa. 61 : 3. This joy, of which Christ is the object, is founded upon his person, his design in coming into the world, the perfection of his obedience, the completeness of his sufferings, the excellence of his doctrine, the virtue of his blood-shedding, the spotlessness and amplitude of his righteousness, the glory of his intercession, the perpetuity of his kingdom, the blessed provisions of the covenant of which he is the surety, the justification, adoption, sanctification, peace with God, access to the mercy-seat, communion with the Father, growth in grace, and final victory accomplished through our blessed Saviour. Truly "this is life eternal, to know God, and Jesus Christ whom he has sent." "Christ was set for a light to the Gentiles, that he should be for salvation to the ends of the earth." Acts 13:47. Would you avail yourself of all the fulness and fatness that are here? "Consider the apostle and high-priest of your profession, Christ Jesus." Set your faith steadfastly in him. Say with Peter, "We believe and are sure that thou art that Christ, the Son of the living God." John 6:69. Your joy in Christ will ever be proportioned to your faith in him. Christ is never truly revealed to the soul of a believer, but he is made more or less joyful in him. It is so in the first dawn of a good hope; it is so in fuller manifestations of his glory; it is so in the day when Christ leads the soul into his banqueting-house, and his banner over it is love. Then its language is, "Stay me with flagons, comfort me with apples; for I am sick of love."

In like manner the third person of the Godhead is an object of joy. So Paul declares that "the kingdom of God is not meat and drink, but righteousness, and peace, and joy in the Holy Ghost." Rom. 14:17. Joy in the Holy Ghost may chiefly signify joy by the power and grace of the Spirit. But even then this language would not be used in a case where one despised that blessed person. No man has joy worth having without the Spirit; and no man has the Spirit who holds him in contempt. The Spirit gives holy delight in holy things.

Christians also rejoice in God's providence. "The Lord reigneth, let the earth rejoice; let the multitude of the isles be glad thereof."

They also delight in the house of God, and cry, "How amiable are thy tabernacles, O Lord of hosts." In the associated people of God, his church, they also rejoice, saying, "If I forget thee, O Jerusalem, let my right hand forget her cunning; if I do not remember thee, let my tongue cleave to the roof of my mouth; if I prefer not Jerusalem above my chief joy." Psa. 137 : 5, 6. In his word too they have great joy. David said, "Thy testimonies are the rejoicing of my heart." "How sweet are thy words to my taste; yea, sweeter than honey to my mouth." Psa. 119 : 103. So God's people rejoice in all that pertains to God, all that is pleasing to him, all that makes them like him.

If these views be correct, then it follows,

1. That the knowledge of divine things is very necessary to the existence and completion of a true Christian character. Charnock says, "Who can delight in God that hath no sense of the goodness of his nature and the happiness of fruition? Who can delight in his ways who does not understand him as good and indulgent in his precepts as he is sweet and bountiful in his promises? If we did know him, we should be as easily drawn to rejoice in him, as

by ignorance we are induced to run from him. Such charms would be transmitted to our hearts as would constrain a joy in them in spite of all other delights in perishing pleasures. Knowledge of God is a necessary preface to spiritual joy in him. 'My meditation of him shall be sweet; I will be glad in the Lord.' Psalm 104:34. . . . What pleasure can a man, ignorant of God's nature and delightful perfections, and that represents him through some mistaken gloss which imprints unworthy notions of God in his mind—what pleasure can such a man take in approaching to God, or what greater freedom can he have in coming to him, than a malefactor in being brought before a judge?" Let the knowledge of God therefore dwell in you richly in all wisdom and spiritual understanding. If you would be more joyful, know more of divine things. "Acquaint thyself with God, and be at peace." "Search the Scriptures."

2. Our joy need not be feeble and sickly, but provision is made that it may be ample. Even when sorrowful, we may be always rejoicing. 2 Cor. 6:10. Men may persecute and defame us; but this is our rejoicing, the testimony of our consciences. 2 Cor. 1:12.

We may be exceedingly glad in the duties of religion, and find it good to draw near to God. If kept from uniting with his people in public worship, he himself can be to us for a little sanctuary. When the springs of earthly comfort go dry, then to the believer "the parched ground shall become a pool, and the thirsty land springs of water." Isa. 35:7. When we are denied the things of the world, we may rejoice in the assurance of a better and more enduring substance. When every thing looks dark and discouraging for the interests of religion, then we may rejoice in knowing that Jesus Christ loves the church better than we do, and that she is graven on the palms of his hands. Our joy may go so far as to make us glory in tribulation. It can keep us from regretting that we have undertaken the service of Christ; so that the more we are tried, the more it will be manifest that we cleave to him with purpose of heart; and though we may be weary in his service, we are not weary of his service.

3. True holy joy is one of the most operative of all the gifts of the Spirit. Nothing will more certainly or thoroughly arouse men to do their utmost for the cause of God. Paul

testifies of the church of Macedonia, that "in a great trial of affliction, the abundance of their joy and their deep poverty abounded unto the riches of their liberality." 2 Cor. 8:2. Yea, he declares that their joy made them willing to do more than it was in their power to do. This holy joy is the animating principle of true obedience. Thus "David and the elders of Israel, and the captains over thousands, went to bring up the ark of the covenant of the Lord out of the house of Obed-edom with joy." 1 Chron. 15:25. Thus in the days of Ezra holy men "kept the dedication of the house of God with joy." Ezra 6:16. So says Isaiah, "The meek shall increase their joy in the Lord, and the poor among men shall rejoice in the Holy One of Israel." Isa. 29:19.

Indeed the human mind is so constituted as to be easily and powerfully moved by all the class of pleasing affections, of which none is more powerful than joy. And so we uniformly find men to be happy whose lives are given up to labor for the good of others. Their holy delight in deeds of mercy leads them to lives of self-denial, and this exercise of their loving dispositions strengthens them. Among the many thousands of letters I have received, not a few have been from missionaries in frontier settlements and in heathen lands; and although some of them have detailed painful scenes, yet I do not remember one that was in a despondent mood. So wherever you find one animated by the spirit of Howard or of Elizabeth Fry, you invariably find them of a happy temper.

Their converts were to the apostles a joy and a crown. Paul says to some, "Now we live, if ye stand fast." Even stripes and prisons and chains could not repress the ardor of holy men of old. They were not sent a warfare at their own charges. God was with them.

4. This subject explains to us how the people of God are brought to bear so well the losses, sorrows, bereavements, and disappointments of life.

> "Joy never feasts so high
> As when the first course is of misery."

The highest joy to the Christian almost always comes through suffering. "No flower can bloom in paradise which is not transplanted from Gethsemane. No one can taste of the fruit of the tree of life that has not tasted of the fruits of the tree of Calvary." God's people know this. If tears are their meat day and night, their sadness drives them to God, and with joy they draw water out of the wells of salvation. Isa. 12:3. The crops may fail, but the covenant stands sure. We and all nature may change, but God is the same. To those who put their trust in him, he is without intermission Father, Friend, God, Redeemer, Saviour, Comforter, Portion, and eternal All; and so he will continue for ever. He who has God for his God, ought not to be cast down because the world casts him out. He who has such joys, ought not to be humbly begging the world for its favor, nor seeking a slice from the loaf of ungodly men. He who cares not for eternal things, may busy himself to be in fashion here; but when the joy of the Lord is our strength, we ought not to grieve at little things. Thus saith the Lord, "Strengthen ye the weak hands, and confirm the feeble knees. Say to them that are of a fearful heart, Be strong, fear not: behold, your God will come with vengeance, even God with a recompense; he will come and save you." Isa. 35:3, 4. In all the righteous is more or less fulfilled the prophecy: "The ransomed of the Lord shall return, and come to Zion with songs and everlasting joy upon their heads: they shall obtain joy and gladness, and sorrow and sighing shall flee away." Isa. 35 : 10.

Nor are they glad for nothing. There are no comforts, no cordials, no delights like those which God gives to his well-beloved. To the blind world all religious joys may seem like enthusiasm; but the human mind is never more sound, its operations are never more safe than when in holy triumph the people of God take joyfully the spoiling of their goods, or are filled with ecstasy at the suffering of reproach for the name of Christ. The hosannas and hallelujahs of the house of God on earth are as seasonable and as reasonable as those of the temple not made with hands. It is an apostolic direction, "Is any merry, let him sing psalms." We have apostolic example also for singing praises to God in the most trying circumstances. Paul says, "We faint not; but though our outward man perish, yet the inward man is renewed day by day. For our light affliction, which is but for a moment, worketh for us a far more exceeding and eternal weight of glory; while we look not at the things which are temporal, but at the things which are eternal." 2 Cor. 4 : 16–18. It has long since been determined in the church that it is better to suffer for

Christ, if he will give strength and joy, than to live in ease and quiet. The hotter the battle, the more renowned the victory. The harder the labor, the sweeter the rest. The darker the night, the more joyous the morning.

5. It is wise to be religious, to be strictly, earnestly, scripturally religious. All the doctrines of revealed religion are true, safe for man, honorable to God. All the duties of true religion are reasonable and ennobling. Christ is no hard Master; he requires nothing degrading. In the progress of revolution, Napoleon Buonaparte judged it necessary to divorce the wife of his youth. In accomplishing this object he required her son to act a part, and publicly declare his approbation of the measure while all the time his heart was burning with rage at the atrocity perpetrated against his mother. Here was real degradation. Jesus Christ has sometimes called his people to die for him, but he never asked one of his servants to do a mean thing, a thing which made him gnaw his tongue for resentment, and yet to profess that all was necessary. No; he imposes no duties but those which will elevate our character for ever.

The prospects opened before the truly pious

are no less pleasing than their duties. It is not denied that there are conflicts and sharp sorrows in the service of God; but even they end in the greater joys. An old writer says, "Give me a man that, after many secret stings and hard conflicts in his breast, upon a serious penitence and sense of reconciliation with his God, hath attained to a quiet heart and is walking humbly and closely with God; I shall bless and emulate him as a subject of true joy; for spiritually there never is a perfect calm but after a tempest. . . . Set me at full variance with myself, that I may be at peace with thee, O God." Nothing but a true and powerful religious principle could have made Paul, in the depths of his sufferings, say, "I am filled with comfort, I am exceeding joyful in all our tribulation." 2 Cor. 7 : 4.

6. It is the duty of all God's people so to live that they may *enjoy* religion. Much has been done for them; they ought to make much of it. Many and great things have been granted them; many and great thanks should be rendered by them. Unless our religion makes us to some extent joyful, it quite fails of its object. From this remark we should except cases of deep melancholy. Poor Cow-

per exclaimed, "I arise in the morning like an infernal frog out of Acheron, covered with the ooze and mud of melancholy." Again, "Could I be translated to Paradise, unless I could leave my body behind me, my melancholy would cleave to me there." Although tempests, earthquakes, and shattered nerves are not under the absolute control of either reason or religion, yet blessed be God that he has spoken many kind things to the timid, the feeble-minded, and the sorrowing; so that if disease allows the mind any fair play, the pious have at least seasons of sunshine.

Jesus Christ said that his teachings were designed to make his people happy. "These things have I spoken unto you, that my joy might remain in you, and that your joy might be full." Again, "These things I speak in the world, that they might have my joy fulfilled in themselves." John 15 : 11; 17 : 3. John says the same: "These things write we unto you, that your joy may be full." 1 John 1 : 4. So that if we have no religious enjoyment, it is either because we have no religion or but little religion, or because we are sadly afflicted and diseased. True piety is as sure to have joy, as it is to have penitence or faith in it.

"The fruit of the Spirit is joy." Gal. 5 : 22. "They that sow in tears, shall," sooner or later, "reap in joy." Psa. 126 : 5. Satan may tempt, providences may look dark, friends may grow cold, faith may be weak, disease may enfeeble and for a time bury the mind in a cloud, but whenever reason reascends the throne and grace resumes her sway, there will be joy. Christians, labor to be happy. Strive to commend your religion by being well "anointed with the oil of gladness."

7. This subject specially invites our attention to heavenly things. God's people have real satisfaction here, but in his immediate "presence is fulness of joy; at his right hand are pleasures for evermore." Psa. 16 : 11. God's people through life long to be clothed upon with their house which is from heaven. And so "when desire cometh, it is a tree of life." Prov. 13 : 12. In that blessed world sin, temptation, sorrow, sickness, and death have no place. Faith is swallowed up in sight, and hope in enjoyment. Ignorance gives place to perfect knowledge. Here the soul had long said of God, "Whom have I in heaven but thee? and there is none upon earth that I desire besides thee." There it sees his full glories

revealed in the person of Jesus Christ, and is satisfied to all eternity in the visions of uncreated splendors. One of the ancients said, "Praise the sweetness of honey as much as thou canst, he who has never tasted it cannot understand the matter." The same is true of holy joys on earth, and much more of the perfect joys of heaven. Of the latter God gives his people a foretaste in the comforts of the Holy Ghost, which he dispenses here. It is true they are but as a few clusters from the vintage of Canaan, but they are enough to whet our appetite for the abundant and unmingled blessings of the spirits of just men made perfect.

Leighton says, "When we shall receive that rich and pure and abiding inheritance, that salvation which shall be revealed in the last time, and when time itself shall cease to be, then there shall be no more reckoning of our joys by days and hours, but they shall run parallel with eternity. Then all our love, that is now parcelled out upon the vanities among which we are here, shall be united and gathered into one and fixed upon God, and the soul shall be filled with the delight of his presence."

One of Bunyan's dying sayings was, "Oh, who is able to conceive the inexpressible and inconceivable joys that are in heaven? None but they who have tasted of them. Lord, help us to put such a value upon them here, that in order to prepare ourselves for them, we may be willing to forego the loss of all deluding pleasures here." Another was, "If you would be better satisfied what the beatifical vision means, my request is that you would live holily and go and see." Bishop Hall says, "My soul, while it is thus clogged and confined, is too strait to conceive of those incomprehensible and spiritual delights which thou, O God, hast provided for thy chosen ones who triumph with thee in heaven. Oh teach me then to wonder at that which I cannot attain to know, and to long for that happiness which I there hope to enjoy with thee for ever."

Meikle thus contrasts the present and the future life. He says, "In this life I may have at times a mortal health; but in that I shall have always eternal vigor. In this life I may have some tainted pleasures; but in that I shall have always pure delights and holy raptures. In this life I may have at times a few friends for a few days; but in that I shall have always all my friends about me for ever. In this life I may have at times some acres of ground; but in that I shall have always an unbounded inheritance in the heavenly Canaan. Here fine clothing of wool; there robes of righteousness and garments of glory. Here a house painted with vermilion; there 'a house not made with hands.' Here bread to eat and water to drink; there the hidden manna and the river of life. Here a portion of the good things of time; there the glorious treasures of eternity.

"As to spiritual good things, in this life I may have communications of grace; but in that life I shall have eternal glory. Here freedom from the reign of sin; there deliverance from the being of sin. Here glances of faith; there immediate vision. Here God in his ordinances; there uninterrupted communion. Here manifestations of love; there all the transports of eternal assurance and everlasting bliss. Here access to the throne of grace; there uninterrupted attendance at the throne of glory. Here I often sin against God; there I shall never offend the eyes of his glory. Here I go mourning without the sun; there my sun shall go down no more."

And so he carries the contrast entirely

through. Whatever evil you have here, you shall have the opposite good in heaven. Whatever good thing you have here, you shall have the same in perfection, or something far better, at God's right hand. To go to heaven is to "enter into the joy of thy Lord."

# CHAPTER XXIV.

## ZEAL.

"Zeal is the fire of love,
Active for duty, burning as it flies."

ZEAL is ardor, and is good or bad according to the principles from which it flows and the end to which it is directed. It is the life of every cause dependent on human exertions. The habits and tempers of men control its modes of operation. In religion its importance is very great, and its nature should be well understood. The Scriptures give precepts and examples, motives and encouragements on the whole subject.

So soon as the word *zeal* is pronounced, some seem alarmed. Men of the world and formalists speak much and feel more against all ardor in religion. "The natural man receiveth not the things of the Spirit of God." Some say, "If the Christian religion is true, why do its avowed friends manifest so little zeal in maintaining and propagating it?" This solemn inquiry admits of but one solution, namely, The best of men are but half awake.

Imperfection mars all human virtue here below. In all things we come short. Yet the very men who start such questions will, upon a turn, put the brand of fanaticism on all who manifest a lively interest in the salvation of men. Cecil says, "The world will allow a vehemence approaching to ecstasy on almost every subject but religion, which above all others will justify it." The real temper of wicked men is unchanged from generation to generation. As in the days of John the Baptist and of Christ, they are still like the children in the market-place. If we pipe, they will not dance. If we mourn, they will not lament. We must look elsewhere than to the world for rules of pious living, for guides to holiness. Even the visible church of God falls far below the true standard of holy fervency demanded in religion.

It is readily conceded that there is *false zeal* manifested for religion. The word of God so teaches. "They zealously affect you, but not well." Gal. 4:17. Of old Jehovah said, "Ephraim hath mixed himself among the people; Ephraim is a cake not turned." Here God admits that in some things his servant was strict and zealous. In others no less important, he was lax and cold. His zeal was partial, and so was deficient. In our Saviour's day, many showed much ardor in tithing mint, anise, and cummin; they passed over faith, justice, mercy, and the love of God. They strained at a gnat, and swallowed a camel. They made much ado about light things, but had no zeal for weighty things. What they did was in itself right, but what they left undone was indispensable. The religion of hypocrites is never symmetrical. It despises divine rules. Its code of laws is eclectic. It never submits to the whole will of Heaven.

All zeal which has for its object any thing forbidden in the oracles of God, as all will-worship and uncommanded austerities, is a false zeal. Something of this nature often enters largely into false religions. Human inventions in religion are multiform, and always dangerous. Admit one as any part of true piety, and there is no end to error and man's devices. God's word condemns a superstitious zeal. Before his conversion, Paul was "more exceedingly zealous of the traditions of his fathers" than "many his equals" in other respects. The world has always been and still is overstocked with a blind veneration for much that has been devised by man. The more of this kind of zeal any one has, the worse man is he. The priests of Baal "cried aloud, and cut themselves after their manner with knives and lancets, till the blood gushed out upon them." They were very zealous, and yet abominably wicked. Many a man is the worse citizen, neighbor, husband, father, brother, and friend, because his spurious zeal has perverted even the generous instincts of his nature.

The Scriptures condemn all blind zeal. They require every man to be fully persuaded in his own mind. Hooker says, "Zeal needeth a sober guide." He who has no "reason of the hope that is in him" is self-deceived. The terrible rebuke of Christ to the Samaritans, "Ye worship ye know not what," should alarm fiery zealots. Ignorance was a radical fault in the ardor of the Jews in apostolic times. Paul gives witness to their zeal for God, but adds that it was not according to knowledge. "For they being ignorant of God's righteousness, and going about to establish their own righteousness, have not submitted themselves to the righteousness of God." They put the law where they should place the gospel. They ignored the merits of Christ.

Sometimes zeal is contentious, and so betrays its spurious nature. Some build churches, endow asylums, defend the truth, yea, "preach Christ of contention, but not sincerely." Good to man and glory to God may be brought out of their labors; but they shall have no divine reward. Their works shall be burned up, and they shall suffer loss. Alas, how many forget that the wrath of man worketh not the righteousness of God. The greatest error of Paul before his conversion was, that "touching zeal, he persecuted the church." No darker sign can attend a religious profession than a cruel, supercilious, denunciatory spirit. "Bless, and curse not." "As we have opportunity, let us do good unto all men." "In meekness instructing those that oppose themselves."

Sometimes zeal is ostensibly for religion, but really for selfish ends. It will serve itself or a party, but not Christ. Men have compassed sea and land to make one proselyte, who, when made, was worse than before. His conversion was not to God, to duty, to holiness, to obedience. Those who plied him with means and arguments never desired his sanctification; they wanted his name and influ ence. In every age are found some professors of religion who rejoice more at making a proselyte than a convert; who are more pleased at seducing an unstable soul out of another into their own communion, than in plucking a brand from the everlasting burnings. This is indeed sad. Let such learn what manner of spirit they are of.

Zeal is often boastful and ostentatious. Jehu said, "Come with me, and see my zeal for the Lord of hosts." The old Pharisees sounded a trumpet before them when they were about to give alms; and for a pretence, they made long prayers. Even in pious men there is often a mixture of motives; and vanity comes in to mar their good works.

Sometimes zeal which otherwise appears well is but temporary, and so proves its spurious nature. At one time the Galatians would, if possible, have given their eyes to the man who was the means of their conversion. They seemed to begin in the spirit, but they ended in the flesh. They were soon turned aside. Their zeal did not last. They did run well for a time, but by and by they were hindered. They counted as an enemy the man who told them the truth. With their ardor they lost also their comfort in religion, so that Paul says to them, "Where is the blessedness ye spake of?"

In some cases zeal betrays its spurious character by the self-righteousness which it engenders. Christ taught his disciples, saying, "When ye have done all these things which are commanded you, say, We are unprofitable servants; we have done that which it was our duty to do." But some come away from the most solemn acts of devotion puffed up with pride, and ready to say to others, "Stand by thyself, come not near to me; for I am holier than thou." Of such God says, "These are a smoke in my nose, a fire that burneth all the day. I will recompense into their bosom." Isa. 65:5. "What hast thou that thou hast not received?" "Not unto us, not unto us, but to thy name give glory." "From me is thy fruit found."

But there is *a true and scriptural zeal.* All fervor in religion is not rash, blind, boastful, contentious, superstitious, temporary, or self-righteous. Genuine zeal is "the wisdom that is from above," and "is first pure, then peaceable, gentle, easy to be entreated, full of mercy and good fruits, without partiality, and without hypocrisy." Jas. 3:17. True zeal has no by-ends. Its principle and its aim are holiness. It leads to purity. For peace it will give up every thing but truth and a good conscience. It wars not after the flesh. It rejects carnal weapons. It is full of courtesy, candor, and kindness. It forbears. It forgives. It pities. It yields to reasonable arguments and suggestions. It is not obstinate. It hates malice. It loves mercy. Its fruits are wholesome and healthful. It pours blessings both on its objects and its subjects, on its friends and its foes. It cares not for vain distinctions which men of the world regard; but without partiality, without respect of persons, it does good to all men, especially to the household of faith. It is un-unfeigned. It feels all it professes, and more. It dotes not "about questions and strifes of words whereof cometh envy, strife, railings, evil-surmisings, and perverse disputings." Its zeal is for the simple truth. True zeal is not light without heat; yet it is modest. If God be glorified and his cause advanced, it is willing to remain unnoticed. It is ready to contend earnestly, but not bitterly, for the truth. If it falls into error, it is not incorrigible. It is moved with alacrity, but not hurried by impetuosity. It leaves a sweet savor on the minds of all the pious. It seeks not its own. Its glory is to glorify God. Its happiness is to make others blessed. It loves rich and poor, and delights in blessing the bond and the free. It weeps over human wickedness. It rejoices in all truth, in all goodness.

Though mild and meek, it is not timid and cringing. When the enemy comes in like a flood, the Lord lifts up a standard against him in the person of his humble people. Then "the righteous are as bold as a lion." The servant of God is firm, not by his natural strength, but through the grace that is given unto him.

This zeal lasts; it is not fickle. It is a fire fed by the oil poured into the heart by the Holy Ghost. It loves its toils, and even its sufferings for Christ and his people. Its meat and its drink is to do and to suffer the will of God. It is different from any principle which governs the men of the world. It is enlightened; it is "wisdom." It hates vainglory. It is strongest when self is most out of view. It finds its aliment in a lively faith in the lively oracles. It hopes against hope. Because it springs from love to Christ, it fears not self-denial. In no case is it indeed perfect. This keeps the most zealous good men in an humble frame. There is probably more true zeal in the church of God than is sometimes supposed to exist; yet there is far less than the miseries of men, the love of Christ, and the glory of God imperatively demand.

The ways in which a genuine zeal may exert itself are many. It does not forget its own immortal interests. He whose heart is warmed with fire from heaven, does not neglect his own soul, but keeps his heart with all diligence, for out of it are the issues of life. Like Henry Martyn, he says, "My first great business on earth is the sanctification of my own soul." The first step towards doing good is to be good. It is a sad spectacle when we see men busy here and there, but caring not to make their own calling and election sure. It is mournful when a man is constrained to take up the lamentation, "They made me the keeper of the vineyards, but mine own vineyard have I not kept." We are never more mistaken than when we imagine ourselves called upon to do some duty which interferes with the cultivation of personal piety. Our blessed Saviour has set us a good example in this respect. Though he was charged with the business of redeeming a world, and though he knew that his personal ministry on earth would be very short, yet he never neglected communion with God. He spent whole nights in devotion. The zeal of God's house consumed him. None walked with God so closely as he. Indeed his personal devotedness to God was the aliment of all his holy fervor. Be wise for thyself.

But true charity looks not only on its own things, but also on the things of others. It takes the beam out of its own eye, but it is then ready to take the mote out of its neighbor's eye. It first weeps for its own sins; it then mourns for the iniquities of others. Thus Jeremiah said to his nation, "If ye will not hear it, my soul shall weep in secret places over your pride, and mine eye shall weep sore and run down with tears." Ezekiel also tells us that when God was about to send his messengers to destroy the land and to waste its people, he sent before them an angel with an inkhorn, to "set a mark upon the foreheads of the men that sighed and cried for all the abominations that were done." Often all that the righteous can do is to weep in secret, and cry, "Oh that the wickedness of the wicked were come to an end!" Matthew Henry says, "The sight of sin either makes a man sad or guilty. If we see it, and are not sorrowful, we are guilty." Blessed is the man who weeps for the wickedness of men, and as he has opportunity testifies against it, and warns men of coming judgments.

Another proper field for pious zeal is the sanctuary. There it makes and there it performs many holy vows. There it swells the voice of joy and praise. There it beholds the King in his beauty. There it is delighted with memories of past mercies, and ravished with visions of future glories. The prayers appropriate to the sanctuary are sure to meet with a hearty response from all who have heavenly zeal. The anthems of praise belonging to the courts of the Lord's house animate the humble soul, and awaken longings for heavenly glories.

True zeal also delights in sustaining sober, practical, and benevolent institutions, whose aim is to enlighten mankind, elevate public sentiment, and bring sinners to Christ. Nor will a true zeal forget the family. A zeal which is warm and active abroad, but cold and formal at home, is not of the genuine kind. He who lets the fire die out on the domestic altar cannot be a useful member of the church of Christ. Could we once see a generation of the friends of Christ duly attentive to the duties of piety at home, it would be a better sign of the approach of the latter day's glory than has yet appeared. Oh that God would now turn the hearts of the parents to the children; and the hearts of the children to the parents.

Another fit work for true zeal is found in direct personal efforts for the salvation of impenitent men around us. Genuine religious ardor watches for souls. Above all things, it delights to win souls. It seeks, yea, it makes occasions to speak a word for God. It is ingenious in devices to do good. It will try a thousand ways and a thousand times. It sows its seed in the morning; in the evening it withholds not its hand. If successful, it greatly rejoices, and gives God all the glory.

In our age and country there is special need of unquenchable zeal in religion. Now and here every thing is active. Evil grows apace; iniquity comes in like a flood. The wicked sleep not except they have done some mischief. Population and wealth grow as by magic. Enterprise is unparalleled. While good men sleep the enemy is sowing tares. Error is rife and restless. Nothing but mighty efforts, owned and blessed of God, can save millions of our people from a worldly spirit, which will, if it prevail, drown them in destruction and perdition. Lord, increase our faith. If a man could say but one sentence to his generation in the assured hope that it would be heard and heeded, he could hardly say any thing better than this: "It is good to be zealously affected always in a good thing."

The interests of society in its present state call for our best efforts. The earth is filled with violence and with the habitations of cruelty. To this remark there is no exception beyond the pale of the church of God and the sphere of her influence. Jewish prejudice, Mohammedan delusion, Popish superstition, Pagan idolatry, and baptized infidelity are crushing alike the best feelings and the brightest hopes of men. General happiness in nations ruled by maxims of wickedness and by men of impiety never has been and never can be secured. The little knowledge and liberty and virtue now on earth are the fruit of the tears and toils and blood of men of whom the world was not worthy.

From the temporal miseries of men who are without God in the world, we readily pass in thought to a death without comfort, a judgment without mercy, an immortality without the life everlasting, an eternity without light, without hope, and without change but from bad to worse. There is indeed something dreadful even here in

> "That cloud of mind
> Which cannot, dares not see the light;"

in those dark and gloomy apprehensions and contemplations which fill the minds of the guilty and superstitious. But it is still more true that bones of iron and sinews of brass will not be able to endure the weight of that sore displeasure which will fall on the wicked in a future world. There is something glorious in the peace and joy of a pardoned sinner on earth; but something ineffably grand and ravishing in the thought of a soul saved, disenthralled, perfected in heaven. Eye hath not seen, ear hath not heard, the heart of man hath not conceived the good things which God hath prepared for them that love him, nor the evil things which he hath treasured up for them that hate him. Infinite joys and infinite woes, fathomless mercy and fathomless misery, heavenly bliss and eternal wrath depend on the course men's souls pursue in time. That course is often determined by means of things which at the time seem trivial. "Behold how great a matter a little fire kindleth." Surely every act of human life may draw after it consequences so vast as to defy all powers of computation, and even of conception. A word may subvert an empire. A word may save a soul. "A word fitly spoken, how good is it." It is like apples of gold in a network of silver.

Nor is any thing in religion more conducive to our happiness than liveliness in the cause of God. Holy ardor is as oil to machinery; it makes every thing work smoothly. God meets him that rejoiceth and worketh righteousness. His most arduous duties refresh his spirit. He comes to them and from them not as a hireling, but as a child who delights in the law of God after the inner man.

Nor should we ever forget that God abhors all services in religion where the heart is wanting. A religion without zeal is offensive to God. Duly considered, it is monstrous to all right-minded men. The insincere will God smite, and there shall be no healing.

A wise man said, "It is better to do a little

good than a great deal of mischief." Very few will attempt a logical refutation of this aphorism. It is better to inspire one man with the love of truth than to bring a whole generation under the power of error and delusion. It is better to convert one sinner from the error of his ways than to make all Israel to sin. It is better to fill one heart with joy at an act of love than to fill every valley with wailing by deeds of malignity.

Besides, it is the plan of God that great results should follow apparently small beginnings. That mighty oak whose trunk has become the keel of the enormous ship was once a small plant, which the tread of a lamb or kid or fawn might have crushed. To plant an acorn is better than wantonly to slay a forest. The necessity of doing even a little good, when we can do no more, arises from the fact that so many and so mighty evil influences are abroad, and from the further fact that life is made up of deeds the effect of any one of which may be apparently trivial. The enemy is always at work; therefore should we be ever diligent. If the friends of truth are inactive, the world will soon be ruined. Destruction wastes at noon-day. Publicity is not to be sought, but neither is it to be shunned, by the friends of God, if he calls them before kings and courts and crowds. And as wickedness distils its influences secretly, so let wholesome truths be taught privately.

The enemy has some advantages. One is, that it is easier to pull down than to build up, to destroy than to create, to corrupt than to purify, to kill than to make alive. The foes of God are also lively. Their industry is worthy of a better cause. It is high time that all right-minded men should awake. For though they are few and feeble, God is on their side. Nothing is too hard for him. None can resist him. None can deceive him. He can bind the strong man, and then spoil his goods. "If God be for us, who can be against us?" If he make bare his arm, all nations shall tremble before him.

Let none of the friends of God forget that a little done every day will in the end amount to much.

> Sands form the mountains;
> Minutes make the year.

This is the secret of a life of usefulness. He who is faithful in the least, is the man whose virtue will not fail him on great occasions.

Christians should endeavor to do good in the least exceptionable way. "Let not your good be evil spoken of." "A good action indiscreetly performed is little better than a prudent piece of mischief." The carnal mind sufficiently opposes holiness without our needlessly irritating it. Cunning is indeed odious and wicked; but prudence is a duty. Trick is despicable. Address is obligatory. Paul's life affords many admirable examples of consummate wisdom in allaying prejudices, in quelling storms of human passion. "Whatsoever thy hand findeth to do, do it with thy might." "No man liveth to himself."

What a blessing to thousands it would be if all who can would lend or give good books to those who will read them. Milton well says that "books are not absolutely dead things; but do contain a progeny of life in them to be as active as that soul was whose progeny they are; nay, they do preserve as a vial the purest efficacy and extraction of that living intellect that bred them. . . . As good almost kill a man as kill a good book: who kills a man, kills a reasonable creature; but he who destroys a good book, kills reason itself. . . . A good book is the precious life-blood of a master-spirit, embalmed and treasured up on purpose to a life beyond life." I had rather be the author of Poor Joseph, a little tract, than of Homer's Iliad; or of the Swearer's Prayer, another little tract, than of Vattel's Law of Nations. To spread the knowledge of God by good books has long been a favorite method of doing good.

Another excellent method of usefulness is giving good advice. Almost all the practical good in this world is the result of good counsel, no small part of which is offered without solicitation, but on a proper occasion and in a right spirit. In giving advice, beware of dogmatizing and of all superciliousness.

In all plans of usefulness, pay due attention to the young. They are alike the hope of the church and of the state. Their habits are not yet inveterate; their sensibilities are not yet blunted. By kindness you may win their confidence. By perseverance you may make an impression on their minds and hearts.

Abound in prayer. Many a time it has opened heaven. Many a time it has opened prisons, opened doors of usefulness, opened the hand of parsimony and the heart of severity. It has both opened and shut the mouth of the grave. By it the cause of righteousness has success and stability. By it the feeble gain the victory and the slow win the race. "What we win by prayer we wear with comfort." Do all you can to stir up a spirit of zeal in your own heart. Get the strongest conceptions you can of the value of eternal things, especially by visiting dying beds and deserted souls, and then flee to your closet and cry mightily to God for his blessing on the perishing. "He who has God's heart shall not want his arm."

God has closely united our duty and our happiness in a thousand ways. In the fall of 18—, a young man was spending a vacation with a friend. He found in his mansion elegance, hospitality, and piety. The grounds were large, and the family was more than commonly agreeable. He could ride or read, or engage in fishing or hunting. For a few days he greatly enjoyed the change. His health needed recruiting, and he felt better. But soon uneasiness followed. He lacked full employment. He was not sure that he could give a good account of his mode of spending time. He began to feel guilty. Killing birds and catching fish, not so much for food as for pastime, seemed to him of doubtful propriety. To ride without an object was uninteresting. In short, he was in danger of becoming melancholy.

At this time he heard of a lot of Bibles in the neighborhood for distribution among the poor. He determined to walk and scatter this good seed. He went from house to house, meeting with various kinds of reception, all of them civil and some of them cheering.

At length he came to a plain house, and was welcomed by a plain woman at the door. He entered, and saw seated around the fire five of her children, not one of whom could walk or utter an articulate sound. As he entered they raised a hideous noise. Their mother said it expressed pleasure at seeing him. Seldom has one beheld a more painful sight. Besides these five was a son of sound mind, but deformed and crippled in his lower limbs. He was a shoemaker. There was also a daughter well-grown and strong, but of a feeble mind and violent temper.

The mother of these children was a poor widow. The visitor introduced the subject of religion, which he found a theme welcome to her. The Bible was there. It looked as if it was well read. When this woman spoke, it was chiefly of the goodness of God. He inquired of her difficulties. She admitted that she had trials, but told him how well the Lord supplied her wants. He found it good to be there. He prayed with them all, spoke a few words of encouragement especially to the widow, and bade them farewell. He has never seen a mother more contented and thankful.

He left the house rebuked for his melancholy, which had in it perhaps much ingratitude. He could not but admire the power of divine grace in this poor woman. He did not inquire to what church she belonged. She gave evidence of belonging to the invisible company of faithful ones who love our Lord Jesus Christ. Soon after he left the house he sought a place for prayer and praise. His sadness left him. That poor woman's behavior and conversation were better to him than many sermons. He then found out that a secret of happiness was to engage in hearty self-denying labors for the good of men, and especially of the poor and afflicted.

The highest motive which can be presented to a pious mind in favor of a life of zeal and devotedness is, that thus we do what we can to glorify our God and Saviour. To be allowed to honor the Father of our mercies, the God of all grace, and the Saviour of sinners, is one of the highest privileges ever bestowed on mortals. So the righteous have always esteemed it. The wants, the woes, the weal of mankind may properly be thought of as motives to a life of labor and usefulness. But they are as nothing compared with the glory of Him who hath made all things for himself, who is before all, above all, over all, through all, and in us all. That his name may be hallowed, his kingdom come, and his will be done, are three of the seven petitions in the Lord's prayer; and they are the first three. Before all things we should endeavor to honor God.

## CHAPTER XXV.

### CONCLUDING OBSERVATIONS.

In closing this work, attention is asked to a few general observations. These may aid in rightly understanding and applying the weighty truths already considered.

I. The symmetry of Christian character.

Whoever has one Christian grace is sure to have others. In the genuine child of God, all the elements of piety are united. He who has strong hope, and no fear of God, will soon become presumptuous. He who has strong fears, but no hope in God, will be desperate. Without reverence, love degenerates into fondness; and without love, dread degenerates into aversion. Faith that is not humble can never lay hold of the most precious truths of the gospel; and humility that does not rely on God is but abjectness. Joy that is not chastened with mourning for sin becomes giddy and trifling; while sorrow for sin that joys not in God works death. Peace which, when called to contend for the faith, refuses to stand up for the truth, would betray the cause of Christ;

while he who loves contention and hates peace, is carnal and odious. Meekness without courage is but childishness; and courage without meekness is forwardness and brutality.

There is a consanguinity between all the qualities that form the Christian character. The elements of one good trait contain the germ of others. Paul speaks of Christian character as a unit: "The *fruit* of the Spirit is love, joy, peace, long-suffering, gentleness, goodness, faith, meekness, temperance." John says the same: "He that loveth him that begat, loveth him also that is begotten of him." No man can love the Father without loving the Son, who was sent by him. He who loves the image of God in the Son, loves the image of God whenever discerned in the humblest Christian. It cannot be otherwise. Any thing contrary to this makes hypocrisy and formalism as precious as true piety.

The great defect in all who make a spurious profession of religion is, not that they have not some things about them that look well, but all is out of proportion. They have zeal, but not gentleness; they have boldness, but not meekness. They pretend to more than they feel. With all their ardor they display vainglory and self-sufficiency. Sometimes they excuse iniquity and smile at sin. Their charity does not "bear all things." They incline to censoriousness. To some they are rude; to others they will not speak a civil word; to others they have real hatred.

In the beatitudes Jesus Christ described but one character. Where poverty of spirit, mourning for sin, meekness, hungering and thirsting for righteousness, mercifulness, purity of heart, and love of peace are genuine, they are found together. Circumstances will call one grace into more vigorous exercise than another. But if we have truly passed from death unto life, God will enable us in due time to exhibit every Christian temper. Human features out of all proportion are hideous. The same is true of any character called religious.

II. A HOLY LIFE ALONE PROVES PIETY GENUINE.

Words are cheap. Edwards.

Actions speak louder than words. Proverb.

Practice is the life of piety. T. Watson.

Even a child is known by his doings. Solomon.

Every one that doeth righteousness is born of him. John.

As the body without the spirit is dead, so faith without works is dead also. James.

If ye love me, keep my commandments.
Jesus Christ.

1. That no man is better than his life proves him to be, seems to be the judgment of all mankind. Even a little child cannot be won by mere words, though it may understand them. The best part of mankind are slow in making professions, because they know how hard it is to perform what we promise. The last to engage is often the first to fulfil. The very existence of such words as truth, candor, honesty, integrity, faithfulness, and their opposites, falsehood, deception, fraud, and faithlessness, shows that the judgment of mankind on these points is harmonious. All men know that words are breath, and deeds only are realities. Profession is not principle. Practice is the best expounder of the heart.

2. God seldom reproves men for being slow to engage, while he constantly guards them against the sin of not performing their promises. Joshua warned the Israelites on this subject. Josh. 24:16, 19. Indeed in so many words Solomon says, "Be not rash with thy mouth, and let not thy heart be hasty to

utter any thing before God." Eccles. 5 : 2. See context. Compare Matt. 7:21–27, and 1 John 3:18, 19.

3. As holiness is not natural to man, the Scriptures say explicitly that whosoever doeth righteousness is born of God. 1 John 2:29. He has a new nature, obtained in regeneration. He has the life of God in his soul. Only that which is born of the Spirit is spirit. When we see a man working righteousness, warring against sin, and heartily doing the will of God, we know that an almighty power has changed his nature. He is a new creature.

4. Whatever does not lead to a holy life is worthless in the sight of God. Man looks at the outward appearance, but the Lord looks at the heart. David walked before God in truth and righteousness, and in uprightness of heart. All religious profession which ends in show is at the best Pharisaism dressed up in evangelical attire. If the heart is not swayed by it, the heart is unchanged. "He that doeth righteousness is righteous; he that committeth sin is of the devil." All pretences to piety which end not in a godly life are utterly vain. Men obey not, because they love not. They hearken not, because their ears are un-

circumcised. There is no folly greater than double-dealing with God. "A hypocrite is hated of the world for seeming a Christian, and hated of God for not being one." All outward religious acts may be performed without a spark of love to Christ. "Two attendances upon public worship is a form complied with by thousands who never kept a Sabbath in their lives." How few heartily engage in the work of mortifying sin. When men are this moment devout, and the next carnal; when to-day they are all zeal for God, and to-morrow all zeal for politics; when they have not respect unto all God's commandments, but seek laxity; when their religious raptures are followed by fleshly frolics, then their religion is vain.

Men should therefore be very careful lest they deceive themselves respecting both the reality and the strength of their own piety. The daily business of a Christian is to resist the devil, deny himself, overcome the world, crucify the flesh with the affections and lusts, imitate Christ, walk with God, and strive to enter in at the strait gate. It is the heartless who, like the "children of Israel, being armed and carrying bows, turned back in the day of battle." "The Christian gains no victories without combat."

On the other hand, he whose life is holy has the fabric of his peace built upon a rock. God cannot deny him, for that would be denying his own work and signet. Although we do not enter heaven for our good works, yet we do not enter heaven without our good works.

III. True Christians are greatly blessed.

As the greatest curses are spiritual, so the greatest blessings are also spiritual. Our great wants must be supplied out of God's treasury, or we must suffer eternal loss and undoing. Paul uses no better designation of the privileges of believers than when he speaks of *spiritual blessings*. God's mercies to his children are sometimes catalogued. In the 103d Psalm David puts *forgiveness of sins* as the first. It is entitled to that place. Without pardon we are under an awful curse. God never bestows saving good on souls left in the chains of condemnation. In more than one place Paul seems to favor the same arrangement.

With forgiveness is always connected *acceptance in the Beloved.* Eph. 1 : 6. So that believers are no more aliens, strangers, foreigners, but sons, heirs, fellow-citizens. We are brought nigh by the blood and righteousness of Christ, and so "have right to the tree of life." Rev. 22:14.

From our justification flows peace with God through our Lord Jesus Christ, by whom also we have access into all needed grace, joy, hope, triumph in tribulation, patience, experience, boldness, the love of God, the indwelling of the Holy Ghost, and salvation full and complete. Peter gives a catalogue in which he mentions "faith, virtue," or courage, "knowledge, temperance, patience, godliness, brotherly kindness, charity." Well does he add, "If these things be in you and abound, they make you that ye shall neither be barren nor unfruitful in the knowledge of our Lord Jesus Christ." Blessed treasury of spiritual good things! Who can tell its value? It is the proof of a godlike temper and a godlike destiny.

Sure of spiritual blessings, men may be poor, yet they make many rich. They may have nothing, yet they possess all things. They may be sorrowful, yet they are always rejoicing. They may be dying daily, yet behold, they live. They may be chastened, but they are not killed. Their affections are set on things which do not perish in the using. Their crown is not the less bright or imperishable because it is seen by faith alone. They are sure of wearing it in due season, if they faint not.

Any spiritual blessing is worth more than the most costly temporal good. A devout thought, a pious desire, a holy purpose, is better than a great estate or an earthly kingdom. In eternity it will amount to more to have given a cup of cold water with right motives to a humble servant of God, than to have been flattered by a whole generation. God gives the common bounties of providence to saints and sinners. Often most largely to the latter. Spiritual blessings are put into elect vessels only. God's people share the good things of this world with the wicked; but the world has no lot nor part in spiritual good things. The sinner has never been pardoned, renewed, sanctified, or savingly taught of God.

The good things of time will soon be gone for ever. The very memory of them will imbitter the future existence of all who die in their sins. But spiritual blessings will last eternally. Though faith will give way to vision, and hope to fruition, yet fruition and vision are the legitimate consequences of hope and faith.

Temporal blessings come in the channel of nature; but spiritual blessings in the channel of grace. The former are of the earth, earthy; the latter are from heaven. God bestows temporal blessings on those who hate him all their days; but spiritual blessings come to believers only, through our Lord Jesus Christ. They cost his life, his toil, his sweat, his agony.

We may form some estimate of the value of spiritual blessings by the promises of the covenant which secures them. Long after his ascension to heaven, Jesus Christ promised to him that overcometh that he should eat of the tree of life, which is in the midst of the paradise of God; that he should be clothed in white raiment; that he should be a pillar in the temple of God, and go no more out; that he should sit with him in his throne; that he should eat of the hidden manna; that He should give him a white stone. How soon our faculties are overcome by attempting to comprehend the fulness of such promises. Let us dwell a moment on the last, "I will give him a white stone." Blunt thus explains it: "It is generally thought by commentators that this refers to an ancient judicial custom of dropping a black stone into an urn when it is intended to condemn, and a white stone when the prisoner is to be acquitted; but this is an act so distinct from that described, 'I will give thee a white stone,' that we are disposed to agree with those who think it refers rather to a custom of a very different kind, and not unknown to the classical reader, according with beautiful propriety to the case before us. In primitive times, when travelling was rendered difficult from want of places of public entertainment, hospitality was exercised by private individuals to a very great extent; of which indeed we find frequent traces in all history, and in none more than the Old Testament. Persons who partook of this hospitality and those who practised it, frequently contracted habits of friendship and regard for each other; and it became a well-established custom among the Greeks and Romans to provide their guests with some particular mark, which was handed down from father to son, and insured hospitality and kind treatment whenever it was presented. This mark was usually a small stone or pebble cut in half, and upon the halves of which the host and the guest mutually inscribed their names, and then interchanged them with each other. The production of this tessera was quite enough to insure friendship for themselves or descendants whenever they travelled again in the same direction; while it is evident that these stones required to be privately kept, and the names written upon them carefully concealed, lest others should obtain the privileges instead of the persons for whom they were intended. How natural then the allusion to this custom in the words, 'I will give him to eat of the hidden manna!' and having done so—having make himself partaker of my hospitality, having recognized him as my guest, my friend, I will present him with the white stone, and in the stone a new name written, which no man knoweth saving he who receiveth it. I will give him a pledge of my friendship sacred and inviolable, known only to himself."

IV. Sinners are poor indeed.

It is a dreadful thing to want bread. Yet man shall not live by bread alone, but by every word that proceedeth out of the mouth of God. It is sad to see a human being without reason. Yet some good people have become insane, and never waked up in their right mind till they were in the presence of the Lamb. But in his unregenerate state, man's case is far more pitiable. Of all such, Paul says they are *without Christ.* They have no Saviour, no infallible Teacher, no atoning High-priest, no Advocate with God, no King ruling in righteousness over them and their enemies. Without Christ, sinners are nothing. He is all and in all. Well did an ancient say, "I had rather fall with Christ than reign with Cæsar." Nonexistence is not so dreadful as a Christless state. "Captives, we cannot be delivered without the redemption which is in Christ Jesus. Fools as we all are, we cannot be instructed without wisdom, and all the treasures of wisdom are hid in Christ Jesus. All plans and hopes not built on him must fall, for there is none other foundation. All working without him is in the fire, where it will be consumed. Without him, all riches make themselves wings and fly away. A dungeon with Christ is a throne; and a throne without Christ, hell." He is life and light, and the delights of the sons of men. Yet sinners are without him.

They are also *aliens from the commonwealth of Israel.* They have no lot in Jacob. Christ's cause may advance, but it brings no joy to them. His kingdom may be set up in a whole nation, but they care not for that. His honor may be great, but they have no share in it. His praise may be sung in high anthems and hallelujahs, but to them it is as the voice of strange minstrels. Prayer may be offered for him, but they never heartily join in it. They are not at home in secret devotion, in public worship, or in the celebration of the ordinances. They would be even less at home in the adorations of heaven. They have no inheritance in the church. They are outcasts, castaways, reprobate silver. They are not sons. They are not heirs. Their prospects for eternity are no better than if God had no church at all.

And so they are *strangers from the covenants of promise.* They have nothing to rely upon for time, nothing for eternity; nothing for this life, nothing for that which is to come. Their heavens are never spanned by the bow of a rich variety of promises, divinely girt together by the faithful word and unimpeachable oath of Him who cannot lie. One of the most gifted among them, even while living in a gospel land, said, "The present is a fleeting moment, the past is no more, and our prospect of futurity is dark and doubtful." Such men are lost. They have no heavenly guide, no safe rules of conduct, no sure word abiding for ever.

Of course they are *without hope.* They may have dreams of future good, but these will all vanish like the mist. Their delusive expectations are constantly failing. They indulge them only to awake to a keen sense of agonizing misery. They are like the vine of Sodom and the fruit of Gomorrah. To hope, as an anchor to the soul, sure and steadfast; to hope, as entering within the veil; to hope, that does not mock our miseries; to hope, that shall not perish, they are utter strangers. One half hour's exercise of such hope as animates the believer would bring more that deserves the name of happiness than all the poor sinner has ever enjoyed. Now without hope, at any moment he may be in total and absolute despair.

Such are also *without God in the world.* A godless man is an undone man, and has a rueful eternity before him, whether he is a godless tyrant, a godless slave, or a godless freeman; whether he glitters in gold or crawls in debasement. He has no communion with his Maker, no confidence in Jehovah, no blessing from the Lord, and no righteousness from the

God of salvation. When nature is falling headlong, or is smitten with wrath, the believer exults, and shouts, "My Lord and my God." The poor sinner cannot do this. He has no God; he knows no God; he loves no God; he trusts in no God; he has no hope in God.

How poor and wretched and miserable and lost is an unconverted sinner!

How rich and free and undeserved is the mercy that saves sinners!

How loud is the call and how great is the obligation to do all we can to save dying sinners!

How inconceivably dreadful it will be to go to eternity an unrenewed sinner!

How infinite is the debt we owe to Him who has given us access to God by his own most precious blood!

Were there ever such wants among mortals as the wants of a perishing soul? Oh, sinner, turn and live.

V. Is there not a low state of piety?

Many answer the question in the affirmative. Some may do so through uncharitableness. But it cannot fairly be called a distorted view of things to say that piety is in a low state generally, and that in many places truth is fallen in the streets. Among the causes of this state of things, we may notice,

1. *The commotions among the nations.* "Wars and rumors of wars" mightily distract public attention from all the concerns of eternity. Piety must have time for contemplation. We cannot profitably wait upon God unless we can do so without distraction. Turmoil may be around us and yet but slightly affect us. When such is the case, grace reigns mightily.

2. *Politics.* Andrew Fuller says that many "have fallen sacrifices to *taking an eager and deep interest in political disputes.*" He speaks of some whose "whole heart has been engaged in this pursuit. It has been their meat and their drink; and this being the case, it is not surprising that they have become indifferent to religion; for these things cannot consist with each other." This is sound speech that cannot be condemned.

3. *Love of money.* This root has struck very deep into many hearts. Nor are its ill consequences even yet fully seen. The worst is probably yet to come. Without checking any sober, lawful endeavor to secure compe-

tence and independence, it must yet be said that a people eagerly pursuing wealth cannot be a very religious people. "If any man love the world, the love of the Father is not in him." "Ye cannot serve God and mammon."

4. *Fanaticism.* Nothing is more opposed to true piety than a wild, heated, ignorant, and furious zeal. It has brought vast discredit on true religion, and has driven many into infidelity and practical atheism. It is like a flame driven by fierce winds through a forest. It consumes whatever it meets. Its unhappy effects are seen and felt for half a century. It brings pure revivals of religion into disrepute. It awakens distrust of experimental piety. It clothes with suspicion every extraordinary endeavor to promote the knowledge and love of God. It creates a necessity for most painful acts of church discipline, and its whole tendency is to disorder and irreligion. To be zealously affected always in a good thing is a great attainment; but a fanatical, fiery, bitter zeal is always followed by ill consequences.

5. *The attention of pastors and churches has been unduly withdrawn from their chief work.* Pastors are often overworked. Consequently

they come not to their work with joyous elasticity of mind. And churches sometimes meddle with things quite out of their line; so that a minister who labors in word and doctrine, who gives himself entirely to prayer and the ministry of the word, is regarded as not up to the times.

6. *A low standard of evidence of Christian character.* It is our duty to "feed the lambs" and to "comfort the feeble-minded." But the lambs should grow to be sheep. A word to the weary is excellent, if it be in season; but the church should never be so addressed as to make her rest satisfied with low attainments. If the babes are fed on milk all their days and never get a taste of strong meat, they will never be strong men, full of vigor. Scriptural marks of a change of heart should be clearly stated.

7. *The neglect of social prayer and conference.* Have not Christians too much forsaken the assembling of themselves together, that they might speak often one to another?

8. *But our greatest lack is in the article of fervent, importunate, united prayer.* Oh for a spirit of strong crying unto God! Would the heavens in so many places be as brass if they

were pierced by the hearty cries of God's people? There is no substitute for fervent prayer. Let that cease and religion must decline.

VI. Time and Eternity.

Formerly it was customary at public executions to bring an hour-glass to the scaffold with the sand all at one end, and when the prisoner had taken his position, to set the glass before him inverted, and the sands of the last hour of his life began to run. Sometimes the executioner and sometimes the minister of religion would say to the unhappy man, "Your sands are almost run." From this the phrase was transferred to the pulpit, and men were exhorted to speedy repentance because their sands were almost run. Oh that men would candidly look at the nearness of death and lay hold on eternal life while it is called to-day.

An old writer says, "I stopped in Clerkenwell churchyard to see a grave-digger at work. He had dug pretty deep, and was come to an old coffin which was quite rotten. In clearing away the mouldering wood, the grave-digger found an hour-glass close to the left side of the skull, with the sand in it." This was telling the dead that to them time was no longer. How much more fit to put the hour-glass before the living, and remind them that their hours will soon all be gone. Why will not men be warned? Why will not the living lay to heart the things which belong to their peace? Between the longest human life and eternity there is no proportion whatever.

"*I have lost a day*" is a dreadful sound in the ears of one who has a tender conscience. Nothing but a slighted Saviour seems to press so heavily on dying sinners as murdered time.

"Remorseless Time,
Fierce spirit of the glass and scythe, what power
Can stay him in his silent course, or melt
His iron heart to pity? On, still on
He presses, and for ever. The proud bird,
The condor of the Andes, that can soar
Through heaven's unfathomable depths, or brave
The fury of the northern hurricane,
And bathe his plumage in the thunder's home,
Furls his broad wings at nightfall, and sinks down
To rest upon his mountain crag; but Time
Knows not the weight of sleep or weariness,
And night's deep darkness has no chain to bind
His rushing pinion. Revolutions sweep
O'er earth like troubled visions o'er the breast
Of dreaming sorrow; cities rise and sink
Like bubbles on the water; fiery isles
Spring blazing from the ocean, and go back
To their mysterious caverns; mountains rear
To heaven their bald and blackened cliffs, and bow
Their tall heads to the plain; new empires rise,
Gathering the strength of hoary centuries,
And rush down like the Alpine avalanche,
Startling the nations; and the very stars,

Yon bright and burning blazonry of God,
Glitter a while in their eternal depths,
And like the Pleiad, loveliest of their train,
Shoot from their glorious spheres, and pass away
To darkle in their trackless void: yet Time,
Time, the tomb-builder, holds his fierce career,
Dark, stern, all pitiless, and pauses not
Amid the mighty wrecks that strew his path,
To sit and muse, like other conquerors,
Upon the fearful ruin he has wrought."

God of mercy, give us grace to improve each hour, so to number our days as to apply our hearts unto wisdom, and to be always doing some good. Let madness no longer reign within us. THE NIGHT COMETH WHEN NO MAN CAN WORK.

VII. HEAVEN.

All the souls that God has made are in heaven, earth, or hell. We who are in earth know something about it. Oh that we may never know by experience the nature of the woes of the pit! If we would be saved, we must learn as we can something of heaven, must breathe something of its spirit, must long for its blessings.

Heaven is a place. Jesus so calls it. It is a city. It is a heavenly country. It is a better country than any known on earth. It has locality. Of its position in relation to the sun, moon, and planets, we have no information; and we need none; but heaven exists in reality, not merely in imagination.

Heaven is also a state, exceedingly pure, holy, excellent. Angels themselves have never attained to a better state. The spirits of just men made perfect can rise no higher.

The inhabitants of heaven have large measures of clear and certain knowledge of the most excellent things. They see God. They see Jesus. They know as they are known. They do not see through a glass darkly, but face to face. They are not liable to errors, mistakes, or misapprehensions. The Lamb himself feeds them, and leads them to fountains of living waters.

The inhabitants of heaven are happy. They are full of joy. They never sin, and they never sigh; they never pity one another, nor envy one another, nor grieve at one another, nor are mortified by each other's follies or weaknesses. Their warfare is ended, their turmoils are over, and their conflicts past. They weep no more. Jesus wipes tears from cff all faces of his redeemed, and the holy angels never did weep.

Heaven is full of variety. It is not all one

house; there are many mansions and many holy characters there. The dwellers therein praise much, they exult much, they admire much. They have rest; they go no more out; they serve God day and night.

In heaven society is perfect, though constantly receiving new and desirable accessions. All unite in loving the Lamb that was slain. Yet there is a great variety in the history and character of its inhabitants. There are angels, who have great power and wisdom and experience. There are patriarchs and prophets and apostles and martyrs and confessors and reformers and kings and shepherds and feeble-minded folk and little children. There the choirs of those redeemed by atoning blood are arrayed in linen white and clean. Among them are infants who knew not that there was a heaven till they saw its pearly gates and golden streets. They knew not that there was a Saviour till they saw him in his glory. Choice spirits are constantly joining this throng above. Let a few words be said of two who have lately passed from earth.

One was a dear, talented little creature. Before her departure she said,

"I am not afraid to die. I have committed all to Christ. There is in the Bible no phrase so precious to me as, 'THE LORD OUR RIGHTEOUSNESS.' My pastor is partial to me. Let him not praise me at my burial; let him exalt the *Lord's righteousness.* When I committed myself to Christ, I did it wholly and unreservedly. I never doubted him since. I may be self-deceived, but of Christ I have no doubt. When I appear at the judgment-bar of God, if I should hear the word, 'Depart,' I should turn with astonishment to Christ, and say, 'Dear Saviour, there must be a mistake here. Did I not commit all to thee?'" Again she said, "Come, Lord Jesus, come quickly." Her last words were, "While I have voice and memory left, I wish to say, THE LORD OUR RIGHTEOUSNESS. It is sufficient for you all. It is all you need."

She was soon followed by another of like spirit. In the year 1839, a family was made glad by the birth of a little daughter. Father, mother, two elder sisters, and a large circle of friends rejoiced together. The babe was a bud, promising beauty and fragrance. Early in life, by her ingenuousness and warmth of affection, she attached many to her. In her teens, her schoolmates saw her worth, admired and imitated. Her education at school being finished, she noiselessly began to move in the best circles of pious and refined society. Here she attracted the love of aged men and women, and of those pressed with the cares of middle life, no less than of the young. Without a dash of forwardness, she was often the companion of people thrice her age. Ere long divine grace began its blessed work, and on this lovely stock engrafted the Rose of Sharon. Still artless and natural, the work of God's Spirit heightened in her all that was previously charming, and sweetly chastened the exultant joyousness of her youth. Elder sisters married and left the paternal roof. She remained greatly to honor father and mother, and light up the boyhood of a younger brother. On a visit to a friend was laid the foundation of the ailment that removed her from earth. Her constitution being good, she buffeted disease for a while; but at last she was shut within doors. Her kind and skilful medical attendant for a season thought the danger slight; but God's will was to take her to himself. Alarming symptoms appeared, and about eight o'clock in the morning of a blessed Sabbath-day her good physician found her sinking, and in the sweetest manner told her that she was entering upon her eternal rest. Surprised, but not terrified, she calmly inquired when the change had taken place. At once the work of life rose before her mind. She thought of the Industrial school and of the Sabbath-school. She said, "I have so much work to do; but God knows best." To her brother, who has since followed her, she made the kindest little address. Then turning to her father, she said, "It is sad for you all." On his assenting, and saying, "Yes, my child, but I feel I shall soon meet you in heaven," she said in a clear, audible voice, "I hope so," and gently fell asleep as the Sabbath bells began to ring. One of her pastors says, "This coincidence reminds us of Bunyan's expression respecting what followed the entrance of Christian and Hopeful into the heavenly Jerusalem: 'Then I heard in my dream that all the bells in the city rang again for joy, and that it was said unto them, Enter ye into the joy of your Lord.' The last earthly sound which echoed in the ear of this dying believer was that of the church-going bell; the first which met her ransomed spirit on high was the peal of welcome from the blood-washed throng before the throne."

Dear child, till the heavens be no more, we shall not again see thy charming face; but thou shalt see the face of Jesus. Our hearts were knit together. I love thy memory. I love thy sincerity. I love the paths marked by thy footsteps. "I heard a voice from heaven saying unto me, Write, Blessed are the dead which die in the Lord from henceforth: Yea, saith the Spirit, that they may rest from their labors; and their works do follow them." The names of these young heroes of the cross need not be given. They are written in the Lamb's book of life.

Into the lips of a glorified spirit in heaven Matthew Henry puts these words: "Would you know where I am? I am at home in my Father's house, in the mansion prepared for me there. I am where I would be, where I have long and often desired to be; no longer on a stormy sea, but in a safe and quiet harbor. My work in time is done, I am resting; my sowing time is done, I am reaping; my joy is as the joy of harvest. Would you know how it is with me? I am made perfect in holiness; grace is swallowed up in glory; the top-stone of the building is brought forth. Would you know what I am doing? I see God; I see him as he is; not as through a glass darkly, but face to face; and the sight is transforming; it makes me like him. I am in the sweet employment of my blessed Redeemer, my Head and my Husband, whom my soul loved, and for whose sake I was willing to part with all. I am here bathing myself at the spring-head of the heavenly pleasure, and joy unutterable; and therefore weep not for me. I am here keeping a perpetual Sabbath; what that is, judge by your short Sabbath. I am here singing hallelujahs incessantly to him who sits upon the throne, and I rest not day or night from praising him. Would you know what company I have? Blessed company, better than the best on earth. Here are holy angels and the spirits of just men made perfect. I am set down with Abraham and Isaac and Jacob in the kingdom of God, with blessed Paul and Peter and James and John and all the saints; and here I meet with many of my old acquaintances that I fasted and prayed with, who got before me hither. And lastly, would you consider how long this is to continue? It is a garland that never withers; a crown of glory that fades not away; after millions of millions of ages it will be as fresh as it is now; and therefore weep not for me."

Grace is glory begun; but glory is grace matured, completed, crowned with the fulness of beatific vision.

NOW UNTO THE KING ETERNAL, IMMORTAL, INVISIBLE, THE ONLY WISE GOD, BE HONOR AND GLORY FOR EVER AND EVER. AMEN.

# GENERAL INDEX.

## M.



## N.



## O.



## P.

## Q.



## R.



## S.

www.ingramcontent.com/pod-product-compliance
Lightning Source LLC
LaVergne TN
LVHW021106110826
845150LV00001B/186

* 9 7 8 1 4 2 5 5 6 5 0 9 1 *